THERE'S SOMETHING ABOUT WREXHAM

*Dedicated to Dad, Uncle Rob and Uncle Rem –
my football-mad family who introduced me to
the magic of Wrexham FC.*

*… And, of course, a special dedication
from us all to the incomparable 'Mr Wrexham' himself,
Joey Jones (1955–2025)
xxx*

THERE'S SOMETHING ABOUT WREXHAM

Great stories from Wrexham AFC's biggest names

DEIO EDWARDS WITH **IESTYN JONES**

First impression: 2025

© Copyright Deio Edwards, Iestyn Jones and Y Lolfa Cyf., 2025

The contents of this book are subject to copyright, and may not be reproduced by any means, mechanical or electronic, without the prior, written consent of the publishers.

Cover design: Sion Ilar

ISBN: 978 1 912631 61 2

Published and printed in Wales
on paper from well-maintained forests by
Y Lolfa Cyf., Talybont, Ceredigion SY24 5HE
website www.ylolfa.com
e-mail ylolfa@ylolfa.com
tel 01970 832 304

Introduction

SINCE STARTING IN 1864, Wrexham FC has developed into one of the most respected clubs in football history. Their highlights over the years include reaching the quarter-finals of the FA Cup on three occasions. Before the 'Hollywood era', their most notable achievement included their famous win over Arsenal in the 1992 FA Cup third round.

There have been countless other highs though, even before that Mickey T moment more than 30 years ago. Twenty Wrexham legends are about to recount some of the magic moments that paved the way to recent successes. In this book, past players will take you into the inner sanctum of the Dragons' lair and grant you an Access All Areas pass like no other. You've seen the TV documentary *Welcome to Wrexham* ... well, peep behind the curtain and find out what happened before the cameras started rolling.

With these exclusive interviews, coupled with photogenic portraits – you're in for a treat, you lucky, lucky people. If you like Wrexham Football Club and funny footballing anecdotes, you'll love this one. *Mwynhewch* (Enjoy)!

About the author

DEIO EDWARDS HAS been described as the 'Statto' of Welsh football. As a Welsh-language writer, Deio has contributed to *Y Cyfnod* and *Y Cymro* newspapers over the years while on teaching duties at Ysgol Y Berwyn in Bala. Deio has followed Wrexham FC for over 40 years and describes *There's Something about Wrexham* not only as a labour of love but also his very own *magnum opus*.

In his own words: "As a lifelong Wrexham fan, it's been quite strange being on first-name terms with some of my biggest heroes. Getting things off the ground hasn't been easy. It's been a bit like a jigsaw, which has come together over time. I'd like to say a special thank you to Mickey Thomas and Mark Creighton who have worked as 'fixers' on this project. There will definitely be a drink waiting for you at the launch party.

"I've often wondered if Wrexham FC is detrimental to my health as my heart's taken some pounding over the years; it's been like an epic game of Russian Roulette. With Wrexham, some days it's like hitting the jackpot, and then, other days, it feels like I've lost it all … but, what can I do when I have an outpouring of unconditional love for something so unpredictable that's on par with my own flesh and blood?

"For as long as I can remember, Uncle Rem – a Wrexham die hard – captivated me with tales of a wizard called Stevie Fox, and a goal machine named Dixie McNeil. In 1984, when I was just eight years old, I was dazzled under the floodlights. 'Freedom' by Wham shmoozed in the background as big Jim

About the author

Steel slayed the Portuguese giants FC Porto. After just one game – I was seduced!

"A few years later, Stevie Massey had me spilling my Bovril while I watched him in amazement; there he was – shooting down the paddock chicken run, clenching his fist as if he'd ripped the heart'n'soul out of Zaragoza. Then came Kevin 'Rooster' Russell, who felt like my very own Diego Maradona (even if we didn't care you had no hair). And then Joey Jones, Mr Wrexham AFC – I only have to look at you and suddenly my heart's thumpin' and I'm screamin': 'C'MON THE TOWN!'

"Mickey Thomas – fancy sending me to orbit with your rocket against Arsenal ... I was only 16, but every time I think of that special afternoon in January – it fills me with pure lovable warmth.

"The list goes on ... Gary 'Psycho' Bennett – you glorious goal machine; Gaz Owen – thank you for the midfield masterclasses; Neil 'Robbo' Roberts – thanks for that goal against Torquay United during the 2007 Great Escape, which had me running on to the pitch and then being chased by stewards. Back then, Benny Hill had nothing on me!

"... Which brings us to recent times: The 'Modern History Boys' have kept my passion for Wrexham bubbling quite nicely. Stars like Ben Tozer, Ben Foster and Paul Mullin. Paul – I just don't think you understand how hoarse you've made my throat over the last few years! Rob 'n' Ryan – I speak on behalf of Wrexham and Wales when I say *Diolch* – Thank you. Thank you for your commitment to delivering on that promise you made a few years ago. Because of you, for people like me, it's always sunny in Wrexham!

"Mold Road is my magical escape, my very own Narnia, as I'm transcended into a world of magic on a field of dreams. I've been blessed to share this enchantment with my own children (Josh, Jacko, and Ellie), and introducing them to the Racecourse is, without a doubt, one of my proudest moments.

I've tried, in vain, to introduce my wife, Debs, to the Mold Road experience, and actually thought I'd succeeded on one special occasion when Josh was a mascot for a match ... only for her to concede that, during the entirety of the match, Debs described me as a 'bloody nutter' as I enthusiastically joined in with every chant, berated every decision against us, and wildly celebrated both goals Wrexham scored during that bitterly cold October afternoon.

"Away from The Racecourse, I am wholeheartedly grateful to Debs for her unconditional love, patience and support during the process of this book, and for her undeniable understanding of me being a Wrexham supporter.

"There is indeed something about Wrexham. Read on and you might just find out what it is."

Contents

	Introduction	5
	About the author	6
1	Mark Creighton – Defender	11
2	John Muldoon – Forward	17
3	Andrew Dibble – Goalkeeper	33
4	Ian Edwards – Forward	38
5	Gareth Owen – Midfielder	57
6	Dean Keates – Midfielder	64
7	Mark Jones – Midfielder	78
8	Mickey Thomas – Midfielder	83
9	Stuart Parker – Goalkeeper	94
10	Lee Jones – Forward	100
11	Glen Little – Winger	120
12	Andy Holt – Defender	129
13	Ryan Valentine – Defender	151
14	Andy Edwards – Forward	156
15	Waynne Phillips – Midfielder	171
16	Billy Ashcroft – Forward	178
17	Steve Massey – Forward	189
18	Danny Wright – Forward	208
19	Andrew Morrell – Forward	232
20	Neil Roberts – Forward	254
	Afterword	270

1

Mark Creighton
Defender

The Beast who liked to feast
2010–2013 (86 appearances, 4 goals)

Affectionately known as 'The Beast', Mark Creighton endeared himself with the Wrexham faithful because of his fearless commitment, and with quotes like: "I'd rather bleed than concede a goal!" he was always sure to cement his hero status. While shoring up the Wrexham defence, the side had a momentous push for promotion but sadly missed out to Luton Town in the play-off semi-final of 2011.

I COULDN'T WAIT for match day, especially at The Racecourse. I can still picture myself standing in the tunnel waiting to go out for the start of a match. I'd look at the opposing players and think to myself – "We're gonna fuckin' BATTER you today!"

Ultimately, that was a special dressing room. We would do anything for each other, the club, and especially the fans. Lee Fowler – what a talented player; Jay Harris – he was mustard for me because he was an absolute warrior – had great technical ability and the first pick in any team sheet of mine; Danny Wright – a bulldozer of a striker; Andy Morrell – absolutely fuckin' fearless and a great finisher; Neil Ashton – Mr Consistent; Curtis Obeng – unbelievably fast as a full back; Nat Knight-Percival – so talented he was converted to a centre back next to me; Jake Speight – a nasty little fucker but technically a good finisher; Adrian Cieślewicz – all GRAVY players.

Suffice to say, team bonding sessions were always a great way to keep the dressing room spirits high.

It was the spontaneous sessions that were the most memorable. A pre-season jaunt at Aberystwyth was a classic example. We'd just beaten Aberystwyth, we were about to go back to these student dorms we were staying in, and the gaffer (Dean Saunders) gives us the green light to go out and enjoy a couple of beers. We're at this bar, beers flowing, jukebox bouncing, and there's the shortest bouncer you've ever seen, and Little Jay Harris has been giving him playful verbal banter, all good fun, no malice ... until Jay gets him in a headlock and they both start rolling around on the floor, neither letting go, like two kids having a fight in the playground. At this point all the lads are on their knees creased up. Next thing, Jay gets naked, starts running around the pub with this diminutive bouncer chasing after him like a scene from *Benny Hill* ... by now we were fuckin' howling!

Eventually, it all calmed down. And just as well, because no sooner had Jay put his clothes back on, in walks the gaffer, Brian Carey and Mal Purchase. They hadn't even reached the bar to order a drink before Jay shouts with his Scouse twang: "EY! FWCHIN 'ELL SAUNDERS, GET THE FWCHIN BEERS IN!"

In total astonishment, the gaffer turns to Brian Carey and says, "What did he just say to me?"

So, Brian Carey pulls Jay to one side and advised him, "Jay, you can't talk to the gaffer like that."

Jay's having none of it, "I fwchin' can, tell 'im to get the fwchin beers in."

As calm as you like, Brian tells Jay to leave. Which he did, with Lee Fowler. Anyway, Jay then spots the gaffer's X5 parked outside and just sprints up to his car, two-foots the front door, leaves a massive dent in it and knocks off the wing mirror the same time, before running off like a naughty kid! Deano never found out who mauled his car ... until now!

Although we enjoyed our fair share of success on the field, we (the players, staff) were fully aware of the struggles and strains off the field. Financially, we (the club) were literally hanging by a thread. As players, there's the danger of living in a bubble and being oblivious of what's going on outside. Perhaps selfishly but also understandable at the same time, in the back of our minds is the nagging voice of, "Shit, we ain't getting paid again ... we've got X, Y, and Z bills to pay, I've got a family to support." And in all fairness, whether it'd be Deano (Saunders) or Mozza (Morrell), the gaffer was brilliant in his delegations whenever there were any issues with our wages. As well as being empathetic and supportive, both discreetly did their best in keeping our spirits up ... Deano was a natural wise cracker, one of the funniest gaffers I've ever had.

So, picture the scene ... It's a Friday morning and we ain't got paid again. Normally, we all loved Friday mornings because we'd kick off with an Old v Young match before we'd have a short sharp session on set-piece routines, then shoot off home. On this particular day, however, the boys, including myself, ain't got paid, so we sounded out Deano before we got our kit on. He assured us, "I've been guaranteed by Geoff Moss, we're all getting paid by this afternoon."

Happy days, all smiles, we bounced out of that changing room to begin training. About 20 minutes into the Old v Young match, we couldn't help notice there was one obvious absentee. Deano loved this prestigious match, always took part, and almost always scored. But not on this occasion. In a break in play, we noticed he was on his mobile ... and sure enough the grumbles began to circle ...

"Fuckin' 'ell! We ain't getting paid!" and all that.

Deano finished the call and whistled the lads over to him. "I'm really sorry lads – we're not getting paid today," he said.

"Fuck sake Gaffer," came a few catcalls, to which Deano replies:

"I know, I know ... I'm down to my last eight million quid as well!" which broke the ice gently, until we all saw a scowl on Mal Purchase's face and half-expected him to rip the gaffer's head off. Big Mal could be fuckin' scary, but genuinely a great bloke.

Ultimately, however, we know why we're here, and imperatively **WHO** we're here for – the diehard fans. These loyal Wrexham fans would literally give an arm and a leg to play for their club. The club that we, the players, are playing for. We (the players) represent them (the fans) because they ARE the club. **THESE ARE THE REAL HEROES** of Wrexham. They're the ones who propped up the club and kept it afloat during those dark, **DARK** periods, when the club was 24 hours away from ceasing to exist. Those unbelievably kind and generous local sponsors that sponsored the club through whichever means they could – **THEY ARE YOUR FUCKIN' IDOLS.** They don't sponsor the club for any internal interest or look to gain any external investment.

Take Phil Salmon from AEC Engineering, for instance.

An absolute legend and a beautiful soul to boot. He couldn't do enough for the club and the players. Sponsoring the club was never enough for him – he'd be in and around the training ground offering his services any which way he, and the company, could. There were times when we'd see more of Phil than our families, such was his devotion! A great bloke and all the staff loved his companionship. We'd talk for hours with him, and on one occasion I simply praised him and showed him a bit of gratitude.

He proudly replied, "FOR THE LOVE, NOT THE GLORY" – and that will stay with me for ever.

I could've cried many times during my time at Wrexham, not for the heartbreaking losses in the play-offs, not for the career ending injury I sustained, but for witnessing the pure devotion these fans have for their club. Yes, that injury was at times soul destroying. But the fans would always manage to pick my spirits up whenever or wherever they saw me – especially when they bellow out "BEEEEAAAAASSSSSTTT". Fuckin' 'ell that's special. And that, in a nutshell, is what this club is all about – the fans. And believe me, there's fuckin' thousands of them! Even before Rob and Ryan, or Mullin and Lee – the core of these fans have always been there. And they always will be. And long may the new fans, the so-called 'bandwagoners' continue along as well. Because at some point every single fan has been 'a new fan' or a 'bandwagoner' – it's only natural to go along with a mate or a family member to watch something that's aroused public interest. And what's especially brilliant about the loyal and hardcore fans of Wrexham is that they will educate the 'new fans' about the club's history, and THAT history is just as important as the future. I vehemently agree 100 per cent with them, because we can never ever forget where we came from.

These same fans helped give us players just as much pleasure as we did for them during one of my favourite seasons as a player, the 2011–12 season. We accumulated a massive 98 points in the league and were somehow just pipped by a Jamie Vardy-inspired Fleetwood, before losing once again to our nemesis Luton Town in the play-offs semi-final. But my outstanding highlight has got to be the Cup run of that season, especially the Brighton games – we were fuckin' brilliant. 'Cheesey' tore them apart at their place to earn a third round replay at ours. I still get tingles down my spine because The Racecourse was rockin' to its foundations that night … and we gave them an absolute tonkin'. Forget about losing on penalties – we outplayed, out-fought, and out-sang a team that were top of the Championship, especially considering we were still a Conference side at the time as well.

I'm loving what's happening at Wrexham at the moment, and hope it continues for a long, long time. I've been fortunate to play and represent the club, the fans, and the whole north Wales area. I've also had the absolute pleasure of going back as a fan in the stands, singing all the songs and chants, dancing in delight when we score, and I've also been lucky enough to attend games as a pundit. Wrexham has been and still is a massive part of my life, and for that alone, I am genuinely grateful.

2
John Muldoon
Forward

The rat, the turkey and the *'cwdyn bach blewog'*
1980–1985 (119 appearances, 19 goals)

Storytelling is a unique artform. Within minutes of his company, you'll realise that John Muldoon possesses this rare gift ... And, better still, he's got a few belters that've been tucked away in his locker (until now). From Mold Road banter, a freezer full of prized turkeys, to European glory – John gleefully shares a few rib-shakin' tales along with a couple of heart-stopping scenes.

I suppose I went into professional football the long way round. The journey which eventually led me to sign for the Wrexham apprentices seemed like an 'A to Z road map' of the north-west counties.

When I was 12 years old, I played for a Sunday League team in Bromborough on the Wirral. After a short spell there, a Tranmere Rovers scout was in at one match and so offered me a trial, 'n' although I was much younger than the others, I continued training with them. Although, at the time, I wasn't aware that you couldn't sign schoolboy forms until you were 13. I even played for a men's side, called Vauxhall's, when I was just 14.

In the meantime, Graham Beacroft, the scout for Tranmere Rovers, had taken a shine to myself and the likes of John Allen 'n' Mark Joseph, and he'd scheduled for me to sign forms at my house on the 21st of November, the day of my 13th birthday. I couldn't wait.

The big day finally arrives, and Graham's sat around our dining table along with other representatives from the club. I've literally got the pen in my hand to sign, when suddenly our phone rings in the hallway. So my dad rushes to answer it, then rushes back into the dining room.

"John – you're wanted on the phone!" So, I put the pen down to one side and walk rather bemused to the hallway, and pick up the phone.

"Hello John, I hope you're fit and well. Sorry to disturb you, but I'm a scout for Manchester United, and I've heard good things about you. I wondered if you'd like to come to United for a week?"

Shitting hell, I didn't expect that! But I was now obviously in fuckin' no man's land. "Erm. Well that's an amazing offer, but I've actually got representatives here from Tranmere Rovers and I'm about to sign for them!"

In the skip of a heartbeat he replies, "Look son, once you sign them forms, you can't go anywhere!"

So I thank him for calling and tell him I'll speak with my dad and the Tranmere representatives and get back with him. After explaining the details of the phone call with the representatives they soon made it clear they weren't very happy at all, especially after I'd decided to go to Manchester United.

Although it didn't work out for me during that week at United, I was soon on the move again, first with Liverpool, then I found myself having a trial at Shrewsbury Town, whereupon I scored SIX goals during the initial trial match! Without being big-headed, I thought I'd done enough to impress 'em ... until after the game, when their coach says I did alright, but he wasn't sure about my height 'n' this 'n' that. But that very same day, my Sunday League manager tells me that we've got a game coming up against a team from Wrexham, would I be fit to play? So of course I played, and we thumped 'em and that's when I got to know a tall scallywag called Andy Edwards! Afterwards, I got offered to go to Wrexham AFC on trial. "Aye, go on then!"

By now, I'd got to know the usual drill of being a triallist and thought nothing different when I arrived at Wrexham for my first session. With this in mind, I'd always remember a piece of advice given to me – be smart and dress tidy – so I turn up in a pristine jacket, trousers, shirt and tie, fully expecting to be in a changing room amongst other triallists ... but how fuckin' wrong was I! Only to realise that I'd be with lads who were already schoolboys with Wrexham Football Club. And the scene which confronted me was like a rogue cowboy strolling in through the saloon bar in a Western movie, and I've got all these new faces looking at me as if I've got fuckin' dog shit on my face! There was Mark Cartwright, Darren Baker, Andy 'Ted' Edwards, Steve Jones, all dressed casually in a pair of jeans and a T-shirt. Well, we might have dressed different, but on the pitch we clicked straightaway and I was in my element as I scored four goals in two games with the lads. "Tell ya wot, I'm lovin' it 'ere," I thought, only there was one tiny little sting in the tail – I was still playing for the Sunday League team, and I'd also agreed with Shrewsbury but hadn't put ink to paper.

The reaction from the Shrewsbury representatives was ferocious, once they'd learnt I'd decided to sign for Wrexham, following an offer from Ken Roberts. Fuming would be an understatement. But, in all honesty, Wrexham showed a greater desire for me than any other club, and more than that, I was loving being with the Wrexham lads, some of them were Welsh schoolboys, so I was learning and developing something new every single day. Flippantly, I gave another reason to Shrewsbury – that Wrexham was closer to home and that I'd be able to be home sooner every day (though logistically, after an evening match, there wouldn't be any transport to ferry me home any time sooner). And I kind of knew they wouldn't buy this – but I couldn't care less – I was happy at Wrexham. And I'd made a mate for life in Andy 'Ted' Edwards.

We were a pair of daft bastards when we were together, me and Ted. He's got a heart of pure gold that fella, but he's an absolute fuckin' nutcase (in the nicest possible way, and maybe that's the reason we hit it off so well – two peas in a pod). Only we were both vying to claim the same position, and quite often we'd both be sacrificed for one another. And I think it's a great testament to our friendship that not once did we ever have a cross word. If I'd played well or scored, he'd be the first to congratulate me, and vice versa – especially when he scored an absolute belter from around 35, possibly 40, yards away to Newport.

Unfortunately, his wonder goal was overshadowed by an incident in the changing room, when around 14 grown men are standing on top of the benches, screaming our fuckin' heads off because of a mouse running around in circles! There was not one foot on the floor until that mouse fucked off out through the door. Crackin' goal that, SuperTed lad. Shame you were upstaged by a little mouse!

With my new-found mates and confidence running high, I'd started on fire at The Racecourse. Doing the chores during the day, having a bit of a laugh and getting up to mischief, as you do, then we (the apprentices) would train in the evening (mainly on the club car park) and always under the tuition and watchful eyes of George McGowan and Brian Prandle. George 'n' Brian were direct with their encouragement, and always ready to let you know if you'd step out of line. They were two amazing guys!

It wasn't all work and no play of though, 'n' I embraced all the elements of being an independent youth. House parties? Drinking in boozers? Driving a fast car? NOT ONE OF THOSE THINGS APPEALED TO ME! Well, OK, I did own a car – a Mini – but by no means was that thing fast! More on the car driving later, because I must confess to never liking alcohol, and our landlady was a strict dear old lady, and one that you most definitely would NOT like to cross.

Even though I was from the Wirral, and not that far from Wrexham, the distance still meant I had to stay in digs and was housed with a few other lads. It was, as you'd expected really, a nice but basic house, good food in the mornin', noon and night to be fair. But I'm not sure if it was the fact that I just hadn't settled or whatever, but I decided to have a look elsewhere. I'd heard off some of the other lads of another digs the club owned so went there to enquire, before I went back home to the Wirral for the weekend.

As I still hadn't passed my driving test, my dad drove me back to digs, and as we arrive, I recognise the car outside and I thought, 'What the fuck have I done now?' because it was the gaffer's car, Bobby Roberts. I get out the car and then notice a load of cardboard boxes on the lawn, full of my belongings. "What the fuckin' hell is going on here?" And before I could open the front door, the old landlady storms out and bashes my eardrum with a volley of how I'd hurt her feelings for enquiring about another digs! During the whole episode, I caught sight of Bobby Roberts, first-team gaffer, sat cosy on the armchair and reading a newspaper in the living room. It later transpired that the gaffer had temporarily moved into our digs while the club were sorting out permanent accommodation for him! The image of him watching me and my dad trying to pile a lawn full of boxes into the car is one of pure comedy gold. Gratefully, I was accepted into the new digs … Or I'd 've been fucked otherwise!

Eventually though, I passed my driving test and got myself a little Mini. Word soon got round the staff at the club I'd passed my test, and lo 'n' behold there were requests of me being the designated chauffeur to here, there 'n' everywhere. At first I declined, as I'd only just passed and didn't want to fuck it up. But then what can you do when the gaffer, Bobby Roberts, requests a favour?

"John!" He calls me over to him. "I believe you've passed you're driving test? Congratulations son! Now, would you do me a favour and take the training equipment in my car to Stansty, and I'll join you in a bit, OK son!"

Oh shit! I couldn't refuse the gaffer, so as ordered, I packed the boot and the back of his car with a sack of footballs, bibs, and training cones. "Phew, right, let's drive this fuckin' thing." It was only when I jumped into the driver's seat that I realised my worst nightmare – there were only two pedals – it was a fuckin' automatic! I didn't have a clue what to do, and just as the panic is settling in, I check to see if any of the lads have fucked off to Stansty, to save me from any embarrassment, but no such joy, there's still a posse of the lads mingling about. So I finally figure something out and gingerly drive towards the training ground, and I'm fuckin' shitting myself, before finally arriving at the car park, with all the lads seemingly waiting for me. I spot Bobby Roberts' parking space and edge in nicely – "Aah, job done" (I thought) then pressed the brake pedal – CRUNCH. "Oh shit." The car only stuttered forward and smashed into the wall with the gaffer's name plaque on it! I can still hear the sound of the impact to this day.

As for the alcohol, well, I absolutely hated the stuff and had no desire to drink it. That was until my 21st birthday, and a few of the lads wanted to make a celebration of it and organised a night on the town. In all honesty, I really didn't want to go, but I begrudgingly joined the lads and had a few drinks, before we all ended up in this nightclub with erotic dancers, or strippers, for entertainment.

However, as the night wore on, I just wanted to lie down and rest my weary head – which is exactly what I did – on the floor directly next to the performing stage. So as I'm minding my own business, and my hand is propping up my head to one side, an erotic performer comes on stage, literally right next to me, and starts strutting her stuff and starts removing her lingerie. So I just I tilted my head towards her, caught sight of her eyes and said to her, "You're old enough to be my mum!" Her soft eyes quickly changed to red hot flames ... she was fuming! And in a fit of rage she literally dragged me onto the stage like a naughty schoolboy and yanked my jeans down with so much force it revealed for all to see, to the sound of all the lads pissing themselves laughing. I've not had a drop of alcohol since!

Back on the field, Ted and myself had started to impress with the Wrexham A, B and the Reserves. And it was a good grounding for us. It hardened us. Especially when we played in the Wrexham Welsh National League. Oh bloody hell, we had some battles with the likes of Bala Town away on a cold, wet and blustery afternoon.

From the first minute, their little centre back let me know in no uncertain terms how he felt about me (not that I understood a bloody word he said), but the growl in his voice was enough. Indeed, so was the fact his studs liked the back of my heel, or his elbow fancied my head. So we get to halftime and I'm in the changing room trying to figure out what's the deal with this growly little fella. As by luck, we had a couple of lads who spoke fluent Welsh, one being Medwyn Evans.

"Fuckin' hell Med, any ideas how I can get this angry caveman off my case? Is there anything I can say politely to ask him just to tone it down a bit?"

"Yes, of course, just tell him – *Cau dy geg, y cwdyn bach blewog,*" he replied.

So, soon enough I got the chance to show off my Welsh lingo, after he'd dug me in the ribs going up for a header, so as I'm getting back up, I say to him politely, *"Cau dy geg, y cwdyn bach blewog!"* Well, it was like a red rag to a bull – he was fuming, frothing, and screaming something at me which indicated his displeasure at my comment. Adding to my misery, Captain Caveman was one of three brothers and all three were on the pitch playing! So, for the rest of the second half, they fuckin' battered me. I couldn't wait to get inside that changing room (for two reasons) – to escape the Three Amigos and also quiz Medwyn on what on earth I'd said to flip this angry little man.

So, once we're inside, I set out to find Medwyn, who smiled instantly. "Basically John, you've just told him to shut up, you small hairy ball bag!" Ha-hah-hah, hey, we had a good laugh about it, and I was just glad to shake them three brothers off my case ... or so I thought, because at Bala Town they had these communal showers to share between both teams, and who should be standing either side of me in the shower?

Fair play to them, the Three Amigos were good as gold, sharing a bit of banter with me, complimenting my play, and it also transpired they were all Wrexham fans and wished us well for the rest of the season. But that's how it was, and that's how it should be – what goes on on the field, stays on the field. And although the three of them loved to rough it up a bit, bloody hell they couldn't half play a bit as well. Talented but fiercely competitive. Which gave the likes of Ted, Steve Jones, Medwyn and myself a taste of what to expect in seniors football, aka the first team. Which we all hoped would arrive sometime in our career at Wrexham.

We rarely saw a first-teamer during our training nights, unless you were called up to train with them in the mornings. Our aspirations were to emulate and play in the Second Division (now Championship) for Wrexham. So to actually speak to, or receive advice from them was pure gold ... and that's exactly what happened during one of our 'knee-scraping' training sessions on the club car park.

It was the usual training regime of plenty of running, then five-a-side. Keep the ball – move it – finish it. Suddenly, the whole training ground came to a halt as Dixie McNeil had come to the ground in his car because, apparently, he'd forgotten something in the changing room. Training continues for about ten minutes, before George McGowan stops training, again.

"Right lads, Dixie's here, and he's willing to speak to you all. Let him know if you've got any questions about being a professional football player!"

At that moment, we were all ushered into the home changing room, and we all sat in a neat square with Dixie stood facing us with the warmest of smiles. One by one we were introduced to Dixie by George and Brian, and then fired a question to him. And one by one he'd answer honestly and encouragingly. Then it came to me, so I was introduced, then George goes:

"John, what's your question to Dixie?"

So I look at George and replied, "Well, I don't necessarily have a question," and then I look directly at Dixie and say, "But I will have your shirt one day!"

For a couple of seconds the whole room descended into an aghast silence ... before Dixie broke the ice with a wry smile and said, "I like a player with confidence, son, so good look to ya!" and then the suppressed laughter from the lads erupted around the room.

Probably the player that visited us most frequently was Joey Jones, aww God bless Joey lad. I loved Joey to bits – we all did. Great character, always wanted to know how we got on in the previous match, and never short of sharing priceless advice. Above and beyond though, apart from Ted, nobody came close to making me laugh as hard as what he did. And we all knew he loved our company as well. We knew he'd do anything for us if we showed his type of enthusiasm towards the club ... even sorting out the rats at The Racecourse.

So there we were, a few of us apprentices putting the finishing touches to cleaning the first-team football boots in the boot room, and Joey's popped in for a chat, and there's a bit of piss taking 'n' that, before you heard the most high-pitched blood-curdling squeal:

"AAAHHH FUUUCKINNN 'ELL!"

Then one of the first-year apprentices legs it towards us and screams, "There's a fuckin' rat in them bins down the corridor!"

So, as cool as you like, Joey takes control. "It's alright lad, sit yerself down – I'm gonna show you how to dispose of a rat – properly!"

Peeping from around the door, we watched Joey approach the bins as quiet as a mouse ... before launching a ferocious kick at the bins and, as he did, this rat fuckin' leaps in the air, and as soon as it lands, starts scampering towards Joey, who's flying down the corridor, heading towards the exit screaming his fuckin' head off with this angry bastard of a rat chasing after him! Joey returned a short while later, and we're still not sure of the whereabouts of the rat, but maybe he noticed Joey's tattoo and thought, "Nah, fuck that!"

But that was typical Joey of being in the moment. A great reader of a room, on and off the pitch. He knew when someone (or something) needed to be dealt with firmly, and if a situation required defusing ... like pummelling a stranger's car with snowballs.

To say it was freezing is putting it mildly, but oh my bloody days it was Baltic. So the gaffer decides that today's the day to improve the lads' fitness – by running up and down the hills of north Wales, albeit with about four inches of snow on the ground. I sadistically sniggered at the rest of the lads when he announced this, because I'd only popped in for a bit of physio following an injury. But Bobby just turns to me in his gruff Scottish accent, "Ahhh John, I think it will do you a world of good to get some fresh air too – you can jump in the car and meet the lads about halfway." And of course all the lads chime in with a chorus of approval to this ingenious idea. Bastards!

So I get to the halfway point up a mountain the locals call 'Land's End' or 'Panorama', and help lay out a few cones up this track for the lads to follow. But when I returned back to the car, I noticed there's another car, partially hidden by hedges and shrubs. It looked unoccupied so I didn't bother checking it out because soon enough the lads filtered past during their gruelling running session. Some of them stopped briefly for a chat and to take in some fluids, including Joey.

"'Who's that over there?" he nods towards the unoccupied car, to which I confirmed that it looked empty.

"You sure about that – 'cos it's fuckin' shakin'!"

So Joey takes a few steps closer, before suddenly retreating and announced, "There's someone shagging in there!"

Within a few seconds, Joey's pummelling snowballs at the unsuspecting amorous couple, and then scarpers off to join the lads, leaving me red-faced and stranded!

Ooohh my fuckin' days, I've never felt so isolated in all my life, because there was no way I was prepared to stay and watch this live sex show, and there was no chance I had the physical capacity to trudge up this arduous track. So there was only one thing for it – walk back down and hope Georgie Showell would offer me a lift back in the car that he'd just taken off in. And after about a mile or so it dawned upon me that maybe Georgie wouldn't be returning along this road, and to heighten my uncertainty it began getting darker and I suspected I could be lost. I was shitting myself senseless. And just as I was wondering if this is where I was gonna perish, I started hearing a faint thudding sound, and heavy breathing. "Crikey! Are them two randy bastards at it again?" Then to my sheer relief, I recognised the voices of the lads – bloody hell – I've never been so glad to see the sight of a large group of sweaty grown men in my entire life! "Alright John lad – wanna lift!?"

Making yourself noticed is one thing, but BEING noticed is another. Talk ON the pitch – keep a low profile OFF it. So when I'd started being nominated for the Young Player of the Month award on a frequent basis, I did begin to wonder, "Am I getting closer to a call up to the first team?" Although I can't imagine how many of the other apprentices were envious of my 'award' – a fuckin' turkey! To this day, whenever we have a get-together with each other, as we're browsing through the food menu, someone (usually Ted or Stu Parker) will shout out, "Anyone fancy a turkey? Cos John's got fuckin' loads in his freezer!"

All that hard work and sacrifices with the apprenticeship, the reserves or A and B sides, started to show a bit of fruition, and I got selected more often for the first team. I finally made my debut away at Preston North End on 28th September 1982, as a skinny 17 year old. We lost 0–3, and I thought, "That's it, my chance has gone." But fair play to Bobby Roberts, he stuck with me, because a few days later we played Bournemouth at The Racecourse, and I scored the only goal of the game for us to win 1–0, after I'd come on as a sub as early as the 29th minute. I scored four minutes after coming on! My winning goal wasn't the only 'introduction' that day, as I was treated to a 'welcome pack' from our captain, Jake King.

I was sat on the changing room toilet when I received my first gift. I'm about to start wiping my arse and I feel something land on my thigh ... it's a toilet paper with shit on it. "Welcome to the first team, John!" exclaimed Jake! My final greeting arrived after the match. While I'm taking a shower (and the showers weren't that warm at The Racecourse), I feel a warm sensation (on both my legs). "Welcome to the first team, John!" both Jake King and Jackie Keay proudly announce as they're pissing on me! Oh, that's very kind of you, cheers lads!

There might've only been just been over 2,000 at The Racecourse for my home debut, but for me it might as well have been 200,000 ... ooohh what a feeling! There's no better place than The Racecourse when them passionate fans are in full voice. You actually can't hear yourself blink never mind think. The flipside, though, is when that passion turns into frustration, which in all honesty I could more than understand – the club they love and adore is financially insecure, and is sliding down the leagues quicker than one of my turkeys on a baking tray.

And so, on the odd occasion (especially if Bobby had decided to play me on the right wing, and there was a sparse attendance at The Racecourse) when I'd be somewhere along the Mold Road paddock, I could hear someone fart, never mind shouting at me. Most of it I ignored, but some of the comments were absolute genius stuff – fuckin' hilarious.

For instance, there was one game where I'd taken the ball down the wing, crossed it in, only for a defender to clear it. But as I'm jogging back into position, I can hear this voice desperately trying to get my attention, and I try not to make eye contact, but still this voice is persistent.

"Oi – Muldoon – MULDOON. Oi! You couldn't cross yer

feckin' legs. D'YOU HEAR ME? YOU COULDN'T CROSS YER FECKIN' LEGS!"

Well, I tell ya what, I didn't know whether to laugh or be offended, but what a fuckin' line though, ey?! At least the crowd around him gave him a chuckle.

But the people of north Wales know their football and they are THE REASON why this football club exists, purely out of pride, belief, and their unconditional love for the club, regardless of who wears the shirt – like Joey always reminded us lads – whenever you wear that shirt, you better be prepared to make sure there's fuckin' gallons of your sweat on it. Ooohhh, wow, what a special guy, and what a special place!

And there's no place like it on those glorious European nights. The Racecourse is literally rocking to the crackling of the acoustics generated by the Wrexham faithful. It truly is a special occasion when the towering floodlights are glistening off the turf and red shirts. So imagine my excitement as a 19 year old preparing to welcome the mighty FC Porto in September 1984. However, my own personal excitement turned into bitter disappointment. Initially anyway.

As with all European Cup rules, the visiting club have access to train at the home club's stadium the night before the match. So, along with all the rest of the staff in the stand, I watched in amazement at the pure class the Porto players displayed in front of us. It was like watching Brazil training in Portuguese shirts. It wasn't spying from our point of view – it was permitted. And it also whetted the appetite. It definitely gave us a clear indication that if we weren't going to be at our best – we were gonna get fuckin' slaughtered! But on the other hand, if we stuck together, anything could happen, and we could all become heroes. I couldn't wait to get to the ground the next day and be a part of this prestigious occasion.

It was slow torture whiling the day, but finally I got to

The Racecourse that evening, and already there was a buzz around the place. Then BOOM! My heart sunk ... Bobby Roberts has just named the team, and Mike Williams was chosen ahead of me, therefore relegating me to the subs bench. Bloody hell, I'm absolutely fuming, and I just couldn't comprehend his decision. "What the fuckin' hell's goin' on 'ere then?"

I tried my best not to show it, but I was fumin', so the best answer I could think of was, "I'll fuckin' show you, yer bastard!" So if I was gonna get my chance, I was gonna show the gaffer that he's made a huge mistake.

As it turned out, it was a classic match – it had everything from chances for both sides, great saves from Stu Parker, shots hitting the bar ... but, it somehow remained 0–0. And the longer the clock ticked, the angrier I was getting. It gets to the 73rd minute, and the gaffer turns to me and says, "John! Get yourself up 'n' get warmed up – you're going on in two minutes!" – and I'm thinking, "Right, this is my chance", and I put one foot out of the dugout, and stood up ready to warm up, when this fella from the paddock behind the dugout shouts:

"MULDOON, YOU'RE FUCKIN' SHIT!"

"Oh," I thought. "Thank you very bloody much." But, not long after I'd come on, I had the last laugh.

I'd always had a good understanding with Big Jim Steel – if he ever received the ball from deep, all he had to do was release me down the wing with his second touch ... and on this magical evening it worked a treat. He's chested the ball down majestically with his first touch and then hooked it out wide for me to run on to, and float one in for him to nod it in with his head to send everyone into a rapturous applause! But something clicked inside me, and although I was ecstatic with our goal, I was still pissed off for being a sub, so immediately after Jim scores, everyone congregates to celebrate, and we're all there jumping up and down with

Jim, and just as he's about to turn around to thank me for the cross ... I just fucked off.

The switch had gone off in my head again, and I was so flaming MAD with the gaffer. As soon as the final whistle was blown, and all the lads and staff are on the pitch celebrating, I've stormed into the showers! By the time they got back into the changing room I'd already fucked off home. Without a doubt I was absolutely ecstatic with the result, but as a young footballer, aged just 19, these are the games you want to be involved in, and I was beyond hurt. In a way, I hope it shows how much I cared and how much I wanted to show exactly what I could do.

I believed that I belonged in the starting line-up, I hoped my two assists away at Porto in the European Cup Winners' Cup was proof. And although we narrowly lost to another famous European side, Italian giants AS Roma, I will eternally be proud of the fact that we gave some much-needed pride back into Wrexham and north Wales, and put them back on the world map, where they truly belong.

From a personal point of view, I will forever count my blessings of playing for Wrexham, because they fulfilled my dreams of playing professional football ... and I couldn't have been happier plying my trade anywhere else other than The Racecourse, because there's no place like home.

3
Andrew Dibble
Goalkeeper

An Indian summer for Chief Dibble
2002–2005 (90 appearances)

It seems Andrew Dibble has always been a bit of a thinking man. While entering the autumn of his career, Andy began contemplating life changes: Swapping keeper gloves for gardening gloves; Wearing zip-up tartan slippers instead of football boots; Or, having a cheeky nap in front of the box rather than diving in the penalty box. And although still relatively young for a goalkeeper, at 37, Andrew was uncertain where the next challenge lay. Or whether 'The Sitting Bull' had enough armour for another season. That was until Wrexham AFC manager Dennis Smith sent him a smoke signal for an Indian summer.

"SHIT! ... WHERE the bloody hell do I go from here?" – that was the daunting thought I had when my contract expired, and wouldn't be renewed, at the end of the 2001–02 season with Stockport County. Yeah, I'd flirted with the idea of coaching but hadn't set a foot on the first rung of the coaching ladder. Spring was a fraught period for us. Until, one evening, my phone rang. I didn't recognise the number, and usually I'd just ignore it. On this occasion I'm glad I didn't: "Hi Andrew, it's Dennis Smith, manager of Wrexham Football Club. I hope you don't mind me contacting you directly, but I prefer to speak with my players personally rather than through their agents."

I was immediately drawn to the person on the other side of the phone. We arranged to meet the following morning for a chat and a cuppa at a service station. I knew from the off that I was gonna sign. Not just for my career. But for Dennis Smith and Wrexham. His pitch was a cross between Martin Luther King and Alan Sugar!

"I want to create a team full of leaders and entertainers to push for promotion. YOU'RE A LEADER! You'll absolutely adore the fans and The Racecourse."

He needn't say another word. It was love at first sight. I fell in love with the gaffer and Wrexham. I was bought! Apart from the brew ... I paid for that pot myself!

"Read the room." That's the advice we're all given isn't it? Well, let me tell you this – that dressing room I shared with my teammates at Wrexham was the bloody best-seller of a book that I've ever read. It was jam-packed with characters: We had the eager youth players like Craig Morgan and Mark Jones. It had quirky lads like Jim Whitley, Hector and Carlos; banter merchants in the form of Trunds and Mozza. In that mix were the leaders – myself, Scary Carey, Fergie, Dennis Lawrence. But essentially, it was also a squad brimming with top pros like Lee Jones, Shaun Holmes, Stephen Roberts, and yer Paul Edwards. Not to mention the galvanising influence of the gaffer, and his assistant Kev Russell.

Wrexham wasn't the only club I joined that summer. I also became a member of the J10 club, named after 'Junction 10' on the M53 near Cheshire. You'll be relieved to hear it wasn't a hooligan firm! Quite the opposite – it was a group of Wrexham players forming a car share to training and home matches. I lived in Wilmslow and on a daily basis would share a car, as well as banter, with Paul Edwards, Captain Darren Ferguson, Brian Carey, and Paul Barrett. We all had our various tastes in music. We were NEVER late. We were ALWAYS early. I mean, would you like to get on the wrong side of Scarey Carey? Or feel the wrath of a tongue-lashing from Fiery Fergie? Bearing in mind his strong Scottish accent left us occasionally bemused and confused! But he was an astounding player and leader for us, and his qualities led the way of the expectations required.

A football match is never won before a ball is kicked, let alone achieving a successful campaign. But in the fourth match of the season, on a baking hot afternoon against Boston United, I was strapping on my gloves and had this overriding sense of invincibility. Not just myself, but collectively as a group. Even though we drew 1–1, I knew we could achieve something special. I knew I was part of a special bond. A bond that existed on and off the field.

I can't emphasise enough the amount of time you spend with each other as a team. As well as training and matchdays, you'll spend a good chunk of your time together travelling on a coach to and from an away match. Sharing a couple of cans of beer and chomping on fish'n'chips on our way back to Wrexham, we'd not only evaluate the match, but it's where we'd conjure up our next team bonding session. So it's just as well we got on with each other, otherwise them long journeys would've been a bloody nightmare.

Evidently, they were more than just a bonding session to

us lads because, truthfully, we didn't need to be forcefully bonded. We just loved each other's company ... albeit even better with a beer or ten. Whether it be to celebrate a birthday, a birth of a child, or a Christmas party, but most of the time we didn't need an occasion – it was just off the cuff. And believe me, they were the best sessions.

We were only meant to have a few jars one afternoon. We were all there apart from the gaffer. One by one, we went round the pubs in Wrexham. Day turned into night. Our group expanded into a crowd, as fans joined us. Including Wrexham superfan, Nigel, who was no stranger to our get-togethers. Anyway, we eventually ended up in a nightclub, where we threw some weird shapes, as well as more beers down us. But someone suddenly alerted us that Nigel was in a spot of bother on his way to the gents' toilets. If being in a wheelchair isn't challenging enough, being in a wheelchair and pissed up to the eyeballs is another level ... and poor old Nigel didn't make it to the toilet in time. So Kev Russell and myself thought we'd save him the indignity and carry him out of the club ... whilst still strapped in his wheelchair. It was like a scene from a *Carry On* film ... we slipped, we tripped and we eventually fumbled our way out of the nightclub, and during the whole comedy routine Nigel literally pissed himself laughing! Anything for Wrexham's No.1 fan, eh Nige!

Those great times off the field were more than matched on it, as we challenged for promotion. And bugger me there were some belting matches. Believe it or not, but we actually fancied our chances in a League Cup match versus Premier League Everton at The Racecourse, and for long periods we held our own ... until some unknown upstart called Wayne Rooney came off the bench for Everton and destroyed us ... whatever became of him I wonder? And who can forget the scenes at derby rivals Shrewsbury Town towards the end of the season – if you thought the noise levels from the Wrexham fans were loud, you should've heard us in the changing room and on the coach afterwards – deafening decibels. Shame Wrexham isn't that far from Shrewsbury because we didn't have much time to savour the bouncing beers on the journey home ... and the bloody chippy was shut. At least we could still taste the sweet flavour of three points. Yum! Please sir, can I have some more?!

Our very own Fagin (Gaffer) ensured we were fed a balanced diet of three points as we marched towards promotion following a masterclass performance at The Racecourse to beat Cambridge United 5–0, and secure an instant return to League One. There were times during that match I caught myself muttering "Fucking hell, this is class" as we totally destroyed a more than decent Cambridge side. The best, in my opinion, was yet to come, as a couple of weeks later we were away at Bury for the final match of the season.

That match ranks as one of the highest in my career. And for as long as I live, I will never forget that warm, special feeling as we headed towards the final whistle, 3–0 up, thousands of our fans singing and dancing, and the lads – my comrades, my friends, my teammates – playing the kind of football you'd do with yer mates at the park with a smile on their faces. Hell, we could've kept on going until they decided to switch the damn floodlights off! But, on a personal level, I was celebrating my 38th birthday the following day, and what a way to celebrate it! I had a huge party at my gaff, and everyone from the club was there ... I'm pretty sure some of the club's cleaners turned up as well ... but what a day! I didn't need any gifts – the gaffer gave me that almost 12 months previous, a priceless gift that just keeps on giving, in the name of Wrexham AFC.

4
Ian Edwards
Forward

I can't explain a fox as mad as a sprout
1979–1982 (98 appearances, 28 goals)

I should've known I was chatting with a former milkman when he suggested we had our chat early the next morning. Within a few minutes, Ian Edwards had me feeling like the cat that got the cream, with his priceless anecdotes from his life as a centre forward for Wrexham Football Club in the old Second Division. Now a hotelier in sunny Criccieth, straight-talking Ian delivers a sharp-witted account of his daily battles with a crippling knee injury. Ian also tells us about a wise old owl, a horse called Nijinsky, a nutty fox, and Joey! As TripAdvisor ratings go, this one's a five-star!

Ian Edwards

I SIGNED FOR Wrexham on the 1st of November 1979, when they were in the old Second Division, the Championship nowadays, for £125,000. Just a couple of days later I made my debut in front of over 20,000 at West Ham, where we lost 1–0 to a Geoff Pike goal. It was a cracking Wrexham squad: Dai Davies, Alan Hill, Alan Dwyer, Gareth Davies, Joey Jones, David Giles, Stevie Fox, Dixie McNeil, Steve Buxton, and Arfon Griffiths.

The previous day, I was introduced to all the staff at The Racecourse, including the mucky buggers in the boot room! And that's when Andy Edwards was tasked with cleaning my boots. Good lad, Andy. Typical lad from the Wrexham area – he had a bit of an edge to him. He was always polite towards me and the rest of the first pros though, but that soon changed once he laced his boots 'cos he didn't mind putting it about during training if he was ever called over to join in with the first team. Joey loved him because he was hard as nails. I always tried to give him a good tip for Christmas ... though I think the best tip should've been on how to clean a pair of football boots properly (rather than tipping him with a bit of cash!). I used to have a joke 'n' a laugh an' tell him he left my boots too slippy and that's why I couldn't bloody shoot straight – there was still a load of mud on them from the previous match!

It was a bit of a dream come true signing for the club that I supported as a young boy. I used to love going to the Tech End with my family or my mates. The roof was only partially covered in the Tech End, but we didn't care, because it was a great atmosphere there. And the move from Chester meant we'd move closer to our families, and we bought a house in Cymau, which suited us no end as a family. My wife at that time had a shorter commute to her work at Iceland food shop, and in my brand-new Ford Capri, or Vauxhall Cavalier XRI, I had a short journey to training at Stansty and also The Racecourse. Cymau was a great little place to live, and we quickly got friendly with the locals, especially the likes of Ray Jones, at the local pub, The Talbot. Ray played a big part in Cymau Football Club – he was the epicentre of the place 'n' he was 'Mr Cymau' 'cos he thought the world of the place.

In all honesty, I'd never really recovered from a serious knee injury playing for Chester City against Rotherham United – so this goalkeeper came flying out, even though he had absolutely no chance of getting to the ball before me, and I was standing on my left leg when he hit it, which caused it to bend backwards. Well bugger me, he didn't even get a yellow card! A slight consolation from the incident was that I managed to get to the ball before him and scored! So not even a scathing tackle from him prevented me from getting one past him. He looked even more pissed off when I continued to play until halftime ... maybe he was scared I'd stick another one past him! But the injury caused me to have around six knee operations during my career, including three big operations where the surgeons cut down the side of my leg, leaving a four-inch gap. This led to me having arthritis later on.

Even at Wrexham I couldn't train full time because my knee would swell up. So my weekly routine was as basic as having a good rest after games, light gym work 'n' then join in with the rest of the lads before breathing through my backside at the end of a game! Although you wouldn't have guessed it! When we pounded up and down them bloody sand dunes in Aberystwyth, I was like a bloody lizard zooming around with sand spraying everywhere!

I absolutely loved going there for pre-season 'cos it was always a good craic, and a great chance of getting to know some of the new faces in the squad. I think the club must've been a bit slow in booking a proper a hotel 'cos we always stayed in student accommodation that was situated about a bloody mile up this hill! Dear me, it was a bloody nightmare after a hard day's trainin' and a belly full of beers ... We'd be absolutely exhausted! Then the following day we'd train at the Aberystwyth sports ground, before jumping on the bus to play Bangor in a friendly, and in the process we'd get battered because we were well and truly bloody knackered.

But that knee injury wasn't the only severe injury I sustained during my career. Whilst I was at Crystal Palace against Leeds United, I went up for a header, and I accidently headed the back of Gwyn Thomas's head just as we went up to challenge their centre half, Kenny Burns. He'd been a bit naughty with me all through the first half, kicking me all over the bloody place. *Iesu mawr*, you should've seen the state of my face – my eye and cheekbone were such a real mess, my eye dropped down, and would you bloody believe it, they made me play until halftime! It was ridiculous! 'Cos not only was I in sheer agony, but I was wandering around like a blind man on a galloping horse 'n' at one point I went up to clear the ball from a corner and I honestly thought my eye had dropped out! Ha-hah-hah, I was on my hands 'n' knees scrambling around along the grass looking for my eye!

Ha-hah-hah, unbelievably, my teammates and the physio were asking me if I could play the second half, and I just warbled, "Igshkyotidkhckhc," which was meant to say, "I don't bloody think so!" A few minutes later I was on my way to hospital, where I later received facial surgery. This entailed drilling into the side of my head to lift my eye back into its place. Anyway, my wife at the time travelled to see me along with a couple of the lads. So she walks in, sees the state of my face 'n' she burst into tears! But then one of the lads said, "Don't worry – she cries most mornings after seeing your face!" Cheeky so 'n' so!

Eventually, you do get absolutely fed up of getting a relapse and being in constant pain. The supporters are unaware and can't understand why you're not producing the goods and, maybe rightly so, they might get a bit disgruntled because they've paid good money to watch a good standard of football. But, in reality, all they're watching is a few cart horses trotting around trying to play football. The truth is, though, these footballers are playing through the pain barrier after taking a load of injections just to help the team and get paid.

And don't get me started on the standard of refereeing, 'cos back in them days a defender could've walked on the pitch and shot me in the knee with a rifle 'n' he'd have only got a bloody warning from the ref! *Duuuw*, some of the tackling goin' on was absolutely scandalous. People always go on about some of Joey's tackling? Well listen, Joey went for the ball first ... most of the time anyway.

Pushing the injuries aside, Arfon must've had a lot of faith in me when I first signed 'cos I failed the initial medical. I didn't get much time getting to know the Wrexham squad before my debut at West Ham. Although, it helped that I knew a few from my time being involved with the Wales international team. Especially Joey, 'cos we'd played against each other at youth level, representing our counties – he played for Caernarfonshire, and I played for Flintshire. Both of us were in midfield back then. As I've previously said, Joey lived and breathed for tackling. I got my kicks from scoring – he had his kicks from ... well, kicking players! If you were lucky, he'd occasionally get the ball first!

And during this youth county match, he's gone in on me so hard, his studs ripped through my sock and sent my shinpad flying about ten feet in the air 'n' about ten yards out of the touchline! So immediately I looked down thinking he'd broke my leg, but somehow my sock's still on my leg with a bloody big hole in it! I turned round and looked at Joey, then quickly turned away, 'cos the look on his face was even scarier than the tackle! Top, top lad Joey, and I know he won't mind me saying this, but he was a dirty so-and-so! Ha-hah-hah, he'll bloody love that I've said that.

Back to the Wrexham squad and, good grief, it was swarming in talent. Arfon was the type that always looked to excite the Wrexham fans with attacking players – even the defenders were encouraged to join in the attacks and chip in with a few goals. Just look at that midfield we had – Les Cartwright was a terrific midfielder that knew exactly what type of cross to supply at exactly the precise moment. Frank Carrodus could run so much during a match he'd wear out the opposition ... and in the meantime he heralded the nickname Nijinsky, after the famous Canadian-born and Irish-trained racehorse – he was one helluva 'n athlete.

Graham Whittle and Alan Dwyer were two great players, but they were more unfortunate than me with injuries 'n' we hardly ever saw them. Such a shame. Graham had an unbelievable strike on him and could score anywhere from 30 yards. But because of his dodgy knees he couldn't even run to get 30 yards from goal. A very funny lad 'n' a typical Scouse humour. And Dixie McNeil ... well, what can I say about Dixie? I think if it wasn't for his knackered knees, he'd still be scoring goals for Wrexham now, because he didn't need speed – his vision was razor sharp 'n' he had this astonishing knack of knowing where to be. Honestly, I swear he had the neck of an owl as he was able to swivel his head 360 degrees and knew precisely where everyone was. So it was just as well Arfon brought me in to be the battering ram and do all the running for him, the lazy bugger! Ha-hah-ha, he'll have a good chuckle at that will Dixie.

Another lad with a great engine was Mel Sutton. Nearing towards the end of his career, Mel was still as fit as a greyhound. But oh, *Iesu mawr*, he could still scream like a town crier! Oh good grief, I still have nightmares of him screaming my name just before he'd knock the ball down the line – "IIIIAAANNN" – expecting me to be on the right wing as if I was waiting for a bus! Running the channels wasn't exactly my game – I preferred to get the ball to my feet from around 20 yards, not

50 yards! Mel also took the training with Arfon, and Mickey Evans. It was never anything complicated 'n' we hardly did much working on set-pieces. Basically, it was about keeping the lads in shape and preparing for the next match. They'd always tell us to be conscious of silly tackles in training. Well … that must've got lost in translation by the time it reached Joey's ears, so, I just tried to make sure I was in his team.

Throughout my time at Wrexham, I picked up on the fact that I didn't think either Arfon or Mel wanted to be a manager, and they were more or less forced into the hot seat. Because, in all honesty, there was nothing flashy or brash about them 'n' they were just two nice fellas. I think, had it not been for Wrexham, they wouldn't have entertained the idea of managing.

As with most clubs there were curfews on which nights you weren't allowed out for a few drinks, 'n' there'd be consequences if you did. By and large, I tried to look after my health to the best I could. I wasn't one for eating rubbish or eating at the wrong time – I was very conscientious like that … but then on the odd occasion I'd be led astray by rascals like Joey! The usual routine of playing a team down the south of England was driving to Crewe railway station in our own cars, catching the train to the nearest station to the ground, then getting a taxi or bus to the ground if we had to. And that was the routine for this particular Saturday game away to Leyton Orient. We lost 1–2, and on the train going back to Crewe, Arfon was obviously a little bit pissed-off and announced that we weren't allowed to go out that night. "Straight home!"

Just after seven o'clock in the evening, we arrived back at Crewe railway station. A few of us were a bit thirsty and fancied a quick couple of pints before going home. Unfortunately for Arfon, but luckily for us, there were a few nice little pubs between Crewe and Wrexham. We already knew Mel and Arfon shared a car, and without making it too obvious, we waited for them to disappear from the railway station car park before we went on our way to the nearest pub. Well, we arrived at the nearest pub and parked in the car park opposite the road. And just as we were crossing the road, a car comes flying towards us and nearly knocks us all down like skittles ... it was Arfon and Mel in the car! Ah well, "Sod it," we thought 'n' we carried on into the pub and had our couple of pints.

Arfon wasn't one for screaming in someone's face. That wasn't his thing – he had a bit of decorum about him. But that's not to say he wasn't an easy touch, either – he could be bloody ruthless! For instance, we were due to play Wolverhampton Wanderers away in the fifth round of the FA Cup, 14th of February 1981. So, very early on that morning of the game, Arfon decided to give me a fitness test before we got on the coach, because of a niggling groin strain I had. It felt OK and Arfon was happy for me to start. Anyway, Stevie Fox gave us a 1–0 lead in the 29th minute, and it was a case of holding on to the lead and seeing out the pressure from the home side. But eventually they scored two goals in quick succession late in the second half 'n' for some reason, which I found unfathomable, Arfon decided to take me off in the 76th minute. Well, I was fuming! So I stormed past the dugout, headed straight into the changing room, and I'd got showered and left the ground with my friends and family.

Monday morning, I get a message – Arfon wants to see me in his office. So I marched to his office 'n' take a seat.

"Right then Ian," he goes. "I'm fining you a week's wages."

"A WEEK'S WAGES?" I squeal. "What the hell for?"

"For your actions after being taken off on Saturday – you didn't come back on the team bus and you hadn't informed me!"

"Yea, well, I just didn't see the point Arfon – we were

losing 2–1 'n' I didn't see the logic of taking a striker off when we're chasing after an equaliser."

"Look Ian, there's been better players than you been taken off in football," he reasoned.

"Oh aye! And I bet they didn't like it either!"

Arfon didn't fine me.

So between the two, neither Arfon nor Mel were especially vocal in the changing room. But, mind you, they didn't need to be – we had Joey going around the room shouting and yelling and then, as we went out to start the match, he'd go towards the crowd and shake his fist as if he's got an opponent's heart in it, like a cat bringing home a rat it'd just caught. But it wasn't in my personality to engage closely or get too intimate with the fans. That's not to say I didn't appreciate their fantastic support or dismiss their value – on the contrary – but mainly because I was perhaps a little bit more introverted being face-to-face in front of a crowd of people ... which may sound a bit strange coming from an ex-footballer who played in front of thousands of fans each week.

I couldn't even bring myself to acknowledge my own family when they were in the stand watching 'cos I just wanted to focus on the game and keep my eyes firmly on the players around me. So I just preferred to get my head down, work my backside off, and hopefully chip in with a goal or two. However, saying that, there would've been a brief interaction with the fans, especially in the Yale paddock, because just as we'd be about to kick off, I'd spit my chewing gum in the air and volley it ... quite often it would land in the Yale paddock and on top of someone's head! I thought it might be useful as a souvenir?

My character wouldn't alter much even after I scored – and although I was obviously delighted, I'd simply (and perhaps majestically) just raise one arm and one finger up and jog back to the halfway line for the restart. This could've been perceived as being aloof, but far from it 'cos I was basically conserving my energy to score more goals. Hey, I always say Alan Shearer copied my cool goal celebration ... just that he performed it about 300 times more than what I did! I honestly don't know where some of these footballers have the energy to sprint around, slide on their knees, or do a bloody cartwheel. That would've finished off my knees if I'd have tried to attempt anything of the sort!

Which is why I chose the nonchalant salute after the goal I scored away at Derby County, September 1980. And had the *Match of the Day* cameras been at Newtown a few nights previously, they'd have caught me scoring an even better volley with my left foot! We were there as guests to celebrate the official opening of their newly-erected floodlights, and during the game a cross was floated perfectly towards me, so I just let fly with a volley so powerful – I was more concerned I'd ripped a hole in the net, than admiring the goal!

So, you could say I kinda practised the volley I walloped past Roger Jones, the Derby custodian ... only this time with my right foot. One of the first faces I saw after I scored was Joey's 'n' before I got mobbed by my other teammates, I simply did 'the Joey' and shook my clenched right fist and continued to jog towards the halfway line. *Duuuww*, I felt like an international superstar with all the lads jumping on top of me! The goal came at a good time as well, as we'd been under the cosh for most of the second half, and it gave us a slender 1–0 lead to battle it out and cling on to a hard-fought away win against a good Derby County side. And even though I'm still proud that the goal was voted Goal of the Month by the *MOTD* viewers, the result meant a greater deal to me. But that smile on Joey's face ... well, I much preferred his infectious smile compared to his snarling growl anyway!

And I should've known he was up to something as soon as we got back into the changing room at Derby. So everyone's congratulating me on the goal, then Joey pipes up.

"Aye, great goal that, Eddie! Just a shame you were trying to trap the ball and it's ricocheted into the top corner!" ... and the whole bloody changing rooms erupts with howls of laughter. So, in fact, Joey wasn't just quick with his feet – his quick-witted mind was even faster! And the bugger got me good again away at Queens Park Rangers, January 1982.

A couple of weeks before the match at Loftus Road, I fractured my scaphoid (a tiny piece of bone in the wrist) and had to wear a protective bright pink cast over it that allowed me to carry on playing.

Just before the match, the referee, Mr A. Grey, came into our changing room and did the usual routine of checking the players' studs (in case the likes of Joey hadn't sharpened his!) and removing jewellery. Then he noticed my cast.

"Hmmmm, yeah, I'm not sure I like the look of that, Ian! I think we're gonna have to consult with the manager of the home side to see if he's happy for you to play."

"Well bloody hell, man," I snapped. "No one's complained about it in the last few matches, so what difference will it make today?" I pleaded.

"Well, if you wouldn't mind Ian, I'd still like to consult the home team manager," he replied quite sharpish before ushering myself and Mel Sutton, our manager, into a little room.

A few minutes later, Terry Venables, the QPR manager, walks in with the referee.

"Awight Ian! Right, let's 'av a look at this cast then." He takes about two seconds to look at it, 'n' says, "Gordon Bennett, Mr Grey! Is that it? Bleedin' 'ell, you were makin' out he had a machete hidden there! Cor blimey! Yeah, don't worry Ian, I've got absolutely naa problems wiv you playin' today, son."

We all shook hands and headed back to our changing rooms. It didn't take long for the news of my eligibility to play reaches all the lads, 'n' sure enough, Joey BOOMS in delight, "OH, EY UP LADS! Terry Venables WANTS our Eddie to play today! 'Cos apparently, he thinks his team's got a better chance of winning with Edwards playing for us! Ha-hah-hah!"

Well would you bloody believe it? Nineteen minutes into the match, me and my bright pink cast scored a goal to put us into a 1–0 lead. The sound of Joey's chuckle when he came over to congratulate me still tickles me, "Well done, Eddie lad – you can play for us again next week if you want?" The cheeky bugger! Anyway, we held on for a creditable draw after Simon Stainrod equalised in the 72nd minute. Yer know what? During the entire journey home, I'd have one of the lads pipe up, "So are you playing for us again next week, Eddie?" or "Ey up Mel, you better sign this blond striker for us, before Terry Venables does!"

But that camaraderie typified our togetherness as a squad. There was never any malicious ill-feeling towards each other and we enjoyed each other's company. Albeit, some would be closer or friendlier to other members of the squad, 'n' that's just life in general, isn't it? This was the case when it came to sharing a lift. Because of their commute from the Altrincham area, Stevie Dowman and Frank Carrodus would arrange to meet me for a few pints in Chester. Nothing too daft, just a few drinks and a quick shuffle on the dance floor 'n' I wasn't a patch on John Travolta 'cos my knees were too buggered for that malarkey!

Anyway, the other lads heard of our jollies at the 'upmarket' establishments of Chester 'n' next thing, there'd be a full squad of us going there. And to be fair, we weren't big drinkers getting pissed and causing mayhem … well most of us anyway.

The likes of Dixie still liked a quiet few in his local, just playing dominoes all night. But, occasionally, he'd join Micky Vinter, Joey and myself for a couple at The Turf after we'd returned from an away game. *Duuuwww*, there was hardly a soul in the place! Not unless Stevie Fox and David Giles had already been in and scared people away with their antics.

Ho-ho-ho-ho, what a lovely fella Stevie Fox was! Helluva friendly soul, but as mad as a bloody sprout! Lord knows who had the bright idea of pairing him up with David Giles to stay at the Crest Hotel – now the Wynnstay – in the middle of Wrexham town centre. However, he quickly had to find permanent accommodation after the club received a huge bill to pay at the hotel 'cos the daft pair had fired shots from an air rifle at pictures they'd hung on the wall as targets! So, it's just as well they could back it up with their football, especially Stevie.

And with no disrespect to Wrexham, but Stevie belonged at a First Division club. He was bloody sensational at training, and during a match. I hated trying to keep up with him 'cos both his feet and legs were frighteningly fast, and he had this frightening ability to trick his way out of a tight space before flying down the wing 'n' cross a beautiful ball in the middle! In fact, he was so fast, I'd still be on the edge of the D busting a gut to catch up with him! Then I'd shout over to him, "BlOODY 'ELL FOXY!! SLOW DOWN, MAN!" and in his native Brummie tone, he'd look back at me with a smile, "Well yaw shouldn't mawve from tha penalty spot – yaw naw oim qwicker than yaw." Then the little bugger would just jog back to position with his shoulders jiggling with laughter while takin' the plaudits from the Mold Road giving him a standing ovation!

And deservedly so, 'cos Stevie was a wizard with them feet 'n' they could've bamboozled Harry Houdini! Well, hey! Listen to this – they certainly bamboozled both of us during one game at home when the ball was going out of play. But I hadn't spotted Stevie travelling at the speed of light towards me 'n' he hadn't bloody seen me either – BASH! – like a pair of cymbals on a drum kit, we smashed into each other, right in front of the fans of the other team wetting themselves laughing, and Stevie gets up and yells at me, "Wot d'yaw think yaw playing at yaw blwdi idiot?" – which I didn't take too kindly to.

So at halftime, to show him I wasn't happy, I gave a look towards Stevie, who's sat down supping on a drink, and I shook my head at him, "Yeah, I naw mait," he says. "Sorry abawt that – ai just didn't see yaw! Oh 'ey, av yaw got tickets to see The Who in Deeside Leisure Centre next month? Oiv got a couple spare if yaw fancy? D'yaw loic their music?" So the following month we both went with our partners and a few others to see The Who at Deeside Leisure Centre, and we had a bloody brilliant night. And that wasn't an attempt to butter me up from Stevie – it was just his kind manner. He was kind-hearted like that and such a loss when he died in 2012, God bless him.

I actually got to know Stevie a little more after he married the sister of a good friend of mine, Nigel Edwards, from the Acrefair area. And it was Nigel that announced their engagement to me.

"Alright Ian, how's things pal? Hey, you'll never guess what? My sister's marrying Stevie Fox!"

"Oh aye," I replied "Bloody good luck with that!"

Obviously it was tongue-in-cheek, but in all honesty, he was just crackers! Not an ounce of malice in him though, just a lovely lad. But he also knew I was into my music, especially the likes of David Bowie, Free, Alex Harvey and Joan Armatrading. I went to see all of them in concerts and also it was how I liked to relax at home – place the needle carefully on the record and let it blast of out the speakers. There was nothing like it during the cold winter months in north Wales.

I must've gone through my expansive record collection during that bleak period when we didn't play a single match from 5th December 1981 to 2nd January 1982, due to the avalanche of snow and ice dumped across the UK. I'd just scored twice when we beat Cambridge United 3–1 away on the 5th of December, and from then on for almost a whole month we couldn't train properly. Instead, we used the Plas Madoc Leisure Centre facilities at Acrefair to keep up with our fitness and play a bit of five-a-side. Then Mel got wind that Llandudno had seen hardly any snow or frost, so we stayed in this posh hotel. Well, this little 'palace' was full of elderly folk 'n' every evening they'd be entertained by this pianist. Anyway, one evening he's playing all the old classics 'n' serenading the old dears. Then, we bundled into the bar! So you can well imagine the capers we got up to with the crackerjacks we had in Foxie and Joey ... so some of them poor old dears twaddled up to their rooms within five bloody minutes!

There must've been something special in that sea air though, because it definitely made a difference when we visited a high-flying First Division Notts Forest, managed by the very successful Brian Clough, on 2nd of January 1982, for a third round FA Cup encounter. Initially, it should've been played the previous day – New Year's Day. But it got cancelled due to Arctic conditions, much to the annoyance of Frank Carrodus.

Living close to Manchester Airport, Frank got very friendly with a number of air hostesses, and sometimes for logistic reasons, if they couldn't meet up, they'd spend hours on the phone. So on this particular New Year's Eve, 1981, I was rooming with Frank in this hotel near Nottingham. And no kidding, the bill must've been extortionate, because they were on the phone all bloody night! And I'd be gesturing to him, "Will you put that damn phone down, 'cos I wanna get some sleep before our game tomorrow!" And finally he hangs up and says quite despondently, "Well, Eddie, I won't get to see or hear from her for another fortnight – she flies out tomorrow," he says with whimper. "Oh dear," I replied sarcastically, "switch yer light off, Frankie lad."

And guess what? The game was cancelled the next day – meaning he could've spent the night with his high-flying air hostess rather than a miserable bugger like me! So we got to spend another night together in the hotel ... Happy New Year!

Against the odds, the Nottingham Forest groundsmen fought against the climatic elements and declared the pitch playable. Well it was either that or they were scared of an ear-bashing from Mr Clough for not getting the pitch playable. Especially as the conditions were still bloody treacherous – oooh, bugger me it was cold. Definitely not the type of weather for a fashion parade anyway! So we've just got off the coach and walking down the corridor towards our changing room, and the sight that greeted us was like something from a Cosmopolitan magazine – dresssed in a long fur coat, smoothly-pleated, tight-fitted trousers and a gleaming pair of spats shoes, was the enigmatic Nottingham Forest centre forward, Justin Fashanu. Bloody hell! He looked a million dollars! Just a shame his boss wasn't as complimentary.

"Well bugger me, young man," Brian Clough spouted just as we were entering our changing room. "If my Barbara was 'ere now, she'd take a picture of you and send it to one of her magazines as a front cover! Now, be a good lad and make the lads a cup of tea, please." That was to be Justin Fashanu's only action of the day, because he wasn't featured in the line-up.

That Nottingham Forest side still contained the majority of players from their successful European Cup winning squad that beat FC Hamburg in the final only 18 months previously. Whereas we were struggling towards the bottom of the Second Division with a squad of players injecting painkillers just to get through a match! Nobody gave us a bloody chance. Only two minutes into the game, our supporters must've had that dreaded feeling of "Here we bloody go" after a Mark

Proctor goal gave the First Division club the lead as early as the second minute.

So we get to halftime, still trailing by a single goal. But slowly we'd sensed that Forest were getting a bit edgy 'n' Joey's on to it.

"You smell that? That's fear, 'cos they've shit themselves! Hey! We can take these second half!"

Well, it transpires, Joey possesses a very strong sense of smell, because we turned them inside out – Stevie Dowman equalised in the 61st minute, Micky Vinter gave us the lead in the 70th, before Dixie rubbed more salt in the Forest wound to make it 3–1! Unpredictable and unbelievable. The scenes in the dressing room were something to treasure, and there was only one question on everyone's lips after the game.

"Any chance we can stop off for a few pints on the way back, please Mel? 'Cos we haven't had a chance to celebrate the New Year yet?"

But, sadly, we didn't have much to celebrate after that, because we lost to Chelsea in a fourth round second replay at The Racecourse, and our League form nosedived drastically after that Chelsea loss, to the extent we were embroiled in a relegation battle with the likes of Leyton Orient, Bolton Wanderers and Cardiff City. As it happens, at the start of that season, the Football Association introduced a new points format: three points for a win instead of two (which had been in place for as long as the Football League was established). And along with a crippling list of injuries to key players, I honestly think they were both big contributors. Without a doubt, them key players could've been the difference in the games where we drew and should've won. I'm no Archimedes, but there's a two-point difference between a single point for a draw and three points for a win.

I know it's pretty hard to imagine it now, but even when we were struggling for form, we'd still beat the big teams like Newcastle at home. There must've only been a handful of games remaining in the season, and they came to The Racecourse in fifth position in the League and looking to push for promotion to the First Division – whereas a win for us would edge us out of the relegation zone. But we bloody well shocked them and won 4–2! You could actually hear the groans from our fans when they took the lead in the seventh minute. But it wasn't long before groans turned into bloody orgasms after I equalised with a bullet of a volley almost immediately after the restart! Dixie put us ahead in the 51st, before a bonkers four minutes saw Billy Ronson increase our lead in the 61st. Imre Varadi got his and Newcastle's second in the 62nd minute, before I got my second, and Wrexham's fourth in the 64th! *Iesuuu mawrrr* it was bloody crackers!! Now that's entertainment! The only negative was a disappointing attendance at The Racecourse – just over 4,500 for a Second Division match against the mighty Newcastle United.

But you couldn't blame the crowds for dwindling – we'd been beset with a shopping list of bloody injuries, and the club was ravaged financially, which prevented us from buying the players we needed for that division. And to be fair to the majority of the diehard Wrexham fans, they were always vocal in supporting us and their passion never hindered … even if one or two did have my chewing gum glued to their hair!

From a personal and professional perspective, getting relegated really hurt me. My last goal for my hometown club was at best a consolation goal, at Newcastle United's St James Park, in front of over 9,000. Going into the changing room was desolate, after we lost 2–4, which meant we'd lost all hope of survival. Bloody hell I was cheesed off and just wanted to get back on the coach and get back home as soon as possible. I just couldn't shake off my dark mood, and a few days later I got sent off, 11th May 1982, at Crystal Palace where we lost 1–2. That was my last match for Wrexham.

Gutted, but still proud of the fact that I managed to play

38 games during that final season with a fucked-up knee and finished top scorer with 13 goals. Despite the heartache of relegation, I honestly hadn't given a second's thought of leaving Wrexham. My initial thoughts were, "Let's get through the summer and come back ready to push for an automatic return to the Second Division." But I hadn't realised just how severe the problems were behind the scenes, and to inject the club with a few quid, I was sold to Crystal Palace. A deal that was delegated without any consent from myself.

A deal that definitely wouldn't have gone through had Crystal Palace seen my medical records, because I know exactly what they would've said, "Don't touch this one – he's not fit to be a milkman!" but that's another story, because I later delivered more milk bottles than Foxie's crosses! Ha-hah-hah, he'll bloody love that.

Diolch Wrecsam – once a Robin, always a Dragon.

5
Gareth Owen
Midfielder

The Ironman with gallons of Gaz
1989–2001 (476 appearances, 45 goals)

For most people, suffering any kind of setback can be deflating and incomprehensible. For Gareth Owen, possessing a curiously scientific yet mischievous mindset enabled him to visualise his progression following a life-changing stroke in September 2023. In the foundations of Gareth's heart are layers of determination, passion and a wicked sense of humour. With such attributes in his locker, it's no surprise that he's widely regarded as a '90s icon for thousands of Wrexham fans.

I've always had this scientific and curious approach to life. I mostly want to know how and why, but most of the time it's a case of "I wonder if?" although it doesn't mean I'm sceptical about everything ... I just want to educate myself and learn more. It's a life skill I've applied since my stroke, as I continue to build my vocabulary and communication skills.

For instance, as a toddler I learnt how to play the piano because I found the beats and melodies to music fascinating. Then, a little while later in life, I learnt how to play the guitar with a good friend of mine, Chris 'Bungle' Williams. Together we became a decent acoustic duo and we even toured a few gigs. Even our debut set at a local bingo hall never discouraged us from performing in front of an audience. We'd done all the sound checks and cleared our throats, so started playing our first song of the gig ... only for the bingo caller to continue calling out the numbers – BANZAI NO.1 ... TWO SITTING DUCKS 22! We were both like, "What the fuck!" and just continued to play our set in front of a bingo hall with a handful of oldies staring at their cards and holding their bloody markers!

Not content with ambidextrous hands and an articulated vocabulary, I suppose it would be rude not to mention my feet with a football at them ... with the added help from my eyes to guide them ... or my big arse to give them that oomph for the perfect ping!

I never saw playing football as a gift. I just loved it so much so that I'd practise day and night. Coming from Connah's Quay, there was ALWAYS football going on somewhere, at the park, on the street, or at school. And I suppose it was only a matter of time before someone was spotted or given trials at a professional club. By the mid-'80s, I was given a chance by Wrexham to attend training on schoolboy forms, for a couple of evenings a week. I loved it. Especially when a first-teamer would join in, either coming back from injury or just gaining experience as a coach ... although sometimes, we'd unintentionally not recognise them.

Just imagine our reaction as we arrived at The Racecourse car park for training, and this guy has just instructed us to form a circle around him. This man then invites every single one of us to strike the ball as hard as we could at him ... without him using his arms to deflect or save any shots at him. Out of respect, I struck the first few with precision rather than power, to which he'd reply:

"Is that it? C'MON, HARDER!"

So I asked our coach, Cliff Sear, "Who's this?"

"That there Gareth, is Dai Davies, legendary Wrexham goalkeeper!"

Ohhhh, wow! After hearing that revelation, I just wanted to knock his head off! Not because I didn't like him, on the contrary, I just wanted to prove to him how good I could strike a ball. So for the rest of the training drill I pelted missile after missile at Dai Davies ... each one cannoning off every part of his upper body like some human shield. He'd literally just lean into every shot like a robot, pinging the ball off him, with his hands behind his back! Just picture it, 16 of us smacking a ball at one guy. Man, he was so-ooo strong. But, thanks to Dai, I was subconsciously practising my ping!

I can't emphasise enough how grateful I am to the coaches I had during my youth, from Cliff Sear, Brian Prandle, Idris Pryce, to the likes of Joey Jones and first-team manager, Dixie McNeil. Each one offering different roles of coaching methods and advice. But then came Brian Flynn, initially signed as a player/coach, before being promoted as first-team manager following Dixie's resignation in November 1989. It was also around this time that I was hovering around the first team. Little did I know that the little man with a huge heart was not only going to change my life, but also the future of Wrexham AFC.

Let's be honest about it – the club was financially on its arse and on the verge of going bankrupt. We needed a miracle ... on and off the pitch. To most people, Flynnie's ideology of breeding a herd of youth players like myself into the lion's den each week must've seemed nuts. But he'd been entrusted by Joey and Cliff that we weren't your run-of-the-mill youth players. We had desire and passion in bucket loads. He knew we'd stand our ground against intimidating opposition who wanted to kick us off the park – we'd simply say, "Fuck you" and give some back. He knew the power of the youthful mentality – NO FEAR!

By the end of the 1990–91 season a group of us youth players had accumulated over 100 matches between us. For Waynne Phillips, Phil Hardy, Lee Jones, Stevie Watkin and myself, we had an unbelievable experience, as we got to play almost week-in, week-out in the League, not to mention against the likes of Everton in the League Cup, or a European Cup Winners' Cup adventure against Danish outfit Lyngby, then Manchester United. OMG ... Manchester United – my team! Old Trafford – The Theatre of Dreams – MY DREAMS! OK ... so we finished bottom of the whole Football League. We all knew there wouldn't be any relegation that season. But Flynnie knew the best was yet to come. He was so clever like that. Especially after summer acquisitions such as Karl Connolly and Mickey Thomas.

I was always confident in my shooting or passing range. It was just a case of selecting the correct 'club' from the 'caddy' I had in the locker. Whether it be a nine iron or four iron! So, with only minutes left on the clock away to West Ham in the FA Cup fourth round, we're 1–2 down. Deep in our own half, I received the ball from Andy Thackeray, just at the time when I was thinking, "Fuck sakes, don't pass the ball to me ... I'm fucked" and suddenly found myself in acres of space and quite a few options. As I said, I was already feeling fucked, but luckily for me I never needed much of a run-up before a ping. So I thought, "OK, time to select an iron from the caddy."

It took around six seconds for the ball to leave my right boot and nestle in the back of West Ham United net, after Lee Jones out-sprinted Tim Breaker to poke the ball past Luděk Mikloško. Truth is ... and please promise not to tell a single soul ... but I'd actually meant to pass the ball to Stevie Watkin as I'd spotted him coming short, and thought I'd simply knock it for him to either take on his chest or flick on ... but I chose the four iron instead of the nine! So glad I did, otherwise we might not have experienced a replay back at The Racecourse – a night that will live forever in my memory.

The scoreline shows we lost 1–0. But there was something far more special than the result that night. To play in front of my family, friends and the Wrexham fans at The Racecourse was always special, but this ... WOW! For me, it was the best atmosphere I ever played in.

Whenever I ran out of the tunnel before the start of a match, I'd always look out for my family and friends. But, on this occasion, I was awestruck by the noise levels ... and the Kop; oh my days! It was a cocoon of noise and all I could see were heads – thousands of heads. I can't even begin to describe how proud I was that night. PROUD of the club. PROUD of the fans. PROUD for my family and friends. PROUD of myself. But also PROUD of the journey that my fellow youth teammates had travelled on towards that night. We were now on our way to becoming established members in the Wrexham changing room.

And what a changing room to be a part of! Built on camaraderie, togetherness and the small matter of fact that we wouldn't allow any dickheads to enter through the door! Not that we ever did, such was the tight-knit group we had, but should anyone have a chip on their shoulders, we'd soon help them shave that chip down a few notches!

Tell you what, with characters such as Gary Bennett, Karl Connolly, and Kev Russell, we didn't half have a lotta fun on and off the pitch. Any chance we had, we'd share a few drinks together. Although personally I didn't like the taste of lager, I actually preferred a glass of Pepsi, so I just went along for the laughs ... and plenty of 'em.

I loved the Isle of Man trip. I couldn't wait for pre-season, just to get on that boat and be with the lads. Especially the 'Three Amigos' – Graham Cooper, Andy Thackeray and Garth (Nigel Beaumont). They could empty the bar as well as all the barrels with their antics. But no one could have yer ribs hurting with laughter like Kev Rooster Russell ... aka 'The Whippet'!

Wherever we went or whatever the occasion, once we'd had enough liquid lubrication we'd start pestering Kev to bring out the Whippet. In all fairness, he didn't need much encouragement! "Go on Kev, it's time for the Whippet!" It didn't bother Kev where we were or who was present ... so out came the Whippet. He'd undress all his bottom half revealing his cock and balls, crouch down on all fours like a dog, tuck his cock and balls to the back of his arse, and trot around looking like a whippet! We would be howling with laughter as he performed his act in front of a shocked public!

So it was hardly surprising we created a special bond on memorable Cup runs and successful League campaigns. We didn't give a shit who we played, we were gonna go for it. West Ham, Man United, Notts Forest, Ipswich, Birmingham or Wimbledon ... bring 'em on!

But of course you need a great captain steering the ship. We were fortunate to have a dressing room full of them. Tony Humes, Mel Pejic, Peter Ward, to name but a few, were rock solid for us. And then there's Joey ... I can't talk about Joey without having a lump in my throat or a tear in my eye, because what he did, not just for me, but for the whole family of Wrexham AFC. There's countless youth players, including myself, spanning decades that would have benefitted from extra tuition from Joey on a cold Monday evening, or a few words of advice. You knew how much the club and its people meant to him. "One hundred and ten per cent effort in every match and show 'em you care for their club – because THEY do bloody care!" was one of his favourite rally cries.

There's no doubt in my mind that without that love and dedication, I wouldn't have had such an amazing career if I'd have played at any other club, at any other level. For sure, there were always rumours that other clubs from a higher division wanted to sign me ... but I didn't give a toss about them. I didn't care about the money they were offering. I didn't really care about any silverware they could've offered ... primarily, I would've played for Wrexham for nothing. Because of that love for the fans and FROM the fans. Their support throughout the period I played was the glue in our bond as a band of brothers. Those same fans are the legacy of the club.

6

Dean Keates
Midfielder

Three men, a mouse and a hay bale
(2010–2021, 184 appearances, 15 goals)

Only a few minutes into our meeting, I knew I was in the company of a leader. Articulated, and politely commanding with a splash of sharp wit – Dean Keates had my uninterrupted attention. Walsall-born and bred, the ex-Wrexham captain and manager was a leader on and off the pitch during the financially insecure times for the club, a period in which he helped orchestrate two play-off semi-finals, a play-off final, was a FA Trophy winner and earned a runners-up medal. With a mixture of humility, honesty and humour, Dean opens the captain's logbook for us.

"HI DEAN, IT'S the REAL Dean here" was the opening line from the other side of the phone. This was the beginning of my love affair with Wrexham Football Club. The previous season saw them finish in a mediocre mid-table League position, and the eternally optimistic manager, Dean Saunders, was busy assembling a team to make a real push for the 2010–11 season. Dean Saunders could sell water to the fish, he was that persuasive. He'd also have a crackin' 'hook' to catch you.

"I'm putting a team together that's gonna get The Racecourse rockin'! We're gonna play with a solid defence, wing backs, creative but nasty as fuck midfield, and big fuckin' centre forwards that's gonna challenge for promotion. Oh, and you're gonna be our captain!" Deano had well and truly set his stall out at winning me over. "You're gonna love this place, Keatesy, 'cos we've even got one of the best training grounds in the UK. In fact, it's probably the best in the north-west – we've had Italian and Spanish teams use it when they're playing Liverpool at Anfield in the Champions League! So, there's no need to worry about clearing dog shit off the grass or finishing training early because people wanna use the field to have a fuckin' picnic!"

I'm yet to get a chance to utter a couple of words together, but I'm already in the palm of his hand, because I'd previously spoken with Kev Russell and Big Bri Carey about the club, so I decide to sign a pre-contract with the club.

Dean Saunders, however couldn't accept my pre-contract decision, so phones me back to arrange for us to meet for 11.30 that night at Chorley Service Station.

"Nah, don't worry about that, you have my word, I'm joining Wrexham, and we'll sort everything out tomorrow."

"No, we'll get it done tonight!"

"Look, don't worry, Gaffer, I'm not like that, that's not what I'm about. We can meet up at 11 tomorrow morning and get it done tomorrow, I promise"

"I'll see you at 11.30, Chorley Service Station tonight, Captain."

"We've got a game later, so I'll drive over straight after."

WOW!' I'm thinking, 'cos he either he really rates me and wants to make sure I'm signing, or he's got a better offer the following day ... like a round of golf.

It didn't take long for me to sign for Wrexham late that night, but we were still sat in the deserted cafe at Chorley Service Station at about 2am, talking tactics with salt 'n' pepper shakers, and dying of thirst because they'd stopped serving a couple of hours previous. I didn't have the heart to tell him it was my birthday when we first arrived at 11.30. So, as we're about to get in our cars at about 2.30am on the 1st of July, he goes, "Oh, belated happy birthday! See you in training." It transpires he'd already clocked my date of birth on the forms. Officially, my life as captain of Wrexham Football Club was now sealed.

Moving to the Cheshire area was something my partner and myself had looked forward to, as it was also closer to our families as well. It was only a short drive from them, and only a 40-minute ride to Wrexham, so it made sense. It was an added bonus we lived quite close to a few of the other lads, which meant car-sharing with Jamie Tolley, Curtis Obeng, Frank Sinclair, as well as Chris Blackburn, and big Gaz Taylor before they both moved on. Good lads, good laughs 'n' good discussions during our journeys. Accustomed to good music, all depended on the driver. We all have different tastes I suppose, I'll stick to my Status Quo.

I couldn't wait to meet up with my new teammates and get to know them individually and personally. As captain, I wanted to know their persona and how to get the best out of them, as we were gonna be sharing experiences together during every training session as well as every match we played. Aberystwyth would provide us with that valuable time together.

It was at Aber I got to know the different types of characters we had in our squad, varying from the Jack-in-the-box characters like Jay Harris and Andy Mangan; the quiet yet ultimately dedicated Chris Maxwell and Curtis Obeng. And then there's ya Mathias Pogba and Joslain Mayebi – totally different characters, but great lads. Spending time 'n' having a few beers with ya experienced pros like ya Neil Ashtons, Frank Sinclairs, Jamie Tolleys and ya Andy Morrells was great, the same can be said with the rest of the squad as well … but the gaffer, aka Dean Saunders, was the stand-out character, as he'd share priceless and hilarious stories from his career. My first taste of the sea salt, beers and laughter left me wanting more of Aberystwyth and my new teammates.

By early December time of the 2010–11 season, we're doing alright in the League. We're in the play-off mix and just signed a man-mountain centre half in Mark Creighton to bolster the defence, and playing some good football. On a personal perspective, I'm enjoying perhaps the best form of my career, and scored one of, if not, THE best goal I ever scored, at home to Kidderminster. The ball dropped to me about 30 yards out from goal, I hit it first time before it bounced and it rockets into the back of net, to make it 2–0 for us! I was totally pissed off by the end of the match as we allowed them to claw their way back to earn a 2–2 draw.

Then came one of the harshest, coldest spells in football I'd ever encountered, which cost Creights some valuable game time because initially he'd only signed on a short-term loan deal, and probably only played around 90 minutes in the space of a month, and we were in danger of losing our momentum because we still harboured aspirations for automatic promotion. If coping with the snow and ice wasn't difficult enough, then the news of the dire state the club was in financially was a whole different ball game.

By and large, as a professional footballer, you've got to go about yourself on a daily basis in an ultimate professional manner. Conducting yourself in the right way, putting in a hard graft and striving to develop yourself and the team. In the same breath, we're all people with other motives as well: families, mortgages and bills to pay. The delivery of that untimely news, that cuts would have to be made, and wages not being paid on time, was still a bit of a kick in the bollocks really. There were bound to be insecurities and uncertainties within the changing room – "What happens if we get injured – do we still get paid? How long is this going to last?" So, posed with these types of questions and all the worries of the lads, I liaised with the gaffer on behalf of the changing room.

As a result of a successful career playing at the highest level, the gaffer was more than financially stable and had never had the experience of depending on hand-to-mouth wages, and was somewhat surprised at the squad's response to the dire situation.

"Yeah, I get what you're saying Keatesy, but you will get paid eventually."

"Look Gaffer, this is the National League, and with all due respects we depend on our wages to support ourselves and our families on a month-to-month basis. I can promise ya we're all doing our best to get promoted, and we'll run through a brick wall for the cause. But you've gotta try 'n' reassure us that we'll at least get some money," I pleaded.

Fortunately for us, we had a fantastic set of lads and coaching staff, as well as an amazing fan base, which was invaluable to us.

Undoubtedly, without those influential attributes we would never have reached the play-offs that season. Falling short in the semi-final to Luton Town was disastrous. We'd only played them the week previous in the last match of the initial League season and played a comfortable 1–1 draw at their place. Stood in the tunnel with the lads before the semi-final first leg at The Racecourse, I can remember thinking how confident I was that we were gonna perform and take us up. About 20 minutes later I was proved wrong and we were 0–3 down. We got caught like deer in the headlights, 'n' it was brutal. We gave it a good go in the second leg, but it was too little too late.

For weeks afterwards that feeling clung to the back of my throat like a bacterial infection, and it left a horrible taste in my mouth. So that summer I went to see the gaffer.

"This can't happen again next season. We owe it to the supporters and we owe it to ourselves ... So, what's in the bank to get some players in that can give us that extra push, Gaffer?"

"I fucking love your enthusiasm Keatesy, 'n' that's why YOU'RE our captain. But financially, we're so fucked, there's talk of the fans raiding their piggy banks, upgrading their mortgages and dripping their life savings out, just to save the club! So you're fuckin' spot-on – we do owe it them. And IF we ARE saved, rest assured I'll talk the birds down from the fucking trees to play for us."

His gift of the gab most certainly did the talk that summer ... but not as loud as the amazing supporters! Absolutely fuckin' amazing what they achieved in a matter of 24 hours, THEY SAVED THE CLUB – THEIR CLUB! And this is when I can remember sitting my partner down to tell her some news.

"Look. You know how much I think of you, but I've fallen in love with someone else as well." She now stands up ready to fuckin' batter me.

"Who is she?"

So I look her in the eyes and tell her. "Wrexham Football Club!" I announced.

"Aw – you soppy sod!" she laughed.

But, in truth, the club and the fans made a huge impression on me as well as the rest of the lads. So much so, we almost felt invincible, especially at The Racecourse. I noticed a bit of swagger in their body language as we're warming up, a detection of steely determination in our attitude, and then, just before we'd walk out the tunnel, I'd take a quick look back, and that's when I saw it their eyes. Fuckin' hell, it was scary at times because I almost felt sorry for the opposite captain, 'cos his team were gonna get pummelled from every corner of the ground. Oh my days, what a season!

We'd found our rhythm from the opening game against Cambridge United, and after that it was just relentless. 'Deano's deals' from that summer had settled in brilliantly. Danny Wright hustling for a goal up front, Glen 'Blakey' Little twisting and turning down the wing ... when he wasn't injured. Awww, I tell ya what, we could mix it up if we wanted to – if it got nasty, we'd go nastier! Take the likes of Jake Speight and Jay Harris, ooohhh naughty little street fighters when they had to be, but intelligent players as well. Lee Fowler, on the other hand, was one of the cleverest footballers I'd ever played with, 'cos he could tell the ball what to do! I wish Cheesey could've talked more to the ball 'n' it's scary to think what he could've achieved if his brain could've run as fast as his legs! What a talent! Literally, during every training session you'd either want to wrap your legs around his to stop him flying past you or wrap your hand across his head just to knock some sense into him! Just a shame Deano received a better deal late September and didn't hang around to enjoy the ride with us. Aahh well, Deano's loss was Mozza's gain, as our experienced striker was named player-manager, and I couldn't have been happier for him, 'cos I knew how much he cared what he could offer as our gaffer. Boy oh boy, did he not disappoint!

Taking Brighton and Hove Albion back to The Racecourse for a third round FA Cup replay in January 2012 was an achievement in itself. But the manner in which we played in that replay was something else that night. Sometimes, during a warm-up, you can kinda get a feel of the atmosphere, 'n' that night our fans didn't stop chanting from the moment we stepped onto the pitch for our warm-up. So I decided to do my pre-match pep talk on the pitch during the warm-up 'cos I could see the lads were feeding off the buzz of the ground, and I made a subtle point of going round every single one of the lads individually and said the same speech.

"WOW! You can actually feel the energy buzzin' can't ya? Special nights like these don't come around that often, so just fuckin' embrace it!" and finish it off with an enthusiastic high five.

Mozza and Wrighty must've had double helpin' off that energy, because they were both absolutely outstanding. Mozza scored an absolute worldie, and OH. MY. DAYS. I actually thought the foundations of The Racecourse was gonna collapse from the almighty eruption – it was SO loud I felt my ears literally POP! I rushed over to congratulate him 'n' Wrighty, and tried to tell them a message.

"Look, we've got them rockin' 'n' if we keep pressin', we'll get a couple more before halftime."

Weeell, it literally fell on deaf ears, 'cos it was all "WHAT?" "EH?" or "I CAN'T HEAR YA!" We'll never know how things would have panned out if Wrighty hadn't fallen badly on his elbow, or if the crossbar was an inch lower, because Brighton wouldn't have sneaked back to 1–1. Or maybe if I wouldn't have missed one of the penalties which resulted in us going out on a penalty shoot-out. On the bigger picture though, we'd showed our qualities to the watching nation that night, and one in which we could draw multiples of confidence to keep us in automatic promotion contention.

Fuckin' Luton Town AGAIN! Only this time they did us good at their place for the play-off semi-final first leg. Back home for the second leg, there was still an air of hope around the ground, as well as our changing room. The atmosphere was soon ramped up by an unexpected source. We were stood in the tunnel, waiting to come on, and suddenly Bryn

Law, Sky TV commentator, has taken the PA microphone and is listing all the legends that have played for the club, 'n' he finishes by saying, "These are the legends of Wrexham Football Club, now let's make some more!" Holy shit, if the crowd were pumped up, then we were bouncin', and I swear we could've ripped our shirts off screaming "FUCKIN' C'MON THEN!"

Oooh, we came mighty close to achieving the comeback of all comebacks. Already 0–2 down from the first leg, they score a first-half penalty to make it 0–3 on aggregate. A mountain to climb, but we still felt we had goals in us. Just that we now needed three just to equalise. Mozza's halftime team talk was absolutely on the money.

"I don't care how we do it, or the consequences, but let's give our fans something to scream and shout about."

We gave Luton a good bashing that second half. Cheesey and Mozza sent the place wild after they scored to make it 2–1 on the day, but we were still 2–3 down on aggregate. The last few minutes were total chaos as we bombarded their penalty box and threw bodies in front of everything like hand grenades. I actually think, had we played another ten minutes, we would've scored. But we didn't. And I don't think I've ever seen so many players sink to their knees at the final whistle in sheer exhaustion and devastation as that afternoon. Even though we lost, I was massively proud of the tremendous effort from the lads and the fans, and so proud to be their captain.

The role of the captain isn't just turning up for a match on a Saturday, slapping on an arm band and shouting at your teammates. As I may have mentioned earlier, I took it upon myself to look out for all the lads, not just on the pitch, but off it as well. I could sense if someone needed a chat, or if someone wanted a few beers, then the rule was pretty simple – A CAPTAIN'S MEETING! Which meant only thing – we're all going out for a few beers, and unless you had a concrete reason not to attend, you had to be at the starting venue on time.

It's not easy choosing my favourite, because we had so many great times, and also because I can't remember much from some of 'em. The Christmas parties were always good, especially the trips to Manchester or Liverpool. The fancy dress dos were also a stomping great time, 'n' I may have dressed as an Oompa-Loompa to one of 'em ... although saying that, judging by the dress sense of quite a few of the lads, it was fancy dress on pretty much most occasions (not naming anyone, Mathias!) and Aberystwyth was a cracking place to get a few drinks down ya. THE BEST, however, was during a mini pre-season tour of bonny Scotland.

It was during that gloriously hot July of 2013, and we'd just played the last match of our pre-season tournament, The Raydale Cup, at Gretna, Scotland. Although I was out with an injury, I still wanted to fulfil my captain's role, i.e. make sure the lads had a good night out, create a positive team bonding and get pissed. It didn't take much of an effort to persuade the gaffer, Mozza, to allow the lads to let their hair down, because we'd had a new group of lads in the squad and it made sense to help them bond together.

That hot summer sun must've had an effect on us, because we soon got pretty pissed, the music got louder from the jukebox, and speeches were gettin' slurred. Like a thunderbolt going straight through me, I had this horrible feeling I'd forgotten to do something – "OH. SHIT!" I'd forgotten to book the taxis back to our hotel. With my blurry eyes, I looked at my watch, "Aww fwckin' 'ell." So there was only one thing to do – walk the couple of miles or so to the hotel. I look around to gather the lads together. "OH SHIT, WHERE IS EVERYONE?" I shouted 'cos I couldn't find a soul. So I frantically look around, and spot Little Jay Harris and Creights and a couple of other stragglers.

"Right, look," I stumbled towards them. "I've forgot to

book taxis for us, so we're gonna have to walk it back to the hotel. Oh, by the way where's everyone else?"

"They've all fucked off," Creights slurs.

"I'm guessing back to the hotel, so just give us a chance to finish these off, and we'll walk with ya," I mumble.

Even though it was now dark, it was one of those summer nights when the stars are out and there's still a bit of warmth in the air. About ten minutes into our trek back to the hotel, Jay screeches in his thick Scouse accent:

"FWCH ME! Lwch at all those hay bales – there's fwchin thousands of 'em! Oooh my God, lwch at the size of 'em, they're massive! See that one over there, the one on top of the hill, I reckon I could roll that fwcher down!"

Weeeeell, by now we're falling over each other pissing ourselves laughing at the sight of Jay stumbling up through this field and up to the top of this steep hill.

"Aaah, fwchin 'ell lads," he screams towards us. "This bastard's heavier than you Creights, g'wed 'n' give us a hand, will yer."

So we hatch a plan. It sounded great at the time, but it's just that we were all pissed! But we'd made our minds up – we'd take it in turns for three of us to push this unbelievably heavy hay bale from the top, another one of us would try and run ON TOP of the bale like a mouse on a wheel, and then a couple of the other lads would slow the tumbling bale down at the bottom.

Because I was injured, I decided to opt out of the pushing and stopping part ... so I was gonna be the mouse on top of the bale.

"Ready Keatesy?" Creights shouts before he helps move this huge bale, but this bale fuckin' flies down this steep hill like a marble down a track. I bounce off and go flying about ten yards in the air 'n' the bale then steamrollers through the lads at the bottom and smashes through onto the road! It was like a scene from a war movie 'cos there were bodies everywhere and everyone screaming "Aaah, my leg" or "Oooh, I think I've bust my fucking ribs" or "Aaah, my fuckin' backs gone, aaah!"

There was no way we could just leave it there 'n' we were still pissed. So we agreed to push and roll this massive hay bale along the road for the mile-and-a-half back to the hotel. How we managed it, I'll never know, but somehow we arrived back at the hotel with this hay bale still intact (even if our bodies weren't).

"Now what?" I asked the lads. "Do we just leave it outside and block the entrance?"

Creights steams in, "Nah, fuck that, I've got a better idea!"

So we wedge the double doors of the entrance open 'n' push the bale past reception, and leave it pride of place in the middle of the dance floor which is full of families dancing in a wedding reception ... and the sight of Little Jay Harris dancing around the bale like a little pixie!

To this day, I'm still unaware of who was responsible for getting rid of the hay bale, because when we all returned to the scene of the crime the following morning it was gone! Nothing was ever mentioned to our coaching staff from the hotel staff or anyone else for that matter ... until now! So sorry, Mozza. (But what a night!)

At the time, I was hoping our little break would be the perfect tonic for us after the heart-breaking end to the previous season.

Hearing our fans chanting to the tune of 'Que Sera, Sera,' "Tell me ma, me ma to put the champagne on ice, we're going to Wembley twice, tell me ma, me ma" towards the end of the 2012–13 season was a bit special, because up until then the club had never reached a Wembley final. But now we had two trips to the capital in the space of about six weeks. They were, however, two contrasting conditions, and two contrasting outcomes.

Reaching the final of the 2013 FA Trophy against Grimsby Town was a massive achievement for the club and the fans. I'd be lying if I said that we, the players, were only focused on the League in the run-up to the final, because we knew we might not get another chance to play in a Wembley final and, above and beyond that, we wanted to experience that feeling of lifting the trophy in front of our fans. Our aspirations were also heightened due to the updates we'd received of the sheer amount of tickets sold to our supporters.

Their dedication and passion for the club got them to Wembley through one of the worst snow storms – even if it was towards the end of March. Amazing. We were already in London before the snow had fallen heavy, and we only got to know via social media how thousands of our supporters had to dig themselves out through the snow.

Hardly a flake had fallen in the Wembley area, but frigging hell it was bitterly cold when we stepped out to warm up, which was confirmed by a message on the Wembley scoreboard "2°C, wind chill feels like –4°C" ... no shit!

I hoped we could warm the hearts of our super supporters as much as they'd warmed ours. We definitely made it exciting by taking the final to extra time, before Jonny Hunt scored his penalty during the shoot-out to create the most memorable scenes. I couldn't wait to walk up the Wembley steps to collect our trophy. However, there was one problem – my little legs had gone 'cos they were shot. Honestly, I didn't think I was gonna reach the top of the steps because my legs were drained of oxygen 'n' I was fuckin' knackered! Then I saw the size of the trophy.

"Fuckin hell Jay, it's taller than you 'n' me put together!" But then the roar of our special fans hits ya. Now, I'm usually not an emotional person, but at that moment of lifting the trophy in front of the Wrexham fans, I came close to shedding a few tears.

From tears to beers, from London to Wrexham, our coach

ran on the fuel of our singing, dancing, laughing and swigging crates upon crates of beers. For a change, I was glad of my diminutive stature, because I'd bounce so high from the rest of lads dancing around, and any taller I'd have bashed my head against the top of the bus about a thousand times. It was rockin'!

It was pretty late by the time we rocked up at The Lodge hotel, just outside of Wrexham. But we didn't care, and neither did the landlord, as the music, the beers, and Jay Harris dancing like a madman to 'Mr Brightside' continued to flow until the early hours of the following morning.

About six weeks later, in the beautiful early May sunshine, we were back at Wembley for the play-off final against another Welsh side, Newport County. Again, thousands of our fans had made the near six-hour trip to London, hoping we'd finally return to the Football League.

We lost 0-2 in the last few minutes. It was a crap game. We all felt like shit after the game. No beers – just tears. It took fuckin' ages getting back to Wrexham. Fuckin' horrible. I honestly felt sick to the pits of my stomach. Oooooohh shit, I felt so bad for our fans.

I stayed on for another couple of seasons in the hope that I could achieve the goal of giving our fans the promotion they so desperately wanted ... and deserved. I then returned twice to proudly become the manager, but again, that precious promotion eluded me, and the super fans of Wrexham Football Club. Special fans for a special club!

7
Mark Jones
Midfielder

The Peter Parker of Rhos
2002–2008 (128 appearances, 22 goals)
2009–2010 (34 appearances, 4 goals)

If you take a quick glance at his CV, you'd notice an eventful life full of childhood dreams – playing football for his boyhood team, moonlighting as a comic book hero, and masquerading as a librarian. Not bad for a shy, softly-spoken lad from Rhos! Wrexham-born and an electrical wholesaler by trade, Mark gives us a candid insight about the highs and lows of playing for the team he supported from The Racecourse terraces.

RHOS IS ONLY a stone's throw away from The Racecourse, where the majority of people are passionate Wrexham fans, so I was always going to be fed on a diet of yer Dixie McNeils and Joey Joneses, then I was lucky enough to watch icons such as 'King' Karl Connolly and 'Super' Stevie Watkin. So, to play for the Wrexham Academy from U8s right through to U16s was just magic. I absolutely loved every minute.

I count myself very lucky with the timing of my breakthrough into the first team, not just because it was full of great lads, but also due to the fact we'd just secured promotion to League One and we're still holding our own in the 2003–04 season. It's much easier learning your trade in a successful team compared with a team struggling for form. I got to learn from THE best player I played with – Darren Ferguson. Not only was he technically brilliant, he could also read the game and pick out a teammate with a sublime pass. He wasn't the quickest on the field, and there was one occasion where someone shouted at him from the crowd, "Fuckin' hell Fergie, I've seen the *QE2* turn faster than you!" In true Fergie style he simply pivoted like an old man, looked at me and said in this deep Glaswegian accent, "Fuckin' *QE2* eh, Jonah!" But still ... WHAT a player!

It was also around this time that I acquired a new nickname. Ever since U8s I've always been called Jonah because of my surname, but anyway it's stuck with me ever since – until I found myself in court for a speeding fine, and as a character reference the court was told that my nickname at the club was 'The Library' for the obvious reason that I was a quiet and shy lad. The latter was very much true – but the former was totally fabricated. I was just grateful that none of the lads were there to hear anything of it. Or so I thought ... I'd only stepped into the changing room the following morning, when I was greeted with everyone 'shushing' and telling each other quietly, "No talking in the library!" to which everyone fell about laughing and absolutely ripped me to bits.

Being quite shy, it took me a little bit of time before I started mixing with the regular first-team lads. I preferred to be with my family or my close mates. Then I went on one of my first pre-season tours with the lads to the Isle of Man. The boat almost sank, and then Chrissy Armstrong caused chaos on the same boat journey, as he started serving himself and the rest of the lads free beer from the bar! Some introduction, but one which would always encourage another 'team bonding' session. Especially the Christmas parties – they were my favourite.

So, one Christmas party, I went as Spiderman. I was only outdone by Danny Williams, who turns up as the Michael Keaton incarnation of the film character Beetlejuice. I swear he looked just like him, teeth and all! Top man Danny, and a great mate of mine. Anyway, back to the party, and we were all in great spirits, so much so that I thought I'd play to my character, so scaled this lamppost … only when I reached the top, and all the lads singing the theme tune, "Spiderman, Spiderman, Spiderman does what a Spiderman can," I realised, SHIT! it's a long way down. So I slowly started sliding down … until I lost my grip and fell to the ground from almost the top of the lamppost! Luckily there was no damage … to me or the lamppost.

I wouldn't have a bad word said against any of my teammates from my time at Wrexham. They were all good lads, with each and every one a little bit different – none more so than Jeff Whitley. Great lad Jeff, and a great footballer to go with it. A bit quirky perhaps, but Jeff would carry this little leather holdall everywhere. We called it 'Jeff's Magic Bag' because it was like a magician's bag full of all different kinds of gadgets you could think of.

One of his favourite 'tricks' was going to Wetherspoons on a night out with the lads. He'd sit there quietly, whilst the old fellas would be watching the horse racing, screaming at the screen … then, Jeff would whip out his universal TV remote, and change the channel from his seat just as the race was on the final straight! The old fellas would be going berserk with the staff, whilst Jeff just sat there quietly sniggering to himself, with everyone none the wiser it was him that changed it over to *Loose Women*!

The LDV Cup run in 2005 is by far my most magical memory as a Wrexham player and typifies the DNA of the club and what it means to be a part of it. Off the field, that 2004–05 season was utter chaos with all that stuff involving Alex Hamilton; the club entering administration, and as a result being the first club to be deducted ten points for doing so. In the space of 24 hours we went from play-off contention to threat of relegation.

Of course we (the players) tried not to let it affect us, and if anything, it spurred us on and made us more determined to give something back to the loyal people who cared so much for the club. The LDV Cup run gave us an ideal platform to repay the fans' faith, with some memorable matches and some cracking Cup ties. I absolutely loved it – we didn't care who we'd play, it was a case of, "Let's fuckin' 'av' a go and send our fans wild," especially when we had Juan Ugarte on fire!

To reach the final was special, but to play it at the Millennium Stadium, Cardiff, was extra special. To see the capital city swarming in a sea of red, and the noise they generated was so amazing.

Dennis Smith didn't have to give us much of a team talk before the game. He simply said: "We know who we're playing for, we know how much this club means to them. These fans ARE the club – let's make sure they're dancing their way back to north Wales tonight," which also struck a personal chord with me being a local lad having all my family travel down to south Wales. And I'm so glad we didn't disappoint in the blazing spring sun, beating a very good Southend United, 2–0, thanks to goals from Juan Ugarte and Darren Ferguson.

The scenes after the match will live with me forever – everyone singing and dancing in the stands and inside the changing room. There was a celebration held back at the hotel for all the staff and their families soon after we'd dried the champagne off our suits ... I just wish I could remember enough to share with you! It's fair to say we had a cracking night led by assistant manager Kev Russell, a seriously funny guy when he's sober let alone pissed! On the whole, though, it was an occasion to treasure for me personally, and even more so for the Wrexham fans. They are the heartbeat of the club.

8
Mickey Thomas
Midfielder

Magic Mickey's Chamber of Secrets
1972–1978 (230 appearances, 33 goals)
1991–1993 (34 appearances, 2 goals)

Once upon a time, thousands of folk from north Wales would skip excitedly towards the enchanted castle, The Racecourse ground, chanting – "We're off to see the Wizard, the Wonderful Wizard of Town!" With a wand of a left foot, a twinkle in his eyes, and a heart full of gold, Mickey Thomas could cause a Racecourse roar as he bamboozled the opposition's defence with his tantalising tricks and pulsating pace.

There's Something About Wrexham

Describing affectionately how he went from a humbling background to filling football grounds ... Mickey's story is certainly one to remember.

IT'S UNCANNY HOW familiar the surroundings were at Wrexham AFC and our own backgrounds when my new best mate Joey Jones and I joined as a pair of young scallywags aged 15 in the late '60s. You see, both Joey and I came from working-class families getting by just to survive. Bloody hell, I even had pieces of cardboard on the soles of my shoes to keep my feet dry. So owning my first-ever pair of football boots was a real treat. But we were proud of our upbringings and the values we'd had. Even if we did only have a shirt, a pair of trousers and shoes to last all year. Hard times. Tough times. Best of times.

And to my surprise, Wrexham wasn't as wealthy as I'd imagined and wasn't in great financial condition at all. We had to make do with what we had ... one training kit for the entire season, and we'd take it back to our digs to wash every Friday.

Our digs were in Borras Park. Eddie May lived next door but one, Stuart Mason lived in the same street. Each weekday, one of them would give us a lift to training and give us a good insight on how to be a good footballer. They both really looked after us. Eddie May was a colossal centre half, a hero of mine, and a stalwart. His contributions to the club were huge.

On the days when we'd be allowed to go home, Gareth Davies, a club legend, would give us a lift sometimes. If we couldn't get a lift home to north Wales (Mochdre/ Llandudno) from him, we'd have to thumb it back home, because we were that fucking skint. We were only on something around £7 a week, £5 of that went to pay for digs, so only £2 to spend on treats like food or clothes. We couldn't afford transport home, so we'd hang around the roundabout near The Racecourse and thumb a lift. Fuckin' hell, we must've looked like a dodgy pair of hitch-hikers in our scruffy pair of bell bottoms and tatty tank tops! Failing that, we'd bunk on a train ... Crikey they were good times!

But them good times wouldn't have been possible if it wasn't for the great John Neal. He changed the club's fortunes with the belief in his vision of the youth structure. In fact, around nine or ten players made it into the first team. Joey, myself, Bob Scott, Graham Whittle, Roger Mostyn, Dave Smallman, Allan Dwyer, Allan Hill ... we all eventually became household names. Awwwwwww ... they were THE BEST OF TIMES. Everyone got on together. Great camaraderie. Yeah, of course we pissed about ... we'd have bets on who could climb The Racecourse floodlights fastest – always in pairs – Joey was as brave as a lion getting to the top, whilst I was struggling halfway up. No 'health and safety' in those days – do what you want. We mixed fun with hard work. It was character-building. We came up the tough way – hard work. Nothing was given to us and we dedicated ourselves to the club.

Which is why I didn't want to let dear John Neal down. He was more than just a first-team manager – he was a father figure. A proper 'people person'. For example, he once gave an interview for a magazine. And in it he says, "Michael (he always called me Michael) is a player that is unique – you have to let him do what he wants to do on the pitch, because that's when you get the best out of him ... off the cuff." OH WOW, that made me feel as tall as them flippin' floodlights!

I never drank a lot of alcohol during the early years. It wasn't my thing. That only became my habit after leaving for Man United. Sometimes we'd go out for a pint with the team, but I'd end up pouring most of my beer into a plant pot. Someone would offer me another drink ... "Yeah I'll have another beer" ... then I'd wait for the lads to turn around, before I'd pour the rest of the beer into the same plant pot. By the end of the night that plant was drooping to one side and more pissed than me!

Tell ya what though, we had some good times on the pitch. Ooohhhh my days, we feared absolutely no one, we took no prisoners, and we shook teams up like they'd been through the fuckin' washing machine in the digs! Cardiff City Welsh Cup final – SLAM! – out you go! Zurrieq and Hajduk Split in the European Cup Winners' Cup – WHACK! – off you go! Tottenham Hotspur and Middlesbrough United in the Cup – POW! – ta-ta! Great times, great goals, with great players. But there was still one title that eluded us – the League.

We should have sealed our promotion waaayyy before the crunch final match of the season against fellow promotion chasing Mansfield Town at The Racecourse in the 1976–77 season. But here we were. Beat them and we're guaranteed promotion to the Second Division. But beat them we didn't, as we lost 1–0. It was a scene of devastation. Inconsolable tears flowed everywhere you looked. Back in the changing room it took an age to get out of the kit ... then into the communal bath, then changed to go home. Some didn't bother. Some stayed rooted to their bench staring at the floor in disbelief.

Good old John Neal went around the whole changing room, putting his arm around every member of staff and thanked us individually for our efforts. What a great man. Eventually I trudged out, got in my car and nudged slowly ... then I spotted a lone young lad, sitting with his head in his hands absolutely bawling his eyes out, so I wound the window down and called him over, trying to hide my own tears.

"You OK pal? I'm so sorry we didn't make it today, but I promise you next season we'll be even better and we'll win the League!"

"Thanks Mickey," he said, still sobbing.

Wwwffff, it took ages for that lump to clear from my throat. And about bloody time – because I had a promise to keep and a league title to win!

Sometimes these things happen for a reason y'know. John Neal left to take charge of Middlesbrough United that summer ... he even took our main striker, King of the Kop, Billy Ashcroft with him. But in came Arfon 'The Prince of Wales' Griffiths as player-manager, and with him he brought probably one of the greatest goal scorers the club has ever had – Dixie McNeil. Now we're talkin'! By the final whistle of most games I'd actually feel sorry for the other teams, because we'd totally smash them! Even the legendary ex-Liverpool manager Bill Shankly would come to The Racecourse to watch us ... so glad he did because he witnessed one of my favourite goals of all time, a delicate chip from around 18 yards to beat the stranded Bristol City keeper. But little did I know that he was waiting for me outside the changing room door.

"Ahhh, Mickey son, I just wanted to congratulate you on your fantastic goal and another outstanding performance – keep it up wee man."

Wee man? I felt like a giant after his amazing comment!

Come April 1978, and we're 7–1 up against Rotherham United in front of a bulging 16,000 at The Racecourse, and heading for promotion as champions. I could hear the crowd baying for the final whistle. So I sprinted towards Mr Newsome, the referee, and pleaded with him.

"Please Mr Newsome, don't blow your whistle, we were heartbroken last year – at least let us and the fans enjoy it for a little longer!"

He just looked daft at me. "But Mickey, you're 7–1 up ... and I'm close to the tunnel."

"Oh please, ref, just a few more minutes?" I begged, whilst all the time just thinking back to that sad lad I'd promised a year earlier.

"Oh, bloody hell Mickey! Right – one more minute – and that's yer lot!"

If there's ever 60 seconds that I could've put in a bottle and kept safe for eternity – that golden minute would be it. But then again ... just over 13 years later, I was back playing at The Racecourse at the young age of 37, following a spell at Man United – and one or two other clubs ... ahem – but this time I was begging the ref to "Blow yer fucking whistle, fer fuck sakes!" Not because I was knackered, or that I'd suddenly remembered I was out of ink for my printer, and not even because I had a bird waiting for me in a layby ... but because we were about to send shockwaves across the footballing globe by sending the mighty Arsenal out of the third round of the FA Cup. As Cup upsets go – this was about to be huge!

It was an absolute joy being back at Wrexham late in the summer of 1991. But what I hadn't accounted for was the dire state it was in. Financially it was in the shit. So much so, I had to wait until the start of the season and for the attendance gates to open, just for the club to afford to sign me. Not that I needed much, because I was itching to get out on The Racecourse turf once again and I would've played for Wrexham for nothing. Sadly though, the famous old Racecourse ground was in a despairing state. Surely these fans deserve more, I thought.

I thank my lucky stars my old mate Joey called me up that summer, telling me his boss, Brian Flynn (my ex-teammate with Wales) was after an old head to take care of the young team they were assembling, along with their fellow coach, Kevin Reeves.

"Oh, and Mickey," he said, "You'd be captain!"

I was already hooked before that announcement, but flippin' 'eck ... what an amazing honour! I'm in! By the time Arsenal came to town on the 4th of January 1992, it was shit or bust for the club and for Flynnie. Although there wasn't any pressure from the board, but again, financially, the club was so fucked up they couldn't afford to keep paying Flynnie's wages. I was desperate to repay those hardcore faithful fans, but also because I knew the gaffer was a fantastic manager for the club.

Now, I'm not religious, but thank God, Ian Wright was injured for Arsenal ... but I also thank the fuck Waynne Phillips didn't take that free kick, otherwise I'd have had to pay for all the free pints of Guinness I've guzzled since! Yes, he'd taken a few during the season, and yes, he'd scored a few, but they were all in fucking training! So there was never any chance he was takin' that free kick (sorry Rushie)! Although, saying that, I'd taken a few free kicks at the end of training the day before. Maybe the balls are still stuck in the trees to this day!

I knew as soon as the ball left my sweet left foot that it was going into the top corner like a torpedo missile ... WHOOSH! And Seaman was all at sea! The next few seconds were like a scene from *Benny Hill* with all my teammates trying to catch me as I sprinted like a gazelle towards our dugout. I didn't give a shit, I wanted to share this special moment with my best mate Joey and, as I leapfrogged on him, he let out an almighty squeal, "Fucking get in ... You crazy fucker Mickey!" Ha! I couldn't help but piss myself laughing, not just at Joey's face, but at the thought that an old timer like me had King Karl and the rest of the young guns trying to catch up with me like lost sheep!

I was still breathing through my arse when Super Stevie Watkin slid in front of the Arsenal and England captain Tony Adams to swivel the ball past David Seaman. Ooohhh SHIT, you'd swear an earthquake had just erupted. WOW!

It still makes me laugh when people say to me, "Yeah but your goal wasn't the winning goal – I feel sorry for Stevie Watkin because he never gets the credits for **HIS** winning goal!" Ha! OK, so let me get one thing straight, I'm good mates with Stevie, and I've ALWAYS been immensely proud of his career and that goal. What a special moment for him and his family. He's a smashing local lad. But, whenever I'm told that comment, I'm already prepared with a reply, "Yeah, Stevie's goal was special, but HEY, without MY goal there wouldn't have been a winning goal! Now, work that out fucking Einstein!" Ha-hah-hah.

I'm often asked if it was my best-ever goal. Hmm ... well, it wasn't bad for a 37 year old, was it?! But in all honesty, that accolade goes to another free kick I'd scored years earlier for Stoke City against Swansea City, when I curled an absolute cracker past my old friend and ex-Wrexham teammate, Dai Davies. Poor old Dai just stood there like a fucking mannequin as the ball whizzed into the top corner. However, as for my favourite goal AND my most important goal, then it is a resounding YES to that free kick against Arsenal.

It certainly made all the back pages in the national newspapers; my mug was everywhere! By the time we played West Ham in the FA Cup fourth round a few weeks later, my face was printed on thousands of copies of different national newspapers, on different types of paper, for something totally different from football (so glad they never used MY printer ... it would've cost me a flippin' fortune in ink!).

So, if you haven't quite guessed it, or heard (if you haven't – then where the fuck have you been!?). But yeah, I'd been charged with producing and handling counterfeit tenners. HEY, I told you, the club was hard up didn't I! So, I was still able to play for the club until proven guilty, and there was NO WAY I was gonna miss out on an away trip to east London to First Division West Ham United. Yeah, I expected a bit of stick from the Hammer fans because of my Chelsea connection, but fucking hells bells, this was something else!

It turns out, the Cockney fans actually hated their own boardroom more than me! Apparently, they'd been in a massive dispute over their own Premium Bonds scheme, accusing the club of ripping off the fans.

This only became more obvious when we went out to warm up before the match. I was doing a few stretches when one of the lads called me over to them and says: "Oi, Mickey, take a look at this!" I couldn't believe my eyes when I noticed a huge banner saying, "WEST HAM BONDS DODGIER THAN MICKEY THOMAS'S TENNERS!"

Well, I'll tell ya, I felt giddy after laughing so hard. But the ode to Mickey didn't end there, because as soon as we ran out to start the match, it began raining paper. Fuck me, it was like Argentina 1978 again! WOW, I thought, they really love their club so much they have a ticker tape grand opening for them. I then noticed a few of our lads stashing wads of these papers down their socks or shorts. I thought maybe they're just keeping them as mementos.

So once we got into our changing room at fulltime, following a heroic 2–2 draw, the banter merchants started calling me out, 'Oi Mickey, your nose looks bigger in this one, or, fucking hell Mickey your hair's a bit thin on this copy!' and that's when I first caught sight of a 'Mickey Thomas tenner' – one of many thousands of copies that were showered onto the Upton Park turf that day with my face on it instead of the Queen's.

We didn't have too long to wait for the much-anticipated replay back at The Racecourse, but just enough time for me to hatch a cunning plan and perform my latest trick. It may have been a freezing cold February night, but the atmosphere at The Racecourse for the replay was RED HOT, and it's by far one of the best atmospheres I've played in – and that includes playing in front 100,000 at Wembley for the 1979 FA Cup final – but this was flaming electric! The attendance may have been just under 18,000, but it felt like 80,000! I'd arrived nice and early at The Racecourse and instantly sought out Kev Reeves from the coaching staff to tell him about the trick

I was about to perform. I didn't ask – I told him! His response gave me an inkling of what lay ahead ... aaahhh fuck it, I'll do it anyway!

Prior to every match, there was the customary captains' meeting with the match officials at their room. So I turn up almost half-dressed around the same time as West Ham United captain Julian Dicks. A quick wink, "Aalright pal", and then it's on to the usual bullshit from the ref.

"Right lads, I want a nice clean game, I don't want any nonsense – we're live on Sky Sports – so make sure you prep your lads to mind their language please. Now, Julian, Mickey, do either of you have any questions?" To which we both politely declined. "OK then gentlemen – enjoy the match," and goes to shake both our hands. But as he shook my hand he immediately pulled it away.

"Now, now Mickey, what the hell is this?"

Aha ... I'd only slipped him a tenner, and a genuine one at that, fucking hell, you should've seen his face. Ha-hah-hah, you'd swear I'd just taken a shit on his boots!

"Well," I quipped, "I had a spare copy!" I had the whole room howling with laughter.

"You're flaming MAD, Mickey," squealed the ref!

Despite narrowly losing 0–1 to the Hammers, collectively, the real winners that night was everyone involved with Wrexham Football Club. We'd instilled a new hope and added another legacy to ensure the soul of the club continued to be the heartbeat of north Wales.

It's not just about success, though. It's the feeling of belonging and sense of being part of a big family and their community. Now THAT is something that all the money in the world can't buy. And it's something that I'm extremely proud and privileged to have as a part of my life since being a member of the Wrexham AFC family. Especially those beautiful Wrexham fans. Their legacy are those magical moments we the players create for them. Our (the players) legacy ARE THE FANS. They know their history. They know the players that helped to shape it. They know how important that history is to the club. So please continue to speak our names with pride forever and always remember that Joey Jones salute and chant – because my mate Joey IS the symbol of Wrexham AFC. Go on Joey lad, show us your fist!

9

Stuart Parker
Goalkeeper

From Acton, with gloves
1981–1985 (51 appearances)

The name's Parker. Stuart Parker. Licensed to Nil (clean sheet). Mission: Preventing the world of Wrexham AFC from another relegation and saving the chirpy Robins from a European slaughtering. Equivalent to an action-packed Bond blockbuster, Agent Parker had to dodge alcoholic missiles, survive physical brutality from a brutal strike force, and evade rockets from a dictator called Dai ... just as well he'd had the 'Marine-like' grounding with the Wrexham AFC ground staff, to heed the challenges of being the club's Number One agent.

How many people can say they were educated for their profession by their heroes? Well, that's my hand up straight away! (Or both if it were a ball.) Known back in the day as ground staff, I got the best grounding any young adolescent could ever wish for: learned a trade, got taught life lessons, worked hard ... and had an absolute blast with some crackin' fellas!

I originally joined Wrexham in the late '70s on schoolboy forms before progressing to ground staff. During a golden period for the club, I got to share my digs with seven other lads in Acton, as well as a training ground with superstars such as Arfon Griffiths – the first-team manager, Dixie McNeil, Les Cartwright, Bobby Shinton ... and not forgetting my training partners and legendary Welsh international goalkeepers, Dai Davies and Eddie Niedzwiecki. Dai, especially, was tremendous with me. ALWAYS ready to offer advice. ALWAYS ready to bollock me if I attempted to parry the ball away! "HANDS!" ... everything was about "HANDS!"

I was also privileged and humbled to clean the boots of a legend in his own right, Joey Jones. What a diamond of a fella. Always chirpy – never chippy. And extremely generous. Whenever he'd come back from international duty with Wales, he'd give me his pair of boots as a gift and say, "I've hardly worn these mate, so you take 'em pal!" Bearing in mind he was a regular for his country at that time, my boot rack at home was full to the rafters!

But it wasn't all glitz and glamour, though. There was also the tough grounding of the daily chores ... and I bloody loved it! Getting stuck into cleaning the first-team changing room or sorting out the kit for the laundry ladies became second nature. We all mucked in ... and mucked about, given half a chance. But if there was one chore I cherished the most, it was tending to The Racecourse pitch. Not only because it was sacred, but mainly due to the fact that I knew how much old Jonny Edwards, the groundsman, cared for that turf. He treated it as if it was his own family. Sometimes we'd arrive back at the ground from a midweek afternoon reserve match for around 6pm, and Jonny would still be tweaking and tendering to *his* turf. Without any commands from our coaching staff, we'd all chip in to help Jonny sort out any of the upended divots or re-lay any patch of grass. We'd be there for hours before being kicked off!

The real hardcore grounding occurred in the Welsh National League. Pitted against hard-knock men, our youth team had to learn quick to withstand and survive the 'dark arts' of football. Back then, we were treated to thuggish tackles, flying elbows, and a good old toe-stomping from opponents that wanted to shake you to your bones one minute, then shake you by the hand and wish you "All the best" on yer way back to the changing rooms. Once again, it was vital grounding coming up against the likes of Marchwiel, Llay, or yer Bala and Llangollen, on pitches you wouldn't let cows graze on – especially during the winter. Though, strangely, after wanting to kick us to bits, most of 'em were Wrexham fans, and most of 'em were more than ready to share a few beers with us in the pub after a game. Youth team or not, it was the culture.

A few years into the '80s, the club had suffered a humiliating back-to-back relegation, and we found ourselves struggling in the Fourth Division without a pot to piss in. The superstars were gone and the inexperienced youth were drafted in. Regular high attendances depleted to ghostly gate receipts.

But then this magical club has a way of clawing itself away from the clutches of doom – with the aid of their unequivocally loyal supporters. Backed with their vociferous support, we qualified for the 1984–85 European Cup Winners' Cup, via the Welsh Cup. We were drawn against the Portuguese giants FC Porto … nobody gave us a hope in hell.

September 1984, and there's no doubt about it, there's

something spectacular about playing a European Cup tie under the towering floodlights at The Racecourse. You can feel the 'crackle' in the atmosphere. It really is a phenomenal experience – especially as a local 21 year old wearing the gloves for the club you'd supported. However, it certainly eased my nerves, the characters we had in our changing room. Ultimate pros and quietly determined lads were yer Jake Kings, Jim Steels, Neil Salathiels; banter boys such as John Muldoons or Stevie Wrights; then you had yer leaders in the mould of Jack Keay and a young Barry Horne.

Our manager, Bobby Roberts, was without doubt ahead of his time with his tactics and approach to the match. "Go out gung-ho and we'll get battered. Go out and play safe and we'll get battered. So go out, be patient, but play to our strengths – be quick down the channels and aim for Big Jim. Stu – any chance you get, also aim for Big Jim, because they won't be able to cope with that type of approach!"

He must've read his horoscope prior to the match, because Porto could've battered us ... but they didn't. They also allowed us to take advantage – which we did! Down the right channel, cross from Muldoon onto the head of Big Jim ... 1–0 in the 77th minute! Our dressing room was carnage after the final whistle, great scenes! But the mission wasn't over yet as we still had the fourth leg at Porto to contend with.

I can cope with rain. But this, this was on a biblical scale, as it pissed down from the moment we stepped off the plane in Portugal on the Monday prior to our fourth leg in early October. In fact, it was so bad, we had to train on a nearby gravel pitch on the Monday afternoon, before eventually being allowed to train at the Estádio das Antas the night before the match. But how we wished we could've brought Jonny Edwards' lawnmower with us, because we couldn't believe how long the grass was! It was so long – much longer than the pitches we were used to even in the Welsh National League!

Another (nice) surprise was the gift hanging on a peg above each player's kit – a gift-wrapped bottle of port, from the Porto officials. It was a class act to be fair. But, at the same time, tempting to crack open just to ease the nerves of playing in front of 25,000 partisan Portuguese. A couple of hours later, and I'm glad we resisted, as we sent shockwaves across Europe by claiming a giant-killing victory, albeit on away goals thanks to a double from Jake King and a dramatic volley from Barry Horne. Back inside the changing room to celebrate, we were shocked to hear there was no players' bar inside the stadium. So, while we waited in the corridor for our team bus, we guzzled down the bottles of port ... just as the Porto players trundled past us. "Never mind," we thought, "We'll have a few bevvies at the airport" ... only to arrive at the airport and there was no power. A delayed flight ensued. No problem – we'll celebrate when we get back to Wrexham ... and that WE CERTAINLY DID. Eventually, as we arrived in the early hours.

We came ever so close to producing another Euro shock against Italy's finest, AS Roma, in the next round, as we conceded a controversial penalty, then a hint of offside for their second in the first leg at the Stadio Olimpico, before agonisingly losing 0–1 at The Racecourse in front of over 14,000.

The bottles theme, however, literally seemed to follow me everywhere. Back in the League, we were due to face our derby rivals on a Boxing Day clash, Christmas 1984. And although Band Aid was encouraging everyone to 'Feed the World' it definitely didn't prepare me for the gift I was about to receive. During the match, our manager, Bobby Roberts, looked perplexed at me, questioning as to why I was standing so far out of my goal. "High press?" you might ask ... but nothing could be further from it. I positioned myself between the penalty spot and the 18-yard box to dodge the miniature bottles of whisky whizzing past my head, launched by the charitable Chester fans! There were bloody hundreds of them. I bet the groundsman, Jonny Edwards, had a cracking Boxing Night! I dunno whether I looked like someone who liked a drink, but sometime later in the season we played Darlington, away. I'd already taken a bit of stick from their fans behind the goal, but after I'd gone down to save a shot before quickly launching the ball for a counter-attack, another missile landed right next to me, but this was no miniature, this was a proper bottle of vodka, launched at me! I was certainly shaken but not stirred!

Bottles weren't the only things hurled at me. Occasionally, you're at the receiving end of abuse. Some of it is vile. Some of it jovial. And it's perhaps the latter that was aimed at me during one match. Bobby Roberts had been a bit critical of me to the local newspaper, the *Evening Leader*, and maybe it was his way of trying to get the best out of me – even if he did question my physique. But as I was jogging past The Racecourse chicken run/paddock for a halftime interval, I heard a voice bellow at me, "Oi, Parker! I'm going for a burger ... d'you want one!?" The next sound I heard was my fellow teammate, Andy Edwards, in hysterical laughter! And still to this day, that's Andy's greeting towards me: "Oi, Parker! I'm going for a burger – d'you want one!?"

However, even though I paid the ultimate price of playing through the pain barrier, I have absolutely zero regrets. Admittedly, it came to the state where I needed to have a course of cortisone injected into my knee just before kick-off, only for it to swell up like a balloon before the final whistle. I'd be in absolute agony and almost unable to stand up straight, let alone dive around like bloody Superman! But I would do it all again. Who wouldn't want to play for a special club in front of their special supporters? I'd jump at the chance! So I'm very sorry Mr Bond, but, you only live once ... not twice!

10

Lee Jones
Forward

Many happy returns of the Jedi
(1989–2004, 140 appearances, 43 goals)

In a galaxy far, far away (well, OK, maybe not too far away), an ensemble of Jedi masters plotted tirelessly to train a posse of young Jedis to defeat the Dark side. Entrusted by Brian Flynn (aka Yoda), Joey Jones (aka Obi-Wan Kenobi), and Kevin Reeves (aka Chewbacca), a young Lee Jones was chosen to play the role of Luke Skywalker to help steer a struggling Wrexham Football Club away from The Dark Side ... the Inland Revenue. With a dazzling glint in his eyes, a head full of magical memories, and a heart full of love, Lee emphatically remembers how the entire coaching staff at the club helped rebuild it from near extinction to a reckoned force. From dressing room dressing-downs to late-night curfew calls, Lee bares all from his four different spells with Wrexham ... and how his X-Wing starfighter jet would always be ready for a return.

I'M NOT ENTIRELY sure if you could call it 'destiny' or maybe even a 'calling', but once I'd got introduced (or could that be brainwashed?) to Wrexham Football Club, I kind of sensed a feeling of belonging (even though my dad was a Shrewsbury Town fan!).

Although I was only at the tender age of between four and five years old, I was taken to The Racecourse for the first time with my family to watch Wrexham v Shrewsbury Town. Luckily, there wasn't any need to worry about car sickness, because we lived in Rhosddu, which is a mere few minutes' walk to the ground. What wasn't so lucky was Wrexham lost that match against Shrewsbury – and we were in the away end with the Shrewsbury fans – with me wearing a red and white Wrexham bobble hat. Even then I could taste that hatred between both sets of supporters.

But it was the action on the field that captured my imagination that day, especially the players Wrexham had around that time. Bloody hell, what a team! And then there was Joey Jones ... Ha-hah-hah, I can still hear the echoing booming sound around the ground whenever he whacked in a tackle, and the massive cheer he'd get from the Wrexham fans! "I'll have some more of that please!" I thought.

I didn't have too long to wait until I got the pleasure of sharing Joey's and the other fantastic staff's footballing wisdom on a daily basis, as I was given a chance to prove my worth with Wrexham during the 1989–90 season (while playing for Lex at Stansty). Fortunately for me, I must've made enough of an impression to be invited for a trial.

Following a successful trial, I was offered the opportunity to sign as an apprentice for the forthcoming '90–91 campaign ... and fuckin' 'ell, talk about a baptism of fire!

Unbeknown to me, and the rest of the apprentices, that hot summer of 1990 would change the course of many of our lives. Having already been introduced to the youth coaching staff (which consisted of Cliff Sear, Brian Prandle, Idris Price, and then Joey of course would join in occasionally), we'd all been prepped of our training programme, our daily duties, and the expectations of us as apprentices at Wrexham AFC. But all that got thrown out of the window the day Brian Flynn, first-team manager, called us in for an intimate chat.

Initially, I was shitting myself, because I thought he was gonna announce that the club was gonna have to let us go because it was financially struggling. What happened next, literally blew us all away.

"Right lads, thank you very much for joining us for a chat today," he started off, which then set me off thinking, "Fuckin' 'ell, here we go, I've only been here five fuckin' minutes and they're getting rid of me already." So I just stared at the floor in front of me.

"But listen," Brian continues, "most of you, or maybe all of you, are going to play the majority of games for the first team this season. It doesn't matter if we win, lose, draw or finish bottom of the League, because no one can get relegated out of this League this season!"

My gaze is now firmly fixed on Flynnie. "So, you're all gonna play around 15, 20, maybe more games, and there's absolutely no pressure on you, so just go out and enjoy your football ... thank you for your time."

And with that he simply smiled at the apprentices, shook hands with our coaches, and goes off to join the first-team professionals, leaving myself and the likes of Jamie Kelly, Gaz Owen, Stevie Watkin, Waynne Phillips and Phil Hardy just looking at each other absolutely fuckin' gobsmacked, but excited. Standing there that day, Flynnie may have looked small in stature, but from then on he was a fucking GIANT in our eyes. Yoda had delivered his first pearls of wisdom.

Over the years since his bombshell decision, there's been countless rumours over his reasons for fielding three-quarters of a team consisting of rookies. Having spent many years with Brian Flynn, from a personal perspective I think it was a reflection upon how he himself operated with his persona and the vision he had in taking the club to the next level.

Whether his hand was forced upon, or if it was a stroke of genius, regardless of the circumstances, there was a lot of work to be done on and off the field. Whatever adversities faced us – we knew we had to be fearless and be ready to stand up to them.

To help deal with such circumstances, we were blessed with the mixture of leaders we had within the coaching staff. Each one of them complemented the 'good cop, bad cop' role, but somehow each one of them had a different way of relaying the same message ... albeit in a different tone. We had a first-team coaching staff of Flynnie, Joey, and Kev Reeves; then they were backed up by Cliff Sear, Brian Prandle and Idris Price taking care of the reserves and apprentices. For the players it was a fantastic blend of a wealth of knowledge mixed with enthusiasm.

Take the reserves and apprentices coaches for instance: Idris Price was the perfect bad cop, and would come down on you like a ton of bricks during a team talk – goin' off his fuckin' 'ead. Then Brian Prandle would play the good cop beautifully and just calm everything down and talk us through all the key points in a cool manner. Cliff Sear, on the other hand, boasted the talent and the ability to perform both roles ... his natural demeanour was gentle, and so he was one of the most softly-spoken men you could ever meet. But fuckin' 'ell, believe me – you didn't want to get on the wrong side of him, because you'd be in big trouble and he would blow his top off – it was that ferocious.

One of the coaches that will forever hold a candle for me is Joey, as he became my very own father figure, a sentiment that still lives to this day. He could be outrageously funny; he could put an arm around you when you needed it; he would spend hours of his time helping you nurture and hone your skills; or when required – he'd bollock you. And let me tell you – you didn't want to be at the end of one of Joey's flips. But we all knew it was because he had our best interests at heart, and also of the love he had for the town, its people, and their club. There was one other personal trait that Joey displayed that made us want to run through a brick wall for him – we knew he had our backs and would not have anyone say a bad word about us. To confirm his desire towards us apprentices – and us of him – there would be an altercation that gripped everyone in the changing room in many ways … and some more than others.

So, it was just over the halfway point of the season and we'd just lost again. We're desperately struggling in the bottom of the League and we'd lost narrowly at The Racecourse. The Wrexham team that day contained the familiar sight of around six apprentices. Attendances are as low as the mood of the supporters, yet still the coaching staff kept their faith in their beliefs and trust with us, the apprentices.

After this particular game though, there's an air of desolation in the changing room, and as I'm sat next to Jamie Kelly, another apprentice, taking my boots off, suddenly the club captain, Jon Bowden, comes storming in and starts ranting.

"These young lads – there not fuckin' good enough. They're FUCKIN' SHIT!"

But just as he's finishing the last sentence, Joey walks through the door and goes, "What did you just say?"

Next thing, Joey just marches up to Bowden and one-handedly lifts him off the bench and props him on the coat peg. As he's clipped him onto the coat peg, you could see his other hand clench a fist. I thought, "Fucking 'ell, Joey's gonna fuckin' BATTER him!" He never did, 'cos in the middle of this pandemonium was the calming voice of Flynnie.

"Joey ... Joey, put him down please."

So Joey lets go of Bowden and tells him, "These young lads ARE the future of this football club!"

Anyway, a few exchanges were uttered back and forth between Bowden, Joey and Flynnie, and after this incident Jon Bowden didn't play for Wrexham again.

At your peril do you ever undermine Joey's cause in ensuring the best interests of Wrexham Football Club, especially when it came to protecting the youth. Because if he felt that anyone had disrespected us, he'd fly at the perpetrators like a fuckin' greyhound ... as one supporter once found out to his cost.

We've just got beaten at home, and we're trudging past the paddock side near the players' tunnel, and there's this one supporter going off his fuckin' 'ead, totally ballistic with us young lads, and comes right to the fence and starts screaming stuff at Joey, "FUCKIN' USELESS" and "Not fit to wear the shirt".

So Joey tells him, "I'll fuckin' see you outside, NOW."

And the bloke goes, "Aye, go then!"

Oooh shit! Next thing, Joey runs through the tunnel, sprints through the main door, still in his kit and football boots, then runs along the back of the main stand and waits for this bloke to come out of the main double gates! In the meantime, Flynnie is unaware of what's going on, so he comes into the changing room, looks around and goes:

"Where's Joey?"

One of the lads goes, "Oh, he's just fuckin' legged it outside to kill one of our supporters!"

And in a flash, Flynnie, Kev Reeves, and Brian Prandle

dart out to see what the fuck's going on, and after finding Joey, they're all trying to drag him off this other bloke – all three of them struggling like matadors with a raging bull! Ha-hah-hah, the other bloke an' his mates looked petrified, but hey, it was funny as fuck! (If the irate bloke is reading this, then let me tell ya – you had a lucky escape!) Ha-hah-hah!

I love the bones off Joey. And that's why we'd give that extra 40, maybe 50 per cent, because his love for us and the club inspired us to want to emulate his passion. There was, however, one occasion when I'd misinterpreted this passion, and boy oh boy, did I get the full treatment off Joey. So one day, I'm just on my way out of The Racecourse car park, and I get this volley of abuse from a lad, telling me how shit I was and "I'm fuckin' crap". So I just turn round and tell him to fuck off and carry on walking home.

Next day I report for training, and as soon as Joey spots me he goes, "I want a word you, in here now please."

I'm thinking, "What the fuck's happened? I think I played alright yesterday."

So he pulls me aside into a quiet room. "We've had a complaint from one of our own supporters about you – saying you shouted abuse at them after the match yesterday."

Showing absolutely no remorse, I said, "Yeah, I fuckin' did, Joey – 'cos he was shouting loads of abuse at me, saying I was fuckin' shit an'all that, so I just told him to fuck off like."

I thought Joey was gonna pat me on the back and tell me I'm a good lad for standing up for myself. Weeell, how wrong was I – he absolutely tears into me.

"Don't you ever do that again. You get abuse – just fuckin' take it. Be the ultimate professional and let your football do the talking ... and also, leave me to sort them out!"

Love him. Thanks Joey!

On the field though, I was loving every minute of it. That's not to say it was a walk in the park – far from it. But it's what you dream of doing. Though I doubt I could've dreamt of the surreal circumstances of my debut.

At that time, during the 1990 season, we were still training at the local rugby club, and on this particular Tuesday morning we were preparing to face Man United in the second leg of the second round of the European Cup Winners' Cup at The Racecourse. Just as we're about to warm up, Flynnie decides to name the team to face United. Bearing in mind it's November, it's north Wales and it's cold 'n' wet, I didn't take too much notice of the team selection because I didn't expect to be included ... and also I just wanted to get going because I was bloody freezing!

So just as we're about to start the warm-up, my mate and fellow apprentice, Kev Jones, jogs up to me and says, "Fuckin' 'ell mate, you're playing tonight – have you realised he just called your name out?" ('Cause in all honesty I didn't hear my name.)

"What d'ya mean?"

"Well," he starts, "he's literally just called your name out."

"Nah, piss off, he didn't" ... genuinely thinking he was taking the piss.

"Seriously," he pleaded, "your name was called out – you're playing!"

But I didn't have enough time to let it sink in because we were about to go straight into a warm-up before a bit of five-a-side to finish off. Nothing too heavy because we were playing later that evening. Training finishes and I still haven't had the time to comprehend my selection, until I'm pulled aside by Kev Reeves, Joey and Flynnie.

"Just to let you know you're starting tonight."

Now it's finally sinking in. "But we didn't want to tell you last night because we didn't want you to be too nervous and we wanted you to get a good night's sleep. So enjoy it!"

There was no time to shit myself, because we were promptly whisked away to our hotel, The Rosset Hall, instead of going straight home. This was due to the European rules stating both teams had to stay in a hotel during a European match. And even though it was a nice and tranquil hotel, I didn't get to relax as much, or get an afternoon power nap, because I was a mixture of nerves and excitement.

Arriving at the ground in the team coach was an amazing experience in itself, because there were already thousands outside the stadium, something we weren't used to, and it took a lot longer than usual going along the Mold Road Crispin Lane side of the ground, it was so packed with supporters.

But if that experience was amazing, what happened next absolutely blew my mind. Quite honestly, it was unbelievable. Just as we stepped out for a warm-up, we were greeted by about 10,000 supporters, already in full voice, under the towering floodlights, and there's still about three-quarters of an hour until kick-off. Bloody hell, to think that I was playing for the reserves at Cefn Albion in front of about 20 people the week previous! Now I was about to play in front of just over 13,000 against my other boyhood team – Man United – in the European Cup Winners' Cup.

Even to this day, that moment still sends a shiver down my spine. Exceptional really, because we were trailing 0–3 from the first leg at Old Trafford, so a high attendance wasn't really expected. But this is north Wales, and the people of Wrexham we're talking about here. These people support each other in adversity. They also love a bloody good Cup upset. There was, however, to be no upset, as United beat us 0–2 on the night, but we didn't half play well and give them a fight. And if I found it hard to sleep before the match, I certainly didn't after it – that buzz left me wanting more, and made me think, surely I'd warranted a regular place in the first team?

The next couple of days in training went as I'd expected: I'd get in, do my duties, work hard 'n' go home knackered. And before you know it, it's Friday – team sheet day. By early afternoon I knew the team sheets for all the teams playing the next day would be up, but at different locations. And for the first time since being at the club, I went straight to check the first team, and I felt a slight lump in my throat and my heart's racing a little bit 'cos I'm not on the first-team sheet, and my head's spinning thinking, "Why's my name not on the team sheet?" So I checked a few more times just to make sure, and then the penny dropped. My name IS NOT on the team sheet! So I walk further down the corridor to look at the youth team sheet for their fixture in the Welsh National League, and notice my name on it – Number 9 – Lee Jones. "Hang on," I'm thinking, "I've just played for the first team against Man United on Tuesday, 'n' now I'm down to play for the youths against Corwen! What?"

Without hesitation, I march down the corridor and knock on the door of the youth team coaches – Idris Price and Brian Prandle. I walk in and look directly at Brian.

"BP!"

He looks back at me, "What's up, Lee?"

"Well, I'm on the team sheet to play for the reserves against Corwen!"

Brian just leans back, nonchalantly, "Yeah, that's right."

"Well, I played for the first team Tuesday, and ..."

Before I could carry on he jumps in and says, "And how d'you think you did?"

"To be fair, I think I did OK."

Again he just sits there as cool as a cucumber and says, "OK ... So why? Why should you be in the first team again tomorrow?"

Bollocks! He's fucking stumped me there, and I start to mumble and jumble, "Er, yeah, well, I dunno, I just thought because, well you know!"

"Look son," he cuts in, "Just because you played in one game for the first team doesn't mean that you've made it, OK son." And he waits a few seconds and then delivers a classic line. "Don't ever forget, Lee – a pat on the back is only six inches away from a kick up the arse," and there's a slight pause ... "So, you're playing against Corwen – be ready!"

"OK, thank you," I said, and as I walk out of the room I think: "Bloody hell, that's one belter of a saying that! I've gotta up my game now!"

Corwen was to be a turning point in my career. I'd already played against them a few times during my time with Lex and was accustomed to that level of football and the challenges you had to get used to. In retrospect, it used to spur me on even more if some hairy-arsed old bastard wanted to kick the shit out of me. "Fuckin' bring it on – the more you wanna' kick me, the more I wanna' score," I'd think. But, to be fair to Corwen, they were a decent side. They could play a bit as well as mix it up with a few challenges. So to come from the game having played well was the perfect tonic.

You never knew what to expect whenever you were called in to see Flynnie – praise? A loan move? A gentle bollocking for not pulling your weight with the duties? "Right then, here goes," I thought when I knocked on his door.

"Ah Lee, good to see you! Please sit down."

"Thanks, Gaffer."

"Now then, Lee. You played against Corwen for the reserves on Saturday, 'n' how d'you think you played?"

"Yeah, I think I did alright!"

And with that massive grin of his face, he says, "From what I hear from Idris and BP, you did more than alright – you played excellent, but what's more pleasing is hearing that your attitude was exceptional! I'm very pleased for you."

I'm now bright red with an awkward gracious smile, "Thank you, Gaffer."

"You see, Lee," he replies. "We couldn't let you think that

you could just walk into the first team, because you have to earn it. So that match against Corwen was a test, and I'm pleased to say you've passed with flying colours! So keep up the good work and keep up the great attitude, because I'm sure you're well aware of the standards we strive for at this club."

Oh yes, we were very well aware of the standards expected. It was drilled into us on a daily basis.

On the day I signed apprenticeship forms for the club, I don't think the ink had dried by the time the gaffer's listing the expectations required as an apprentice as well as a member of the playing staff. Then he properly goes into Yoda mode.

"There are two key rules I want you to abide by please, Lee. Firstly, you've got to put £5 from your wages in your pension. And secondly – starting from today, I'm gonna call you at 10.30 one night to make sure you're at home. It might be tonight, next week, next month, or maybe even next year! But if you're not in, there's gonna be trouble, OK Lee? Because in any walk of life, punctuality and dedication are vital life skills. They show that you care and that you're willing. OK? Good lad. Enjoy it, and good luck with us at Wrexham Football Club."

Let me tell you – I made sure I was early for everything. From team meetings and away games departure to every training 'n' every match – I made sure I was one of the first, if not THE first, to report for duty. As for that phone call? Well, at the time, fortunately my girlfriend only lived down the road from my house, so each night would mean glancing at my watch constantly – 9.15, 9.30, 9.45. "Right, I'm gonna have to go," I'd tell her. "See ya tomorrow," and then I'd peg it home just in time to hear the chimes for the *News at Ten* on the telly.

So ... a week goes by after that initial conversation, 'n' there's nothing. A month? Not a tinkle. A few months? Nah, nothing. But each night I still make sure I'm home by 10pm.

And during all this time though, you'd hear the other lads say in training:

"Hey, guess what? I've had the phone call from Flynnie, 'n' guess what? It was fuckin' bang on 10.30! I fuckin' shit myself 'cos I'd literally just got through the door!"

And every time I'd hear that someone else had received the call, I'd start thinking, "Right, I'm next." But that call didn't arrive until towards the end of the season, when I was an active first-team player, and it was the same old routine – check the watch: 9.45. OK, quick peck on the cheek for the missus, then leg it home. "BONG! This is the *News at Ten*." And suddenly BRRRINNG. So I check the time and fuck me it's bang on 10.30! So I answer it.

"Hello?"

"Hi Lee, it's Brian."

"Oh hi, Gaffer, you OK?"

"Yes, I'm fine, thank you Lee. I'm just checking you're in. And you are, so I'll see you tomorrow morning in training. Good night," he announces before he hangs up.

"Yeah, see you in training tomorrow, Gaffer," I reply sheepishly.

Punctual and dedicated. So if the gaffer's setting the standards, then so should we. But I wouldn't have liked his phone bill though!

As apprentices we had these same principles engraved into us. Whether it be in training, cleaning the boots, painting the Kop barriers, or laying out the first-team kit, the mantra was always, "Good enough is NEVER good enough," because everything had to reach THE standard or else Phil Hardy, our apprentices' steward, would be on you like shit on toilet paper.

Phil made his first-team debut whilst still a first-year apprentice against Hartlepool United in May 1990, and received a lot of respect from everyone having made such a good impression. In that respect, Phil deservedly became the head of the apprentices, our steward, and our spokesman. For instance, if anything was wrong, or needed sorting out, then Phil would be the main delegate. This would also mean him having to bollock us, the apprentices, after he'd had a bollocking from Cliff Sear.

"Look Phil, you need to sort these fuckers out – these jobs haven't been done, they're not doing this 'n' that properly, so it's on you. Just fuckin' sort them out!"

So then Phil would gather all the apprentices and lay into us. "Listen lads, I'm gettin' it in the ear from Cliff, because you haven't done your jobs properly – DON'T TAKE THE PISS OUT OF ME! I want the jobs DONE!"

And not one of us back-chatted him, because of the respect we had for him, and we also didn't want to get him into any more trouble with Cliff. However, we eclipsed ourselves one Friday afternoon when we were handed a very important lesson.

We'd already started on our cleaning duties, when Cliff walks in. "Right lads, we need to **DEEP CLEAN** this place 'cos it looks a shithole. I want everything and everywhere cleaned spotless by five o'clock this evening … or else!" Then he looks at Phil, "OK Phil, thank you!"

The second he walks out, we worked and cleaned everything like Trojans – the place was immaculate. At five o'clock on the dot, Cliff walks through the door.

"Phil! Are the jobs done?" Cliff asks.

"Yes, Gaffer. It's all done."

"OK. Well look, I'm gonna go around and make sure it's right."

So off he goes. In the meantime, we're sat there talking amongst ourselves and feeling quite chuffed with ourselves. Twenty minutes later, Cliff comes back in and we all fall silent.

"Right, I've been round everywhere, it looks OK." Then he runs his finger along the top of the door frame, and with it about an inch of thick dust was embedded on his finger. He looks round every one of us and goes, "You fuckin' wankers! Monday morning, we're not training, you're gonna do everything again. Phil, I wanna a word with you, NOW!"

So Phil follows him out, then comes back about 15 minutes later, looking exasperated. "Lads? You fuckin' killed me!"

"Why, what's up Phil?"

"Fuckin' hell lads, you said all the jobs were done."

"Well fuckin' hell, Phil! It's only the top of a door frame!"

"Well, Cliff says that if you miss that one per cent or any other amount of per cent here and there, you'll miss it on the pitch, or start taking shortcuts on the pitch. So yeah, it does fuckin' matter!"

Another valuable life lesson from another Jedi master.

That period was without a shadow of a doubt THE best 12 months of my entire footballing career. And if I could relive another year in my life it would be that era, because it was with the best group of players, the best staff, and I've gone from being a first-year apprentice to being a regular first-team player and making my debut against Man United; League debut away to Northampton Town on a cold arse miserable Friday night, and scoring my first, and second, goal for the first team at home to Rochdale United. And it's just as our own Yoda said, "The harder you work – the greater the reward" – and each training session was hard work, let me tell ya.

By a country mile, THE day every single one of us looked forward to was a Friday. Fucking hell, I couldn't wait to get in and get changed into my training kit, because I knew, just like everyone else did, there was a full-scale match between Wales and the rest of the world. And let me tell you this, it most definitely was NOT for the faint-hearted.

If you were born in Wales or had a legitimate link to being Welsh – you played for the 'Wales' team. If you didn't, then you played for 'The Rest of the World' team. Now, without being biased, but we had two seasoned Welsh internationals in our team – Joey and Flynnie – and regardless of their age, they were still a class act. That Wales team also boasted the likes of myself, Stevie Watkin, Waynne Phillips, Gaz Owen, Chris Armstrong, Mark Morris. We even acquired Graham Cooper due to a member of family with Welsh heritage, before we had two more ex-internationals join the Wales club – Mickey Thomas and Gordon Davies.

The Rest of the World team would have Kev Reeves – ex-English international – and then the other English, Irish, or Scottish lads, like Mark Sertori, Gary Worthington, Brian Carey, Jon Bowden, Vince O'Keefe, Phil Hardy, Nigel Beaumont, Geoff Hunter, Sean Reck, Andy Preece 'n' the rest.

The rules were simple – TRAIN AS YOU PLAY ON A SATURDAY – NO HOLDS BARRED – FUCKIN' ANYTHING GOES!

During that Friday treat, you would never have guessed we were all teammates, or that we had a match the next day, because not once did Flynnie ever say, "Right, we'll take it easy today lads, we don't want any injuries before tomorrow". Nah, fuck that, it was play to the DEATH! It was like a WAR ZONE! Joey and Flynnie instigating it all – Joey flyin' into tackles like he'd do on a Saturday. Flynnie was much more astute but would still leave a deft little elbow or a knee in the side of someone's back; there'd be a scuffle breaking out on one side of the pitch after a nasty little challenge from an apprentice on Mark Sertori! And just as the dust would settle down, there'd be another fight breaking out between the likes of Jon Bowden and Kev Jones because of another heavy tackle! Regardless of who you were, there'd be a fight breaking out between two apprentices, two professionals or an apprentice and a professional. It was never on a personal level, just that desire to win and a sense of personal pride. No wonder there'd be someone unable to play on a Saturday because of an injury sustained in the Friday grudge match.

God help us if we'd lost the Friday match, because we knew Joey would go mad for starters, then Flynnie would pipe in and go fumin' 'n' there'd be lads pointing fingers at each other.

"YOU! YOU FUCKIN' SHITHEAD, PASS THE BALL SOONER" or "YOU FUCKIN' COWARD – PUT A FUCKIN' TACKLE IN!" Because the reality was, if you put the effort and attitude in during training, then you'll put them in during the match on a Saturday. "Good habits" as Joey used to tell us every day. But it was a great place to be if Wales won because Joey and Flynnie would set us off with renditions of 'Delilah' or 'Bread of Heaven' … heaven forbid if the Rest of the World won, because they'd be belting out the likes of 'Swing Low' or 'Flower of Scotland' or 'Danny Boy' and Joey would go fuckin' berserk and run around the pitch chasing after the likes of Andy Thackeray 'cos he was gonna fuckin' deck him! Ha-hah-hah, good old Joey lad!

Those training ground clashes were again another integral part of the learnin' process of how to deal with the culture of football. Mix that up with a huge dollop of camaraderie, and the end result should be the perfect recipe. The coaching staff were brilliant at this. Take the annual pre-season trip to the Isle of Man, for instance. It was a crackin' short break for everyone to get to know each other properly and share a few drinks and a few laughs as well. But, of course, there'd be a curfew on us apprentices.

"Right, go out and enjoy yourselves. Apprentices I want you back at the hotel by 11 o'clock – senior professionals back by midnight, please."

Weeell … we literally bounced to the first pub and spent a few hours with the first-teamers, and it didn't disappoint us. 'Cos, fucking hell, we laughed to the point of breaking ribs, it was that brilliant, and it gave you chance to think, "Actually, he's alright, him", or a case of airing any grievances that perhaps hadn't been resolved. But the clock was always ticking.

We knew we couldn't be late because we didn't want to let Flynnie down. And we also knew Joey would kill us, so we made sure we arrived back at the Ascot Hotel for bang-on 11 o'clock. Perched in reception, and looking at his watch as were walking through the reception is Flynnie.

"Exceptional timing, lads! Get yourselves to bed, and I'll see you in the morning" – life lessons!

West Ham United away in the fourth round of the FA Cup was to prove another test and life lesson. I didn't feature in the historic win over Arsenal in the previous round, but I was still there to cheer on the lads 'n' danced 'n' celebrated with them in the changing room after the game. But, deep down, I desperately wanted to play more of a part on this magical journey.

So, Flynnie's named the team. I'm in the matchday squad as a substitute. Going out to warm up before the game was a range of feelings for me – I had goosebumps from the atmosphere and thought, "Fuckin' 'ell, I wish I was starting, but if I get a chance I'm gonna show you," to the utterly bizarre and surreal sight of seeing thousands of £10 notes flying around the place, with Mickey's face on them. What the fuck was goin' on there?

By the 74th minute, Trevor Morley's just scored to make it 2–1 for West Ham, after Waynne Phillips scored a cracking equaliser for us in the 61st. Within a minute of Morley's goal, Flynnie looks at me and says, "Lee, get warmed up." Like a whippet I'm off down the sideline. I hadn't really realised how close the sidelines were to the crowd, and suddenly I'm within a yard of the West Ham fans, and they're pelting me with pies and Mars bars, before I'm soaked with a gobfull of phlegm spat at me. The hatred directed at me was off the scale.

"Fack owf you fackin' sheep shaggin' bastard" or "Don't

stand too close son or we'll fackin' do you, you fackin' sheep shagger."

Then Joey's advice kicked in and I thought, "Right you horrible bastards, I'll ram that shit down your vile throats with a goal" and legged it like the Road Runner back to our dugout 'cos I couldn't fuckin' wait to get on.

"OK, Gaffer, I'm ready," I said.

"Listen Lee," he says in my ear, "you've got one thing to do for me – go and score! Just score a goal 'n' that's all you've got to do. Nothing else in the game, just score a goal."

So, we get to the 81st minute and West Ham have just had another period of pressure in our half, then the ball runs to Gaz Owen, and instinctively I'm thinking of peeling off from their defender, Tim Breaker, expecting Gaz to knock the ball for Stevie Watkin to bring it down and then release me through on goal. But Gaz pings it over Stevie, and the West Ham defenders and my instincts led me towards Luděk Mikloško, 'n' the ball takes a knock off my shin and rolls past him. FUCKIN' HELL, I'VE SCORED! I'm now screaming my 'ead off with my arms aloft in front of the ecstatic Wrexham fans! Bloody hell what a feeling! We ended up drawing 2–2 and earning a big pay day replay at The Racecourse. The scenes in the changing room after my late equaliser was of pure joy and elation. A whole world away to the home changing room ten years later.

Like the prodigal son, I'd returned to Wrexham for my fourth (and last) stint at the club towards the end of the 2001–2002 season. The club was in a battle on and off the pitch – fighting relegation and fighting off the administrators. Dennis Smith had taken the managerial role after Flynnie left and had a mammoth task on his hands of keeping the club going. We only had a handful of matches to avoid relegation, but results had to go our way as well.

Cambridge United at home, first week of April, was a game we had to win and hoped results elsewhere were favourable.

I knew, from the very first touch in the match – "'Ang on, I could have a couple of goals here today." And by the 74th minute we're winning 5–0, and I've scored all FIVE! But I'm thinking, "I could get a couple more here." Then the ref whistles to bring on a sub, for us, and I see the number 44 go up ... SHIT! That's my number! Well, I'm absolutely blazin' as I'm going off to be replaced by Hector Sam. Obviously, I wasn't pissed off because it was Hector, but I was enjoying my football and wanted to score more!

I'd cooled down a bit after the final whistle, and as I'm shaking the referee's hand he gives me the match ball, and I'm waving at my family in the stand, before Les Evans, the official club photographer, wants a picture of me with the match ball. I get back into the changing room absolutely buzzin' again. However, I'm greeted by a deathly silence and everyone staring down at the floor. It transpires the results elsewhere hadn't gone our way. We were relegated.

Thankfully, I signed a permanent contract during the summer of 2002, and both Dennis and myself made a vow to each other that we'd get the club promoted straight back up. And that we certainly did, in emphatic fashion! Bloody hell, we had goals in us from all angles thanks to the likes of Lee Trundle, Andy Morrell, Hector Sam and myself. Boosted by a creative midfield in Darren Ferguson, Paul Edwards, Carlos, Scot Green. Propped up by a solid defence with Brian Carey, Stephen Roberts, Dennis Lawrence, and Andy Dibble in goal.

In a sentimental way, I sensed it was the perfect way for me to repay the club and its amazing fans for all their love and support during what was an extremely difficult time for everyone involved. But that's Wrexham in a nutshell – we'll get knocked down, but you better be ready for when we get back up 'cos we're gonna fuckin' batter you, Joey-style! So have no fear, my X-Wing starfighter jet is ALWAYS ready to burn the skies and land on The Racecourse. Fancy a ride?

11
Glen Little
Winger

Snakey Blakey and the Vegas road trip
2011–2013 (43 appearances, 2 goals)

If ever there was a hat made purely from the old adage 'quality not quantity' then it would fit perfectly on the head of Glen Little. Statistically a Wrexham player for two years but clutched closely in the hearts of the fans for a lifetime, the chirpy Cockney could captivate an entire stadium with sensational sorcery and literally levitate thousands of bums off seats ... once he'd got his own backside off the subs' bench. From bench-warmer to crowd-pleaser, Blakey could generate enough power to light up the old

Glen Little

pylon floodlights at The Racecourse with his snake hips slaloming towards the opposition goal. A popular figure with the Wrexham faithful while on the pitch, the super sub soon became a popular local resident off it. With his bombastic Cockney charm, the maverick winger shares some of his highlights while at Wrexham ... and tells us how he became a resident in a house called VEGAS!

I WAS INITIALLY invited by the gaffer, Dean Saunders, towards the end of 2010–11 season to do a bit of training and play a couple of reserve games. I loved it. So, I came up again to meet up with Deano, and listened to him giving it the big one, "We're gonna do this 'n' that," so I kept a close eye on how the lads were doin' and could see they were forcing themselves into the play-offs and thought, "Ey-up, there gonna bloody well do it!" But, it didn't happen that season as they got done in the first half against a smart Luton Town in the first leg at home. So, promotion was on hold for another season.

Frustratingly, my signing couldn't materialise straight away. Because of the club's dire financial issues, there was a transfer embargo. Then things went from bad to worse in the blink of an eye, and at one desperate point it actually looked as though the club was gonna be extinct. But deep inside I always knew it wasn't gonna get to that at Wrexham because of their supporters. So in came the good old Wrexham Supporters Trust to save the club and become the club owners. Sure enough, the blower goes, and it's the gaffer. Fucking 'ell, he could charm fish out of the river he could. "Yeah, we're gonna get promotion, and we've got a proper team 'ere now, fantastic fan base, great ground ... so all we need now is for you to sign and it'll be like stealing the moon from the Russians, mate!"

Anyway, after all the upheaval, eventually I signed because I thought we had a good chance of promotion – I didn't see the point of signing for a mid-table team so late in my career – but I knew by looking around the changing room and seeing the squad we had, I thought, "We've got a bleeding good chance of doin' somethin' 'ere," and I backed myself to be a part of it. It was a perfect team – bit of experience who'd played at a higher level; lads in their prime; and some crackin' young players who were hungry to prove themselves. Put together like a jigsaw. Bloody hell, we got 98 points and still it ain't even enough. Nine times outta ten that accumulation's enough – but not this time!

Another big selling point for me were the fans and the noise they could conjure up, because I'd played against Wrexham at The Racecourse years previously for Burnley, and stone me, once them fans warmed their tonsils, it was like cranking up the wind machine AND the speakers at a rock concert at the same time. And suddenly you'd notice the Wrexham players morphing into possessed aliens like something supernatural. So once Deano had finally finished yackin' on after about an hour or so, and I'm there noddin' away like that bleedin' Churchill dog, I'd already made me mind up because I knew from my previous experience of The Racecourse roar … "I fancy a bit of that, son".

Even in training, I'd think, "We ain't 'alf gotta crackin' set of boys 'ere." Because I could see first-hand, with the likes of Mozza, he had goals in him; Speighty was a goal machine; Westy a classy centre half; Creights, a man-mountain centre half, Keatesy – an inspirational captain; Jay – a little terrier; as well as Cheesey – the Polish wizard, Wrighty … he may have looked like a clothes hanger what with his shoulders 'n' that, but he was a bloody good striker for us; Pogba was as enigmatic as a fackin' lightbulb; then you look at the little genius Lee Fowler, before Fleetwood nicked him off us midway through the season. Though truthfully, he shouldn't have been playing at that level, he was far too good to be playing in the Conference. We also had Curtis Obeng playing exceptional at right week-in, week-out, so we were bloody gutted when Swansea came in for him.

In between the posts we had Chrissy Maxwell who was first class and was probably playing at a level far too low for his talent. Quiet boy, but sooo talented. We also had Jossy ... who was a totally different creature to Chrissy. Yeah, he might've come across as someone a bit different, but most goalkeepers are, aren't they? But he could win us a few games with some of the stupendous saves he made. He was a bit like a knitting needle was Jossy – drop one, pearl one!

One of the first things Deano sorted out for me was accommodation. He says to me, "Right, Blakey, there's a lovely little gaff for you in a lovely town called Rhostyllen. It ain't far from the ground or training. It's ideal! Oh, by the way, you'll be sharing with a couple of other lads!"

Well, for two years I stayed in the house, which we called Vegas ... because what happens in Vegas stays in Vegas. My housemates varied over a period of time. Danny Wright was the only housemate that started and finished staying in the house the same period as me. Lee Fowler came and went within a few months. Then we gained young Declan Walker (Trigger) because he was injured, so he needed somewhere local to live. Ha-hah-hah, poor mite didn't know what hit him, or where the fuck to look!

The club then took on an influx of Brummies, and let me tell ya, them boys were rum lads on AND off the pitch. And where d'you think they wanted to stay? Yep – fackin' Vegas, baby! They'd be offered other properties, but oohhh nooo! They wanted to have a bit of Vegas! We then had the likes of Martin Riley, Westy, and Joey Clark, kipping with us whenever they fancied a night on the tiles in the town. Blow me, there were more people coming and going than a fackin' bus shelter! From the outside you'd think, "How you gonna get five or six of us in there?" But it was like the Tardis.

Soon enough, the reputation of Vegas gathered at a faster

pace than Cheesey's twinkle toes! So, we'd go out for a few beers, and sure as shit we'd have all sorts of people coming over and goin', "Oh, is there a party going on at Vegas tonight?" Well, it would've been rude of us to refuse anyone!

Listen, I ain't saying that Vegas was some kind of seedy brothel, or Party Central, but we didn't 'alf have some blindin' times there. And to be fair, we looked after the house 'an' all, by keeping it domesticated and hygienic. We'd all have our chores and we'd all muck in. Bearing in mind we'd all prefer the shopping duty compared with cleaning the bathroom, especially if we'd 'ad a big one the night before!

There was one duty I absolutely loved. I hadn't long joined up, so as I'm walking in through the door, Gaz Taylor's walking out. And so he leaves his duty of helping out with the reserves. So after training one day, Mozza asks me if I fancy jumping in and helping out! I weren't too sure straight away, until he says that I'd be an assistant to Joey Jones.

"Ah fack me Mozza, why didn't you say that in the first place! I'll tear yer bleedin' arm orff to be wiv Joey!" And that's when my bromance with an absolute legend of a fella and a footballer began. What a geezer! And on top of that we had a great set of lads in the reserves. To be honest, I'd go as far to say that there were times when the reserves played better football than the first team and pulverised teams just for fun! Oooh, I tell ya, I loved every minute with them boys, and of course with my partner – Joey. Still to this day we call each other partner! He knew how to mix it up, of when to have a laugh and when to do the business. It's people skills, innit? But Joey would always drum it into all the boys how important the club was to the area of north Wales, and the people of Wrexham.

Little wonder we were able to produce the goods on the pitch with the first team then, innit?! And although we didn't even have a sponsor on the kit for the start of the 2011–2012 season, after only a few games in and we'd bashed a few teams about like a rag doll, I get a text message one morning from my mate John Oster, who's at Doncaster Rovers, and he says, "Deano's turned up at our place!" and I thought, "What?? What's goin' on 'ere then!" He hadn't let any of the players know absolutely nothing.

Crikey, the night before we'd played Southport away, and we were on the coach on the way back home, and Deano's chatting away as he did, but didn't mention a thing ... fack me, we wake up next morning and he's gone! But probably, reading between the lines, he's gone because he thought he'd save the club a few bob by not having to pay his wages. But I thought Deano was alright, and to be fair he'd put that together on a shoestring so short you couldn't hang a bleedin' conker on it. But he had that effect on people, ya know. He could talk the talk, and yer know what? We'd run through a brick wall for him. We all loved him. And considering the financial side of things, he did a bloody good job. So, you couldn't blame us the players from the initial shock of his departure.

In all fairness, we all adapted naturally to Mozza progressing from being a teammate to being the gaffer. But, typical Mozza, he got all us experienced lads together in a room with him and asked us our opinions and thoughts, and he took every single feedback on board, again proving the top geezer he is, and because of his nature and character we would be behind him and do absolutely anything for him. But fair play, he took it on and took us on a 20-game unbeaten run.

It was bloody frightening how teams couldn't handle the crowd at The Racecourse. No matter who we played we always had goals in us. Hard side we were an' all. Fucking horrible to play against. We could mix it up with a bit of pace, an' brute when we had to as well. Teams would try to intimidate us when we started to roll them over a bit, but we weren't 'aving any of it, so we'd give 'em some back (and a bit more) just to make sure they got the message – 'You ain't goin' from 'ere today looking nice 'n' pretty' and because of that togetherness, we'd know as we were walking out of that tunnel that, if we were on it on that day, we could score five or six. Yeah, some team that. Even today, I still get the 'ump and think, "How the fuck did we not get promotion with that team we 'ad?" Perhaps it had something to do with someone called Jamie Vardy slammin' goals in for Fleetwood Town? Didn't help that they stole Lee Fowler from us, neither! Ninety-eight points and STILL NOT GETTTIN' PROMOTED ... yer 'avin a laugh!

Staggering the amount of points we accumulated in the two seasons between 2011–2013, and still didn't get the big one – promotion! Saying that, we didn't 'alf tear it up a bit – we had the FA Cup run in 2012, play-off semi-finals 2012, FA Trophy winners 2013, and play-off final 2013. But at the end of it all, it still shows we ain't got a promotion – the Holy Grail. You haven't done what you really wanted to do. Strange to look at it as a failure – but that's what we did – failed to get the club rightfully back into League football.

"We should've given Championship side Brighton a good whippin' in the FA Cup third round replay back at ours in January 2012. Cor blimey, they didn't know what hit them. Cheesey had already given 'em a taste after he smacked in a cracker at their place to earn a replay, so all our talk on the way back on the coach was how we would be ready for 'em at The Racecourse. Considering we were a Conference side, we had that belief that we could still sort 'em out.

And it was one of them games when every single one of us was on top of their game. I could feel in myself and in my legs that there was an unstoppable energy. And we had the perfect start an' all, after Mozza caught out their keeper with a diamond of a curler. We could've and should've put a few more past them, but it just didn't go in for us. Mozza tried to hide how delighted he was with us at halftime, before he eventually caved in and gave out a wry little smile and said, "Fucking hell. Whatever happens tonight boys, I just wanna thank you for making our fans happy. I can't tell you how proud I am." I know we lost on pens, but I think the gaffer got it spot-on with his halftime assessment, because that performance was from another planet that night.

And what about that run we had in the FA Trophy in 2013? Wembley final! Have some of that, please! We used to joke about it with the lads in the changing room that the FA had fixed the draw – we all said they'd fixed the draw so that the FA could get more money because they knew the Wrexham fans would almost fill Wembley and line their pockets. Semi-final first leg against Gainsborough at home, comfortable leading 2-1. Neil Ashton makes it 3-1. Everyone's thinking about planning their trip to Wembley come end of March – nice sunny day, early spring and all that. Beautiful. So, second leg their place, Wrighty scores a worldie, and we're all starting to smell the hot dogs outside Wembley ... but those Gainsborough boys dug their heels in, got a couple of goals and, all of a sudden, it's time to get the brute force into action, innit! Just as well because we held on to book a spot for a Wembley final against Grimsby Town.

So much for that nice sunny day in early spring down London way. It only dumped one of the biggest snowfalls in decades. Stone me, it was bleeding Baltic! I'm just so glad and grateful that we gave all those thousands of Wrexham fans, that travelled all those hours through treacherous conditions, a bit of silverware and a load of precious memories to stay with them for ever. And ours, the players an' all. Corker of a game, weren't it? Could've gone either way at one point, but it was us asking all the questions and doing all the pressing in the end. Thankfully, it was our turn to win on pens. Good ol' Bagpuss scored from the spot to equalise during normal time. But it was young un Johnny Hunt that sent the Wrexham fans into a delirium with his winning pen.

We had a bangin' night to celebrate on our way back to Wrexham an' all. And it's those magical moments that will stick with me – the singalongs, the bus literally bouncing down the motorway, beers flowing, every one of us laughing and smiling. Great times. Now all we needed to do was get the big one, weren't it? Promotion.

Newport play-off final was just a bad game. Nothing felt right. Mozza admitted he got it wrong in the last game of the season before the play-offs – when he played Danny Wright – when in hindsight he should've rested him for the play-offs, after Danny sustained an injury to his elbow. Just a horrible day. Oh yeah, it was a sunny day in late spring. Can't please everyone, I suppose.

In a nutshell though, Wrexham's one of the best times in my career, but also one of the biggest regrets, because we didn't do it and get promotion. But tell ya what though, they were two unbelievable seasons, playing for an unbelievable town. Because, in all honestly, Wrexham FC is the Colosseum of the town. Now that's what you call history! Because a club's history is the blueprint of its future, and that's what Wrexham's all about!

12

Andy Holt
Defender

Only food and workhorses
2004–2006 (98 appearances, 10 goals)

Northern Soul was a popular music genre with the Wrexham folk back in the early '70s. In 2004, a different kind of Northern Soul became just as popular with them. The signing of Andy Holt gave the folk of Wrexham a left-sided workhorse – a figure of resemblance to themselves: A grafter with a bit of flair. From Balti pies to offending an evil emperor, in his typical 'northern gusto', Andy lifts the lid to his box of goodies on how a playboy ate himself, and the shark that gobbled up 20 chicken nuggets.

As league debuts go, not even Disney could've scripted such chaotic scenes as my welcome package. I made my debut against Swindon Town at home, 7th of August 2004, and during the game, the club's chairman, Alex Hamilton, had consumed a few beers, and went into the middle of the Mold Road Kop to explain exactly what was going on. On the pitch, we didn't know what the bloody hell was going on! We were aware of a commotion, and I was just thinking, "What's going on?" so just presumed some Swindon fans had sneaked into the Kop, got found out, and trouble flared between the two sets of fans.

It wasn't until after the game we found out the truth, that our troublesome chairman had inexplicably wandered into the lion's den – the Kop – and thought he could simply reason with thousands of Wrexham fans. Surely, he was aware, that those same fans had just marched in protest against Hamilton, prior to the match? But in the process of his whimsical idea, he caused a riotous scene with the fans, stewards, and the police! "What a bloody idiot!" were my initial thoughts on him.

But I shouldn't have been too surprised, because over a period of time I would briefly come into contact with Mr Hamilton 'n', I must say, he came across as a strange character and a really odd person. Conversations between us were always limited to a short and very brief scale. Not once did he mention any plans of building a B&Q, nor did he ask if I was any good at decking … but I bet he wished I could build a wall to protect him from the protesting Wrexham fans outside his house in Hale!

Wow! Welcome to Wrexham! I already knew the Wrexham fans were very passionate from my days of playing against them for the likes of Oldham Athletic. But, oh my Lord, I hadn't realised just how much they cared for their club, and I also wasn't aware of the background noise coming from the accountant's office. It was quite strange, because the noise wasn't a true reflection of what was happening on the forefront – the actual football. What a fantastic and strong group of lads – all brimming with quality, and a fantastic attitude. We kinda just tried to ignore all the background stuff 'n' just tried to focus on the football and getting promotion to the Championship, because we knew we definitely had the personnel to achieve it.

Transparently, the club's financial struggles became glaringly obvious when our wages consisted of receiving cash in envelopes. We were later informed the cash was from the gate receipts after each home game, which meant we had to wait until after each home game to get paid instead of the usual route of getting it paid straight into our bank accounts. A true reflection of the club's hardship, because there was no meaningful external investment other than the hard-earned cash from loyal fans walking through the turnstiles, and the magnificent support from local sponsors – which meant the world to us players – not just in a financial manner, but also in a footballing sense, because it gave us that extra pride and incentive to give them the joy they so truly deserved.

Dennis Smith sounded like the calmest person in the world when he phoned me in the late spring of 2004:

"Hi Andy, you OK, son? ... Listen, I'm really interested in you, and I want you to come and play for us ... we've already got the makings of a good squad to push for promotion 'n' there's a great set of lads you could car share with, if you like?"

"Yeah, that could be really useful. Is the training ground near the stadium?" I reply.

"The training facilities are by far the best outside the Premier League! Colliers is based near a place called Gresford, just outside Wrexham ... I think you'll love it 'ere son 'n' I reckon you'll love our fans. Oh and hey, they'll love you, 'cos you're just their type."

Flippin 'eck!! I didn't need to hear any more from him.

"Brilliant, let's meet up and let's get the deal done!" I said excitedly.

Living in the Manchester area, I got to car share with good lads like Darren Ferguson, Jim Whitley and Brian Carey, so in fact it was more like a 'car school' because of their vast experience and their knowhow 'n' I loved it! Car school rules were dead simple – the driver was in control of the temperature settings and the music. And if you weren't happy as a passenger, well tough! But who on earth would want to argue with Darren Ferguson and Brian Carey!?

I'd come across Big Bri earlier on in my career when I played for Oldham Athletic against Wrexham. At that time, Oldham had a big centre half called Shaun Garnett, a Scouse lad and, bloody hell, him and Big Bri had the best battles! 'Cos it really was a case of 'Clash of the Titans' as they're both headcases, they're both hard as nails, and neither of them giving a monkey's if they got battered in the process! So his moniker 'Scarey Carey' sums him up perfectly. Honestly, he was such a massive presence, and a magnificent player to go with it ... but just be careful not to cross him, especially with a lackadaisical attitude 'cos he couldn't bear piss-poor attitude.

But ooohhh myyy – I've never heard anyone whinge as much as Darren Ferguson! Man alive! He'd peck yer head like a woodpecker on a tree 'n' he was even worse with the opponents – he'd just hammer them all through the game like an annoying fly in their ear 'n' get in their heads so much they'd eventually snap! And when they eventually did, you kinda noticed a wry little smile creep up on his face, saying, "Yep, got ya!" You what? He was exactly the same in training, until someone would bravely plead with him, "Ooohhh come on Daz, just give us a break!"

It's just as well he was able to back up his constant whining with his technical brilliance and perfectionist attributes ... ranging from whatever attire you were wearing, to setting the standards on the field. And if you didn't reach those high standards, he'd let you know instantly, before you'd start hearing the murmurs from a few of the lads. "Oh no, 'ere we go." But it's that drive 'n' desire that accelerated everyone's standards 'n', deep down – we loved it.

Tactically, I was a bit of a novice in the wingback role. I wasn't really an out-and-out left winger, and not an out-and-out left back, but running up and down the wing, pummelling crosses into the middle I was more than accustomed to. Once Dennis revealed the team formation, and with my new-found role of a wingback, I was really excited. Carlos Edwards, one of the Three Amigos from Trinidad and Tobago, was to play the wingback role on the opposite side, with the three centre halves providing cover for Andy Dibble in goal.

We had a pretty decent start, keeping in touch for play-off contention, playing some good football 'n' I'm thinking, "I'm enjoying this!" regardless of the background distractions of the club being taken to the courts. An old adage, I know, but as soon as we put our training gear on, or wore the Wrexham shirt on a matchday, we just tried to get on with it – we had a match to win, and we aimed to achieve that with hard work and a bit of entertainment.

I know it's another strange cliché, but the saying 'You can smell the atmosphere of a changing room' is absolutely spot-on. It doesn't convey the smell of a mixture of body odour, farts, or aftershave but, in actual fact, it's the sense of an amalgamation of characters. And I'm the type of person that loved to absorb the changing room ambience – it gave me a good sense of where we were as a team and the characters within it. Looking around, listening to the vibe in the changing room at Wrexham, there was always a sense of hope and togetherness. A bit like a tin of Quality Street, 'cos there was a varying choice on offer – each one suiting an acquired taste ... some sweet, some strong, and a bit nutty! But as for quality? Well, we had a tin full of it!

Chris Armstrong, Andy Dibble, Jim Whitley, Danny Williams, Dean Bennett, Stephen Roberts, Shaun Pejic and Craig Morgan were just a few of the names that formulated our changing room vibe and provided that quality! I'll let you decide which were the nutty ones ... quite a few to choose from, to be fair. That push for promotion, however, suddenly became an even harder achievement, as we became the first club to be deducted ten points for entering administration. This punishment sent us from promotion hopefuls to relegation battlers at around the midway mark of the season. A proper kick in the goolies. Shortly after the announcement, we played Scunthorpe United away in the second round of the FA Cup, where we beat them 2–0. On the coach journey back, I just had this reassuring feeling of "D'ya know what, we're gonna be OK!"

Undeniably, I always felt we had a good enough squad to survive, or even mount a challenge to climb up the League. But time became our enemy, and a match away to Swindon Town confirmed our worries, as we let a 2–1 lead slip, and eventually lost 2–4 to a ten-man Swindon Town. Visibly, you started to notice lads thinking, "SHIT! We really are in the SHIT!", which was hard to comprehend, given the characters within our changing room – a changing room packed with strong characters. There was no 'airs and graces' with them 'n' you wouldn't see an arm around someone if they weren't doing something right – instead, you'd have a bloody good bollocking! Personally, I loved that, 'cos it's what spurred me on to play better and improve. Yes, it wasn't pretty, and the language would be colourful. It wasn't for everyone, but it bloody worked for me.

This would be the case during a match, or on the training ground especially when we played the big Friday training match, ooohhh they could be tasty 'n' feisty! Airs and graces? Pffft, more like handbags and punch-ups! I'm pretty sure there were many times we'd have lads injured for the Saturday match because of the feisty Friday match in training! Honestly, it was pure madness! We played and trained to win. Anything less was not tolerated.

Unless, however, you're the ultimate enigma, and your inspirational performance in a match gets you out of jail for your inept performance in training. But that's exactly what our goalscoring talisman, Juan Ugarte, did week-in, week-out. Watching him in training, we'd turn round to the other lads and say, "Ooohhh my dear Lord, what is he doing?? How on earth has he missed that?" There were other times when we'd play five-a-side or a practice match on a Friday. You didn't want him in your team – quite the opposite – you'd just palm him off to another team, because he was sooo bad. But then, come matchday, he'd be unbelievably sharp, a nightmare for the others to mark, and a machine in the box to score goals for fun! Quite frankly, he was the definition of 'chalk and cheese'.

Kevin Russell, aka Rooster, was another character 'n' a bloody madman of a person. Sometimes he'd have you second-guessing if he's a genius or an escapee from a lunatic asylum! One minute he could play the good cop role, talking softly and giving advice, 'n' then flip the coin to be the bad cop, totally losing his head and screamin' at someone, before flickin' another switch and be an absolutely raving lunatic and have the whole squad wheezing with laughter! I'm sad to say I got to meet Rooster's whippet on many occasions – the first time was when I was with Oldham on the Isle of Man tour, and Wrexham were there as well, and we all happened to be in the same bar 'n' I start hearing shouts of "whippet!", "Get the whippet out!" – 'n' there's Rooster on all fours performing his whippet ... I just looked at the Wrexham lads 'n' said, "I just don't understand what's going on 'ere?"

Firmly pushing the whippet aside, Rooster was a class footballer, and I'd had the pleasure of playing against him whilst I was with Hull City, and then in the Friday matches at Wrexham. If I was to liken him to another player, it would be someone like Paul Dickov of Man City, 'cause he'd run you to the ground, a bloody workhorse who just wouldn't stop, and you'd be pleading with him, "Rooster, will you please stop bloody running." And, oh hey, he could be a horrible shit sometimes an' all, 'cos he'd stand on yer toes or catch his studs on yer calf, even though the ball's on the other side of the pitch! And yes, he'd do this on a Friday – my own bloody assistant coach! Adding more salt to the wound, he'd pop up in the last minute with the winning goal – and most likely to be worldie – stick his hand up and yell – "YEP, I'VE STILL GOT IT, LADS!" and if you were on his team you'd be screaming and celebrating with him! But you'd want to tell him to piss off and throttle him if you were against him.

Ooohhh deary, deary me, talking of worldies, there'd be days when we'd be wondering what the hell is Hector Sam on? Honestly, there were times when he was amazing, like his performance against Oldham when he scored a hat-trick, and looked a different class to the rest of us. The same in training when he looked untouchable, and I'd be like, "HOLY SHIT! This guy's unbelievable!" But the very next day you were like, "NO WAY!! This cannot be the same person? Surely, Hector's got a twin brother, because one is masquerading as a footballer, and the other is a footballing genius!"

And then there was Carlos. Well, bugger me, he could play. He was a pretty quiet character, but once he laced his boots it was a different story. Which I found out in one of my first training sessions.

"Right ... Holty 'n' Carlos, you're gonna be doing some one-on-ones against each other, just to test each other out – attacking and defending."

"Yeah, OK Gaffer, no problem," I said to him. Then came the one-on-ones, and I was like, "Holy shit, he is incredible," 'cos I honestly couldn't get near him! He'd be driving on my inside and going on to my weaker foot, my right foot, then going outside on to my left, and I'd end up twisting my legs! What a brilliant player, and genuinely a great guy, but then all three of the Trinidad and Tobago guys were so easy to get on with.

On the whole, I got on with all the lads 'n' staff 'cos there was a genuine camaraderie and solid team ethic there. And if perhaps the gaffer or Darren noticed the morale was a bit low, they'd insist on a staff bonding session ... not that we needed a valid reason to be honest. They were always a great occasion, especially the few times we had in Manchester, when Darren had arranged for us to visit some various bars and clubs. They were always great fun 'n' always good banter flowing just as quick as the beer.

It was probably through Darren that we acquired a truly fantastic goalkeeper in Ben Foster. Only 22 when he signed, he is still the best goalkeeper I have ever played with, or against. You just couldn't find a weakness with him – he was good at catching crosses, he was vocal, and bloody hell he could kick the ball an absolute mile! His first training session with us, the gaffer wanted to practice a set-piece 'n' tells Ben:

"So this position of play, Ben, you aim for Holty, he wins the header, then we can feed it down the middle to Juan ... OK Ben?"

Ben just gives him the thumbs-up, "Yeah, got ya Gaffer." He looks up towards me and shouts, "HOLTY – GO FURTHER BACK!"

At this point, I'm stood on the halfway line, and I'm like, "what's this kid doin'?" So I go back about five yards 'n' shout back to him, "No worries, mate" and give him a thumbs-up. But then he starts waving his finger.

"NOOO, GO FURTHER BACK!"

So I go another ten yards back and I'm like, "Here we bloody go", and then BOOM! He launches the ball perfectly onto the top of my head 'n' I go, "HOLY SHIT!! we've got a keeper here, boys!" Because his accuracy was sensational, and it was no surprise really when Darren's father, Sir Alex Ferguson, came in to sign him for Manchester United on the back of the LDV Vans final.

Sunday, 10th April 2005, is a date and an occasion that will live for ever with me and everyone else connected with Wrexham. To reach a final, when all hope is against us in the League, really showed what this club is all about. But to reach the LDV Vans Trophy against Southend United, in Cardiff, on Welsh soil … well, it beats the heart even harder, doesn't it? So we reached Cardiff on the Friday, two days prior to the final, and it was a lovely spring day when we got to our hotel, the Vale of Glamorgan Hotel. A stunning location and we really just chilled and chatted for hours. The next day we got whisked away for a tour of the Millennium Stadium, Cardiff, where we had the chance to walk around the pitch and go inside our changing room. It was a great idea, because we had a good feel for the arena, which perhaps would've been overwhelming on the day of the final.

However, the morning and pre-match couldn't have gone any more bloody awkward for me and, in all honesty, I could've easily found myself out of the squad, and possibly out of the club! It all started the week leading up to final, when a journalist from *The Sun* newspaper got in touch and asked if I could give a short 'tongue-in-cheek' briefing on all the lads in the squad. "Yeah, of course," I accepted 'n' never in a million years thought any malice would come of it, especially as it was only meant to be a bit of banter.

Ooohhh blooodyyy hell's bells! That 'tongue-in-cheek' bit me harder than bloody Jaws! 'Cos, just as we're tucking into our breakfast on the morning of the final, one of the lads gestures towards me, and starts laughing in an evil manner:

"You're in deep shit, Holty! Tee-hee-hee. Hey, the gaffer's gonna kill you mate", and passes me the *Sun on Sunday* newspaper.

"HOLY FUCKIN' SHIT! Hey, make sure the gaffer doesn't get a copy." Too late!

"HOLTY! HOLTY? Come 'ere, son, I wanna a word please."

Yep, the gaffer's collared me and he's sat down holding the *Sun on Sunday* newspaper in front of him.

"Care to explain yourself, son?" he goes.

"Well, Gaffer," I stammer, "I didn't think they'd print everything I said, honestly! I never meant to cause any offence ... genuinely, it was done tongue-in-cheek."

Throughout this whole episode, the gaffer is holding a double-page spread of his face superimposed on to the body of Darth Vader, after I'd likened him to the Evil Emperor on a typically wet training session, when the gaffer would walk very gingerly (due to his several hip operations) towards the training pitch, dressed all in black waterproofs ... the only thing missing was the 'Imperial March' theme tune!

Thank God, the gaffer forgave me and, only a few short hours later, I was warming up with the rest of the lads on a baking hot south Walian early spring Sunday afternoon. Even then, I had a hunch it was gonna be our day as our fans poured in and in fine voice. 'Dakota' by the Stereophonics played in the background just as we were making our way back to the modern Millennium Stadium dressing room. OOOHHH MAAAN, the overriding sense that something special was gonna happen was soo powerful, it gave me goosebumps as I was putting on my No.19 Wrexham shirt. Then a hush descended, 'n' it was the gaffer's final words:

"There's thousands of our fans out there – we represent them – they represent us. We've been there for each other all through the season. Give them something to shout about and send them dancing back to north Wales tonight. And hey – no one remembers the losers – we only remember the winners ... so let's get out there and be winners!"

HOLY SHIT! Lining up with my teammates, I stood

behind Ben Foster in the tunnel, waiting to walk out for the match 'n', flippin' hell, the 'Imperial March' had nothing on the cocoon of noise of our fans chanting, "WREXHAM, WREXHAM, WREXHAM, WREXHAM." It sent shivers down my spine, so I just said to Ben:

"Just get me out onto the pitch, Ben. Oh, my days, I've got so much goosebumps, I just wanna get out there and play."

He turned and looked at me, "Fuck me, Holty; we've gotta bring it home today mate!"

Inside of me was a burning ball of excitement and passion. Darren Ferguson took one last look at us before we marched out and barks:

"FUCKIN' C'MON, BOIS!"

It's probably just as well we had the fireworks when we walked out onto the pitch, because there were none during the match. Whether it was down to the sheer heat, or just the occasion, but it definitely failed to live up to the atmosphere created by both sets of fans, especially ours, because they were tremendous. They just didn't stop singing, and there's no doubt it gave us that extra impetus to keep going and keep hoping that we'd find a breakthrough. Oh my days, it was really draining though, and it was such a massive relief when Juan reacted quickly to head us into the lead in the ninth minute of extra time. Our celebration is one of my favourite photos during my career, as I'm jumping onto Juan, who's wheeling away to celebrate in front of our ecstatic fans. WHOOSH – talk about an injection of serotonin – BANG! Straight away you feel a huge wave of vitality rushing through your body, and all that fatigue is instantly forgotten.

Darren must've had an extra dose from somewhere, because in the last minute of extra time he sprints (and believe me, Darren wouldn't sprint if there was a leopard chasing him!) on to a loose ball to prod it past the Southend United keeper Darryl Flahavan. But his cameo isn't finished, as he then performs a schoolboy attempt at a roly-poly 'n' as I'm running towards him, I'm shaking my head shoutin', "WHAT THE HELL?" No sooner had we got back for the restart, the final whistle blew! Aaah, thank you referee for your kind offer of another shot of serotonin, WHAM! BUZZIN!

Pure scenes. Lifting the trophy in front of our ecstatic fans was so special. Not just because we'd won the final, but also because of all the shit they'd been through that season. And it just felt amazing to see 'em 'n' hear 'em singing and dancing in the beautiful sunshine. Even to this day, whenever I hear 'Is this the way to Amarillo' by Tony Christie, I'm instantly transported back to that glorious day, and we're all just soaking up this enormous wave of high emotion. And once we'd jigged our way back to our changing room, there was only one thing on all our minds – getting in touch with our friends and families – so we switched on our Nokia phones! We ran back out onto the pitch to get a better signal to speak with our families, who were sat high up in the Millennium Stadium. Ooohhh mate, that was an emotional moment, speaking, crying, laughing and waving to our loved ones.

"Right, OK then, we'll see you back at the Vale of Glamorgan Hotel later! Errrmmm, not sure how long we'll be 'cos there's a few crates of Budweiser waiting to be emptied in the changing rooms 'n' there might be a whippet prowling around!"

Soaked in sweat 'n' beer – soaking up the dressing room spirits, I found myself sitting back and just enjoying the view of this momentous occasion … because the moment passes you by ever so quickly, and there's always a danger that you're not 'present' enough to just feel the moment – 'n' out of the corner of my eye I thought I recognised someone globally famous enter the room in an immaculate grey suit. "It can't be? Nah … oh bloody hell, it is an' all!" Sir Alex Ferguson was walking around shaking everyone's hand and congratulating us on our fantastic success, and he particularly shook Ben Foster's hand a lot longer than anybody else's! Fair play, he was obviously there to cheer on his son, Darren Ferguson, but I thought it was a class act of him to make his way down to our changing room to congratulate each and every one of us. Magic moments.

Still singing and dancing, we arrived back to rapturous applause and cheering from our families and hotel staff at the Vale of Glamorgan. "Yes please, I'll have another shot of serotonin!" – and so the joyous occasion continued to flow all through the night, with everyone hugging and dancing. We even had our very own musician, as Stevie Roberts tinkled the ivories on the piano and serenaded us by singing a few songs, which really encompassed the entire day. A great piano player, but an even better centre half. Although, usually, it would've been Jim Whitley that would've sat on the stool and played a few tunes, because Jim is THE most talented person at everything – he's a phenomenal artist and paints official portraits for the PFA, he performs an unbelievable Sammy Davies Junior, 'Mr Bojangles', and plays off a three handicap at golf … just a super-talented person.

Ooo, what a great night! I wish I could tell ya what time I went to bed, but I can't! But what I do remember is the sun rising, just as I'm straggling along up to my room 'n' still clutching my winner's medal in one hand, the match programme tucked under the other arm, and my club tie wrapped around my head. I've kept all three as precious mementos. Without a shadow of a doubt, that special weekend is the highlight of my career.

The icing on the already sweet-tasting cake, for me, was the presence of someone who became very dear to me during my time with Wrexham – my pal, Joey Jones. No one deserved that victory more than Joey – because he lives and breathes Wrexham Football Club. Oooh mate, Joey would be at the training ground every single day, without fail, and just outside the doors to the main changing rooms, there's a wooden plank, like a fence, and every single day we'd be doing pull-ups with him on this plank, because he was just a machine – such a naturally fit and strong guy, who would never give up. Such an inspirational person. Them pull-ups and sit-ups though ... och! He made Joe Wicks look like an amateur!

Being introduced to Joey has been one of the special moments in my career 'n', in all honesty, I hadn't realised just how famous he was, and how much he was endeared by everyone from all the clubs he'd played for. So I only found out properly by searching him on Google, and my reaction was like, "Holy shit, this guy is a proper legend." That for me really typifies Joey to a tee – never one to laud himself up and be arrogant, never big-headed and showing off – he just loved being one of the lads, he's got a wicked sense of humour, very much a down-to-earth guy, a heart made of pure gold. I always saw Joey as like being with one of your best mates in school, where you'd have a laugh 'n' do anything for each other. Even now, I can still hear his voice talking to me, "Right Holty, this is how it's going to be – we're gonna run through brick walls together, and if you come with me, we're gonna be alright." Ooohhh – I flippin' loved that mentality.

We instantly blossomed and kinda latched on to one another because we both played in the same position – he was a left back and so was I, and we just clicked and got on so well. I could just talk and listen to Joey until the cows came home, because he loved football 'n' he loved being with good people around him. And because he was such an approachable person, he'd always make time for anyone seeking advice.

I knew I wasn't technically blessed with any outstanding skill, but what I did have in my tank was stamina. I loved a tackle, I'd never shirk a tackle, and could deliver a decent ball into the middle. I just loved that aspect of being in a battle and putting an honest shift in. And that's where Joey saw that comparison between ourselves, because Joey's persona was all about being an honest person putting in an honest shift ... just that he could do it a little bit better than me. And perhaps, in that sense, I would always seek his advice, or perhaps a bit of feedback from a game, which was always invaluable.

"Keep looking for that inside, Holty," he'd say or, "Just pick your head up a fraction sooner and look to clip it down the line pal, OK?"

And I'd be like, "Yeah, I like that, I see where you're coming from mate, thanks Joey." It made sense because we both shared the same traits and mentalities of being a left-footed left back and getting the ball out of our feet, down the channel and peg it to follow it up. It sounds ever so simple, doesn't it? But it made sense because of the way it was delivered to me by Joey.

By no means was he a softy, and at the drop of a hat he could take the piss out of someone one minute, and then put them in their place if they needed it. There was never a chance of someone having a comeback either 'n' you'd be like:

"Well that's Joey! 'Cos not only has he got the medals to back it up, he's also as hard as bloody nails, so I ain't gonna mess with him." Bloody hell's bells, Joey didn't half fill his boots with the likes of Matty Crowell. Oh. My. Days. 'n' holy shit! I tell ya what, if he was a chocolate bar he'd eat himself! Honestly, what a character. Matty was from that generation of looking as if he'd auditioned for a part on *Footballers' Wives* 'cos he loved that playboy image of a flash car, expensive dodgy clothes, wacky hairstyles. Honestly, he spent more time in front of the mirror pissin' around with his hair, longer than yer granny would in a hair salon! Bloody hell fire!

And don't get me started on his fake tan!! Gee whiz, there were days where he was about five different shades of mahogany! Ohhhh he was a flash bugger, and sometimes in training you'd wanna teach him a lesson and two-foot him! But, in all honesty, he was a great lad, and on his day he would be unplayable.

Sharing large quantities of hair gel with Matty was Chrissy Llewelyn. But owww, hey, you wouldn't want to mess with Izzy, not unless you liked being battered and chopped into tiny little pieces. In fact, I'd liken him to Rooster, because I'd hate to mark him 'n' he's one of those that's quick, naturally tricky with both feet, and you wouldn't have a clue which direction he's going. Just an absolute bloody nightmare to defend against. Talk about clinical! Pffft! Hey, once he'd get his eye in, weeell, you might as well tell the keeper to start bending his back 'n' collect the ball from the back of the net. Helluva good lad Izzy, 'n' always up for a good laugh. But just be careful of his angry eyes ... because that was the warning sign and signal to book yourself a taxi home!

For whatever reason though, it just wasn't happening for us in the League, which was really hard for me to comprehend, especially with the talent we had at the club. Of course you do feel the air of angst filtering from the fans, and rightly so. But I was perplexed at how on earth we were still struggling in the relegation zone, and eventually it did start to have an effect on my home life. As a footballer, you know, when things aren't going your way, even though you're trying your damned best, and you start hearing the odd jeering from your own fans ... and it's a sound that still rings in yer ears when you walk through the door to your home later that day. As soon as you're in the house, you just crave solitude 'n' you just wanna be left alone.

Which was hard for my family to understand. And because they weren't massively into football, they'd say stuff like, "Never mind love, there's always next week" or, "Ah well, as long as you enjoy it." Ooohhh mate, that used to drive me mad, so I'd instantly reply with, "Look, it's my job, I need to win these games," but they'd always be at a loss trying to understand what the implications of a result meant. The worst one was always, "Don't worry – it's just a game." WOW! Thanks, you've just made things a hundred times worse!

Inevitably, we succumbed to relegation. Years later, I still look back and wonder how we would've fared if we weren't deducted that ten points. The implications of our relegation to League Two did, however, provide the fans and the club with a chance of playing in some spicy derby matches. I kinda knew the hatred between Wrexham, Chester, and Shrewsbury, but I honestly hadn't realised just how much the Wrexham fans despised them. My first taste of derby-day hostilities came when we beat Chester at their place in the run-up to the FA Trophy success. I hadn't expected a big attendance because it was the third round. But as soon as we stepped out, I felt this massive wave of hostility and noticed over 1,700 of our fans chanting and screaming their 'eads off. HOLY SHIT! This was like nothing I'd ever been involved in before. Then Juan nicks a goal for us to win 1–0, and it was a case of shut-up shop, let's get showered and let's get the hell outta here.

That was like a garden fete at the vicarage compared with the fixture at The Racecourse in March 2006. It was tasty before we'd even kicked off, but it got a lot tastier after Jonah walloped one in from 25 yards, and then Danny Williams made it 2–0 heading from a corner. Bloody hell, there's absolutely nowhere else like The Racecourse on derby day against Chester … pure theatre. The atmosphere was so loud you couldn't hear Rooster or the gaffer screaming instructions.

In the meantime, all our families are in the main family stand, hearing our fans screaming at the Chester fans, "FUCK OFF YOU ENGLISH BASTARDS!" and the Chester fans retaliating with, "AAAH, FUCK OFF YER SHEEP SHAGGIN' WANKERS!" Our families were like, "Eeerrrr, OK, this is interesting." So it was quite inevitable I'd have to sit in the 'Mastermind' chair at home 'n' explain to my family the rivalry, and how much it meant to the fans because of the cross-border hatred.

My most abiding memory from any of the derbies was Jonah's torpedo missile against Chester! Boy oh boy, could he strike a ball! Oooffff! I tell ya, his boots should've had a 'toxic' label on 'em, 'cos they were lethal! Jonah was something of a silent assassin, 'cos he'd literally ghost around the park and then, WHAM! The ball's ripped the back of the net a split second after touching the lace of his boot. Ha-hah-hah, anybody else 'n' they'd be screamin' their 'eads off 'n' chuckin' their shirt in the crowd ... but not Jonah. He'd just smile 'n' giggle 'n' utter, "Aye, not bad that, hee-hee-hee." Such a talented and skilful player, especially in tight areas. Not that you'd known he was there, he was so quiet. Unassuming, yet lightning quick with his one-liners, Jonah would just float around the place, before causing a massive eruption with one of his classic one-liners. Lovely lad, and very funny. I'd always assumed the reason for his nickname, 'The Library', was because of his quiet nature ... but I presumed wrong, 'cos apparently it was a character reference towards him in a court case!

But Jonah was most definitely the shining light on an otherwise fairly dull season. We were neither here nor there in the League really. We just couldn't mount a good run of wins together to really push to get straight back into League. We lost a few good players just to plug the ever-sinking pit of money we had. And although the new players weren't to blame for that lack of spark, we simply weren't cooking on gas ... more like an air fryer cooking chicken nuggets on low heat. Which then brings me on to another teammate, Lee McEvilly. McEvilly was yer typical character who loved a challenge, could bulldoze his way past defenders, and was able to produce a stunning goal that left you in total disbelief. So could his lifestyle conditioning as well! A pre-match diet of 20 chicken nuggets and a Coca Cola absolutely bombed my brain. I'd just look at him and say, "Lee? Are you actually for real, mate?" And without batting an eyelid, he'd just carry on munching his way through this family-sized box of chicken nuggets! Bloody hell's bells! But another great guy 'n' a great character to have around the changing room that was always involved in the mickey-taking.

Lee was the type of character that could give 'n' take the piss, and I think it was a testament to his character that he didn't take himself too serious. Which was just as well during one match at The Racecourse that season, when things weren't going particularly well for him, and you kinda sensed our fans weren't pleased with his work rate, especially compared to Izzy's, who was just a bloody workhorse. Then came a break in play, along the Mold Road stand, and the ball's gone out for our throw-in opposite their 18-yard box. I'm jogging down the line to take the throw, but Lee's already there, and just as he's about to pick up the ball, one of our fans shouts, "OI FATTY, FANCY A BALTI PIE?" and stretches their arm out to hand over their pie to Lee. Without hesitation, Lee takes a bite out of this pie like Jaws 'n' gives a thumbs-up to the shocked fan and says, "Mmm, that's alright that – cheers!"

I just stood there, with the ball in my hands 'n' I'm shaking my head thinking, "What in the world of hens and chickens is going on?" I then take the throw 'n' send the ball straight to Lee's chest. He then swivels like a ballerina and hits it on the half-volley 'n' it crashes against the bar! I'm jogging back to the halfway line still shaking my head again. Maybe I was pissed off because I wasn't offered a bite of that Balti pie!

Driving home that evening, it dawned on me like a flash of lightning 'n' got me wondering perhaps the lyrics to my own fans' chant wasn't the threatening, "HOLTY, HOLTY, HOLTY, HOLTY", and after all this time it was "BALTI,

BALTI, BALTI, BALTI", because of the fans' favourite savoury snack? Well, bloody hell!

Another really funny character was little Alex Smith. Technically brilliant and a brain as sharp as a kitchen knife, Smithy would come up with this really clever 'n' very funny idea of spicing things up in the post-match interviews after a game. So each week he'd invent a new word – a word amalgamated from two totally different words, and whoever did the interview had to use it, and if they didn't, they'd have to face the consequence of a forfeit. And, on one occasion, his word of the day was 'terrocious' which was an amalgamation of 'terrible' and 'atrocious'. Ooohhh, let me tell ya, the strange and puzzling look on the faces of all the journalists was priceless! They were so flummoxed, they asked me to repeat it several times 'n' each time I'd repeat myself. Eventually, to save themselves from any more embarrassment, they'd fluster 'n' nod, "Right yea, of course, yes ... terrocious, thank you Andy! Good luck for the next match," before packing away their Dictaphones. Phew! No forfeit for me then!

But they were just the little nuggets of joy I experienced as a player. There's a lot of highs 'n' lows during your career, and you've really got to dedicate yourself and be ultimately sacrificial to be able to experience more highs and lows. Even my own brother's wedding played second fiddle, and it just wouldn't sink in with my family again.

"Andrew, your brother's getting married middle Saturday of this November, d'you think ...?"

And before they finished their sentence, I jumped in ahead of them, "No!"

"Ooh! But why not?" they'd come back, looking absolutely stunned.

"Because I'm playing football – that's my job, and look, it's the first round of the FA Cup, so I'll get to the night do."

And then that classic phrase rears its ugly head, "Oh but Andrew, it's just a game."

FLIPPIN' HELL! Could you imagine going to the gaffer asking him, like a little schoolboy with a note from his parents: "Dear Mr Smith, Andrew Holt will not be able to play football in the first round of the FA Cup this year because he has to attend his brother's wedding ... oh, and he might have tummy ache."

Ooh my FLIPPIN' days! The thought never entertained my head so, as it turned out, I played the game and then went straight to my brother's wedding night.

The only time I ever asked the gaffer for some official time off was during our pre-season tour in Belfast, late July 2005, because my wife at that time was due to have our baby around that time. So I made a deal with the gaffer, where I stayed at home and trained with our physio ... but while the lads were in Belfast, the gaffer rang me and said, "Look, Holty, you're gonna have to play a game." So the club arranged for me to fly out to Belfast, for one game, then straight after the game finished I flew back home. Honestly, I felt like an international superstar!

But that was just how being a part of Wrexham Football Club made you feel. It has this way of getting into your heart 'n' it just stays there, like the beat to your favourite song. However, I still get that taste of an unfinished wedding cake – 'cos I was another ingredient, along with the other ingredients, trying to mix and gel everything together to bake a cake for Wrexham Football Club. 'N' the only thing missing was the icing – someone to have the cash to splash ... all good things come to those who wait, eh! Savour the flavour, my dear Wrexham fans.

13

Ryan Valentine
Defender

More than a feeling ... on Valentine's day!
2006–2008 (48 appearances, 2 goals)

After 100 years of Football League status, the club was on the brink of extinction; over 10,000 desperate fanatics baying for hope; 12 yards was the distance between desolation and salvation. Local lad and boyhood supporter of his beloved Wrexham AFC, Ryan Valentine had only one thing on his mind in the midst of May Day madness ... to do his job and put the ball in the net. Here, the former Wrexham full back gives an authentic account of a season full of fraught, and frivolous frolics.

There's Something About Wrexham

ONLY SEVEN DAYS previous, I was dressed as Fred Flintstone, suppin' a few beers with my teammates. Now ... things are far from yabba dabba do. We're 1–0 down to Boston United in a winner stays up last match of the season clash. We've just been awarded a penalty. I'm the designated penalty taker.

I should be a bag of nerves. I'm about to take a few strides to save the club that I've loved and supported since I was aged eight. More about 'that penalty' in a bit.

As an eight year old, I watched that Mickey T missile and Super Stevie Watkins strike sink the Mighty Gunners of Arsenal in 1992. Like a leaping salmon, I was hooked on following The Town. I went to as many matches as I could, mainly with my dad's mate, Peter, in car-fulls or coaches to some memorable away matches – to the likes of West Ham United, Manchester United or Blackpool. I absolutely loved it. And it's a period in my life I'm so grateful to have experienced as I got to know just how much the club means to people and why it attracts the staggering amount of attention it gets. In the summer of 2006, I finally got the dream move to play for them, after a spell at Everton and Darlington.

I couldn't wait to meet up with my new teammates on a pre-season excursion to Belfast. The squad included players that had previously played at a higher level, such as Chris Llewelyn, Michael Proctor, Neil Roberts, Matt Crowell and club captain Darren 'Fainter' Ferguson (earning the moniker Fainter following a night-out in town with the lads, he got his fingers jammed and slammed in the entrance door into the Horse and Jockey, "Aaahhh fffaaaccckkk" he shouted, before fainting and falling to the floor like a sack of spuds!).

There was a sense of local pride to the squad, as it boasted six members that hailed from the Wrexham area and North Wales, including Mark Jones, Danny Williams, Stevie Evans, Simon Spender, Neil Roberts and myself. Which may have been a factor why things got a bit lairy and tasty on a night-out in Belfast – let's just say we guzzled gallons of beer, our tongues loosened and lost any kind of filter inside our heads! You can take the lad out of Wrexham, but you can't get Wrexham out of the lad! Luckily, these were the days before social media ruled the world, and we were even more grateful that the local press hadn't travelled along with us.

Fortunately for us, we had a great coaching team in Dennis Smith and Kev Russell. As long as we performed in training and on a matchday, they would allow us to let our hair down from time to time. The gaffer was a top bloke and had a real aura about him. Hard but fair. Kev was just a great person, our go to guy who could have a laugh with you but also give you sound advice.

League positions don't lie. Teams are in their positions for a reason. But if you'd have told me in early September that season that we'd be fighting relegation by around February, I'd have looked daft at you, as we got off to a good start. After our humbling at Accrington, we never really recovered.

Dennis Smith and Kev Russell were sacked and replaced by Brian Carey, already part of the backroom staff. The fans were desperate for us to drag ourselves away from the drop and we were desperate to repay their loyal support. Shrewsbury Town away, midweek, towards the end of April, a tasty local derby, and we came away with a 1–0 win, after Michael Proctor scored near the death. Buzzin' by our huge win, Neil Roberts announced on the team bus, "Right lads, were havin' a barbecue at my house this Sunday, every single one of ya is comin'. Bring yer partners … oh, and by the way, it's fancy dress."

Whether it was proposed as a loosener for team bonding, with the knowledge that we needed just a point to survive and just one home match remaining, or a gesture of goodwill on Robbo's behalf, but it was a bloody party! I went as Fred Flintstone and had a yabba dabba do time. Some others, however, must have come as magicians, as they disappeared for a few days – only resurfacing and returning to training around 48 hours prior to the crunch match against Boston United, following a monster session.

Trailing 1–0 at halftime in the biggest match in the club's history, I wanted to rip everyone's fuckin' head off on our way to the changing rooms. My mood hadn't altered once we got in, as I launched the kit bag with my left boot like a fuckin' rocket! In no certain terms I fumed at everyone.

"Fuckin' disgrace, shower of shit performance. A club's history hangs in the balance and we play like a bunch of pricks. FUCKING RAISE OUR GAME!"

By now, most of the lads also piped up, and it was total chaos with everyone shouting and swearing. Luckily, the coaching staff let us say our piece, before settling us down and calmly reassuring us that if we stepped up a gear and kept the ball tighter, then we'd be OK.

Their prophecy unfolded early in the fourth quarter, as we were awarded THE penalty. So here we go, back to the main story. Like a fish in a goldfish bowl, I shut out all the white noise. It was only after smacking the ball in the back of the net that I was able to release all the tension that had built up inside me in the week leading up to the match. With the pressure seemingly off our shoulders, we were now unstoppable as Chrissy Llewelyn and Michael Proctor sealed our victory but, more importantly, the club's proud League status remained.

Thousands swarmed upon us on the pitch after the final whistle. We were their heroes, as they signalled an official declaration for a party! And that we did – in true Wrexham style! Personally, I was so overawed by our last day escape and getting the club out of jail, I went out to celebrate again the following day ... only to find myself in the clink, for a bit of mischievous antics! Special times indeed.

And that, is THE fitting word to describe Wrexham AFC. Special. For me, there's no club, town, city, or area that generates and captures this insane amount of imagination, as what Wrexham does. It's as if it's a national football team representing north Wales. They all go, not just for the match, but for the whole occasion: the buzz of the journey, the hum and hub of excitement around Mold Road. Families and friends clinking and singing in their favourite traditional pub. Then, the 'Men of Harlech' theme tune, 'Wrexham is the name', booms out. Magic. I'm so proud I've had the privilege to have been a fan and a player for my favourite team. C'mon The Town!

14
Andy Edwards
Forward

Is it an eagle, is it a plane? No, it's SuperTed!
1980–1986 (154 appearances, 35 goals)

His personality traits mirrored those on the field – direct, fearless, entertaining and dedicated! Proudly hailing from Queens Park (a stone's throw away from The Racecourse) Andy Edwards, aka SuperTed, was and still is yer typical 'sound lad' from the Wrexham area who's devoutly in love with the club. It's been said that – "Andy takes no nonsense off anyone". Here, he tells us in his own words about not holding back and pulling no punches (although he threw a fair few in his time). Andy recalls with pounding pride of playing for The Town, and how a man in a boy's body looked after himself (on and off the field). So, strap yerself in, and get the throat lozenges ready ...

BACK IN 2017 I suffered a massive bleed on the brain. Coming round on the bed in Walton, I felt as though I'd been cracked on the head by Dixie McNeil's flaying elbow again! But it felt 100 times worse. However, I'm the lucky bastard really, because I survived. I've had the chance to spend quality time with my family and my mates down the pub. I can also count my blessings that I've still got a sharp as hell memory, especially the precious memories of my time playing for my team – Wrexham. Bloody hell, there's thousands of lads from north Wales that would give anything to wear the shirt with the Wrexham crest embroidered on it, and actually playing for them on The Racecourse turf ... and I did. So, for me, every day is a great day!

It doesn't matter where you've been brought up, it'll always leave an imprint on you. It'll always play a part in your personality. I was brought up surrounded by tough council estates, plenty going on, bit of mischief here and there, and we'd always stick up for each other ... until someone pissed you off and you'd end up cracking them on the nose and causing a mini riot to erupt! Ahhh, happy days la'!

So, that's why I'll always be grateful to Queens Park, for making me the stubborn but good-natured little nutcase I am! I'd like to think that my heart's full of gold, but my head? Well, let's just say that when the surgeons at Walton operated on me, even they didn't come across a fuckin' filter!

I guess I'll always be grateful to the fact that I was pretty decent at football. Playing for Queens Park Youth Club, I didn't know anything about anything, playing in the Wrexham and District youth leagues and all that – but I knew I could play a bit.

Then one night there was a knock on the door, so I answered it, and there was two men there.

"Can we speak with your dad?"

I thought, "Fuckin' hell." So, I shouted for Dad, "Dad, there's two fellas wanna speak to you here."

"WHAT THE FUCK 'AV' YER DONE NOW?" he shouted back.

"Nothing Dad, HONESTLY!"

So, being a typical grown man from Queens Park, my dad just looks at these two fellas and says, "What d'ya want?"

"Mr Edwards," one of them said. "We're from Wrexham FC, and we'd like to sign your son as a schoolboy at 15."

"Oh aye," my dad replies. "Is he any good?" 'Cause the thing was, my dad had never watched me play.

"We'd like to sign him as a schoolboy and he's exactly what we need," they said.

I thought, "Fuckin 'ell." And so I signed for my hometown club, my heroes!

A few weeks later, I'm in the Wrexham baths, and there was a message on the PA system, "Can Andy Edwards come downstairs, please." So, I looked around confused, I go downstairs, get changed, and my dad's standing there with my football boots.

So, as I'm walking closer towards him, I said, "What?"

"Well, you're playing football!" he snapped back.

"Well, who for?" 'Cos by now I was confused as fuck.

"For someone at the Stansty."

So he takes me to Stansty. And the staff there then sent me to The Racecourse! When I finally arrive there, you should've seen the looks I had ... I was wearing a big pair of Doc Marten boots, army pants, and a Sex Pistols T-shirt! I was then shown into the changing room, and fuck me, there's John Muldoon looking dapper in a tie and suit, and as soon as the rest of the lads clock me, they said, "No, we're not playing against him!" Unbeknown to me, this was gonna be my trial match and we were playing against Rochdale Reserves. Apart from a few butterflies early on, I absolutely loved every minute, and I must've done alright because after the match they invited me to join the first-year apprentices on a trip to Eindhoven, Holland.

Of course I was a little bit nervous, but I soon settled once I got to know a few of the lads, especially the likes of Stu Parker, Steve Jones, and John Muldoon. I must've made a good impression, because on our way back home, the club offered me a chance to stay on as an apprentice – fuckin' magic! Wrexham were in the old Second Division at the time, now the Championship. For me to be catapulted from standing next to my mates on the Crispin Lane terraces to be sharing a training pitch with my absolute heroes like Gareth Davies and Dixie McNeil, gave me a massive boost. As it happens, I got my first piece of vital advice from Dixie, only it wasn't my pride that got hurt this time.

Whether you were a 17-year-old apprentice trying to make an impression, or a seasoned pro still trying to prove you've still got it, during training nobody literally gives a fuck, because everyone wants to win everything, and no one wants to show any weakness. Me and Dixie were no different. Sadly, he was coming to the end of his career, whilst I was putting my feet on the first rung of the career ladder. And this particular training was no different to any other – fuckin' anything goes – and there's an aerial battle to be won between me and Dixie. CRACK! Dixie's elbow has just whacked me in the face.

"Ooohhh, fuckin' hell," I yelled!

Dixie just looked disgusted at me and says, "Well, get yer elbows up then, son," showing absolutely no remorse, whilst I've got a black eye looking like something from fuckin' *Looney Tunes*. Fair play though, at the end of training he sought me out and pulled me aside for a quiet friendly piece of advice.

"You alright, son? Look, football can be a brutal game, and them defenders ain't gonna be nice with you, they're gonna want to batter you to get the better of you – so as you go up for a header, use yer elbows for two reasons – to jump higher, and to protect yourself – OK son?"

It's only decades later that I'm able to appreciate and realise how much of a massive deal it was at that time; a fuckin' tearaway from Queens Park training with super Dixie McNeil? YOU'RE TALKING BOLLOCKS MATE! But hey, that's exactly what I did an' it was class.

I signed as an apprentice when Mel Sutton was in charge. But then he got sacked after another relegation. So in 1982 Bobby Roberts took over, and initially I wasn't sure if he liked me or rated me to be honest. Then, on Tuesday, 31st August 1982, the first team had a home game that night, in the old Milk Cup against despised rivals Shrewsbury Town in a big derby match, and I was getting ready for a driving lesson. So, I went to find Bobby.

"Boss, can I come back in for seven o'clock so I can go to my driving lesson first?"

And before I could carry on he snaps back in his gruff Scottish accent, "No yer fackin' can't – yer here for six o'clock!"

Typical me, I answered him back. "Well fuckin' 'ell, it's usually 'alf six!"

By now he's just staring at me. "Bastard six o'clock – be there – or NOT!"

So I got back to The Racecourse just before six o'clock, and I've only just got one foot through the main doors, and Bobby Roberts spots me, like a fuckin' radar.

"Get in my office!"

And straight away my mind's going faster than a greyhound. "Ooo shit, what 'av' I done wrong!?"

As calm as you like he looks me dead in the eyes. "Yer playing tonight!"

My 17-year-old arse was going like a bloody fruit machine. I'd got my big chance after Dixie had twisted his ankle in training.

"Can I phone my dad?" were the first words that flew out me mouth.

"Of course you can."

Only thing was, we didn't own a telephone at that time, so I had to phone our next-door neighbour, and after a little bit of time trying to track him down, my dad gets on the other side of the phone, and goes, "What's up?"

"Dad, I'm playing tonight!"

So, I left him two complimentary tickets to the match in reception. The time that elapsed between that phone call and sitting in the changing rooms with the rest of the lads passed me by in such a blur, you'd swear I'd been with the smackheads on the common in Queens Park.

There was one aspect I definitely wasn't allowed to forget … or bloody escape. Even though I was starting for the first team, I still had to do my apprenticeship duties – which was laying the kit out neat an' tidy – only this time, I got to put my own kit on, which was surreal as fuck, to think I must've laid that kit out on dozens of occasions, but now I was the recipient. Ooohhh, the material on that shirt felt fuckin' amazing against my own skin! And them smackheads must've sneaked into the changing room again, because I can't remember much from the match, apart from winning a few aerial duels, especially on one occasion when I outjumped both their keeper and centre half to win the ball and almost scored before it was cleared off the line! But by far the best was hearing The Racecourse erupt after we scored. We eventually won 1–0, thanks to Simon Hunt finding the net. A bit of a change from spending the night with my mates playing snooker above the old Hippodrome Cinema, I suppose!

I've already mentioned a couple of heroes of mine – Dixie

and Gareth, but there's one that will always have a special place in my heart and soul, and no doubt in tens of thousands of other Wrexham fans – Joey Jones. He may have a Liverpool tattoo, but he has Wrexham FC in his blood. Oh God, what an absolute legend! He made you want to run through a brick wall just by looking at him, but at the same time lose the feeling to yer legs by pissing yerself laughing! I owe a lot to Joey (even my nickname).

I was with the second-year apprentices, getting stuck in to the daily chores, and Joey walks in an' starts chatting with everyone, as he always did. It was also around this time that *SuperTed* was on the telly, and he literally just looks at me and goes, "Fuckin' hell, it's Teddy Edwards, aye, that's you – SUPERTED!" And it's stuck with me ever since – even to the extent of it being my email address!

But what can I say about Joey? Well, to start with, we're both from similar backgrounds, and as soon as we clocked eyes on each other we clicked like mad. He knew how to make me laugh, and I knew how to please him 'n' make him proud of me. I never wanted to let him down. Not through fear, but for my utmost respect for the man he was. Although, saying that, he'd always remind me with one of his sayings, "Don't be fooled by the frame, Ted," because even though he was built like a zip, he could kick his way through a brick wall. His influence would ooze through me.

For instance, there was a midweek match away at Preston North End and, because the club was totally skint, five apprentices were selected for this first team match, consisting of John Muldoon, Steve Jones, Medwyn Evans, Darren Baker, and myself. Bobby Roberts told us he had every faith in us to stand up for ourselves and be ready for a battle. He showed this by naming John Muldoon and myself up front. I always backed myself against anyone, but on this occasion I needed a bit of encouragement from Joey to help me sort out their ageing centre half, Alan Gowling. I tell ya what, from the first whistle, this old fucker, Alan Gowling, just wanted to kick the shit out of me and John.

Then I heard Joey shouting towards me "TED! TED! JUST FUCKIN' DO HIM!"

I just checked with Joey. "Really Joey, because ..."

"JUST DO THE OLD BASTARD, TED!" he immediately ordered me.

And, there's no way I was ever gonna let my Joey down. Soon enough, Stevie Jones knocks a ball over the top and, as I'm hanging up in the air for a header, I throw my elbow in his face, win the header, and I suddenly feel a sharp pain on my elbow. "Fuck me, my elbow's killing me!" I look around, and Gowling's on the floor screaming his head off, he's pissing with blood. I quickly realised why. I've got his tooth stuck in my elbow! Even to this day I've still got a scar of Alan Gowling's tooth in my elbow. Cheers for that, Joey lad!

By chance though, a few weeks later I attended a meeting with the Combined Insurance company, with an American rep. Basically, it was a company that looked after you if you weren't paid your wages or if you felt in any way mistreated financially. However, I'd only popped my head around the bloody door, and whose toothless face greeted me? Alan fuckin' Gowling! I thought, "Oh shit, how am I gonna get a contract off him?"

I know a lotta people thought I was a dirty bastard, but I wasn't – I just looked after myself in the right way – aggression was part of my play. It's how it was in the early '80s. You HAD TO look after yourself, or else it was curtains! And possibly due to my aggressive attributes and chipping in with a few goals, Bobby Roberts continued to select me to play up front with the Scottish giant, Jim Steel. Oh, he was a hard bastard once he crossed the white line was Jim. Typical Scotsman off it though – as tight as a gnat's chuff with his wad, and miserable as fuck if we lost! But I loved him. He was right up my street. Especially when we were on the pitch together. And I reckon Bobby Roberts sensed this partnership blossoming, and we became a regular feature in the old Fourth Division ... as well as for a few European appearances.

Wrexham v FC Porto. No one gave us a fuckin' chance. According to the press and the media there was more chance of Big Jim Steel buying a round of drinks at Peppers nightclub than us getting a result. They all thought we'd get fuckin' battered: A skint Welsh football team on its arse, struggling in the Fourth Division, with home crowds so fuckin' low I could hear a fan sneeze on Crispin Lane.

As for Porto ... Portuguese Cup winners boasting NINE internationals, a club with enough money to buy the whole of north Wales with whatever cash they had in their pockets and massive home attendances you could hear as far as France! But people should NEVER underestimate the love and courage this town and north Walians have. Especially in times of adversity.

I dunno if it was because most of the squad were so young, but the closer it got to kick-off, the more we sensed that we could cause an upset – not in an arrogant or cocky way – but when you get that Wrexham crowd behind you, you really do feel fuckin' invincible, even with a team consisting of five apprentices in the matchday squad. But Bobby showed faith in us and, tactically, got it spot on that night! Even if it meant that I knew I wouldn't play the full 90 minutes. It was a tactic he used most of that season for any of the big games. He'd start me on the right wing, knowing I'd wear their left back out so much he'd be begging me to fuck off; then Bobby would replace me with Muldoon and he'd cross the glory ball for Jim Steele or Barry Horne to score. GET IN! Looks like that dip in the Atlantic Ocean I had the previous day with Muldoon in Porto worked wonders, eh! But fuck me it was Baltic splashing around just in our Speedos!

Preparations for AS Roma were simplistic, at best. The

day of the match and we were having a chat with all the lads, and Bobby Roberts pulls aside Neil Salathiel and myself.

"Ted, Sal, come here. I've got a nice job for you big bastards." And as he pauses and looks around, his voice hushes, "Bruno Conti! About a hundred caps for Italy and regarded as a god in Rome. You's two are marking him today – DO A JOB ON HIM!"

And like a seasoned hatchet man I replied, "How bad, Boss?"

And just as Bobby was about to open his mouth, Sal says, "Ted, you kick him, and I'll volley the Italian bastard!"

True to form we did as we were instructed. Bruno Conti trudged off at halftime. But fuckin' hell, it was hard work chasing him around and trying to kick him. It worked though, because collectively as a team we played bloody well that night. We dug in and could've nicked a goal with a couple of half-chances.

The Roma players looked a little bit embarrassed at the final whistle; either that or the sheer stench of sweat on our shirts put them off wanting to swap shirts with us at the end. Which we couldn't have done anyway. It was the only kit we had, and the boss would've gone ballistic with us! Even if we had put a bloody solid shift in that night.

But that was typical of Bobby Roberts' persona, he was old school. He was a gruff Scotsman, with a sharpness to his voice. He could get hard on us because he wanted us to be the best version of ourselves and he desperately wanted us to be successful. Success, according to Bobby, was something you had to work your bollocks for. There had to be an element of pain before gain, hence the thousand press-ups and sit-ups he had all the apprentices doing every afternoon! And it was during one of these gruelling sessions that he growled like a proud father at me:

"Fackin' hell son, you're a man in a boy's body, yer bastard ya. You'll do fer me."

Proper man-manager material that also liked a drop of whisky. So much so, he decided to share some with us. Just before we kicked off against Sheffield United in a Cup match at The Racecourse. It happened just as we were all in the changing room, chatting away and slowly putting our kit on. And in he walks and slams this bottle of whisky on the table. Everyone stops and just stares at him.

"Right, yer bastards, you're all having a shot of that."

An eerie silence is then interrupted by John Muldoon, "But I don't drink, Boss."

And even though Bobby was yards away from John, his eyes literally bulged out of his face and butted John in his head, "YOU'RE FACKIN' DRINKING TODAY, SON!"

Poor John must've only had a sniff of the stuff before he was spewing up before the game! Bobby didn't try that trick again though, because we got battered 1–5. To this day, my old mate John Muldoon is still teetotal. Probably just to piss the boss off!

Smashing fella, John, and he didn't get the credit he deserved for his time with Wrexham. 'Cos fuckin' hell, on his day he could work as hard as a sheepdog and cross the ball as sweet as Beckham down that right wing. And, to be fair, if he'd played for the club at a different period, he'd be lauded! Even if the little shit did cause me to have a fuckin' hidin' for something he'd done when we were apprentices.

As part of being an apprentice, we all had to attend a day release in the Tech, and we were doing painting and decorating. So every lunchtime, one of the apprentices were sent to get ham rolls for the Wrexham professional players from the Crosville Café in town. It was John's turn this particular day, and being the typical charming Scouser, he starts chatting up one of the girls there. The very next day, it was my turn to get the grub for the pros, and as I walk in I spot these girls that John was on about. "Hello," I thought, so I quickly pick up the ham rolls ... and just as I'm about to introduce myself, WHACK!

"That's for shagging my missus, John Muldoon!"

Oooh yer bastard! I've only been smacked across the side of my head by some big ugly skinhead! So I walk back across to give these bastard ham rolls to the pros. My ear's pissin' with blood, and soon enough I spot Muldoon.

"Oi, you, yer prick. I fuckin' warned you to be careful with them girls in the café!"

John looks at me, not a fuckin' clue what's gone on. "Bloody hell Ted, what the fuck's happened to you?" he asks.

"One of their boyfriends has just twatted me in the ear!"

There's one aspect of this incident that I'm really proud of – I didn't drop the fuckin' rolls when I got whacked! And later that same day, I caught up with the skinhead.

"Oi you, you got the wrong one – I'm not John Muldoon – yer prick!"

However, apart from the Cup runs in the Welsh Cup, and Europe, the club was still strapped for cash (much to the frustration of the hardcore faithful). Them suffering fans loved the club and, for the majority of the time, encouraged us lads on the pitch. But sometimes, during a match with only a sparse crowd in attendance, you would still hear the odd comment – some you'd ignore – some though, would make you piss yourself laughing.

A match at home to Exeter City was a prime example. At the time, we were struggling for form, and Exeter came to The Racecourse boasting two ex-England internationals, Gerry Francis and Stan Bowles. And there was a bit of a hype before the match regarding these two, and how good they used to be 'n' all that. But, in truth, they were two knackered old pros 'n' it was a shit of a match, full of niggles and grudges. I remember havin' a tussle with Stan Bowles in the middle of the park, and he's landed on the deck. I've gone to pick him up, but as I'm extending my arm to help him, he spits in my face, so I cracked him in the eye, BOOM – "Fuck off!"

He's there screaming, "Aaahhh, fackin' hell son, what's that for?"

I just towered over him and said, "Don't spit at me then!"

This got the crowd goin' absolutely bananas, and you could really feel their passion rippin' through their tonsils … until Exeter scored and then the fun from the fans came to life. Stuart Parker got offered a burger from a fan because of a comment from Bobby Roberts; and shortly after the restart, the ball goes out of play for a throw-in for us, a few comments get thrown at John Muldoon just as he gets closer to the old Mold Road and, as he collects the ball from the ball boy, the ball boy says;

"You are SHIT, Muldoon!"

It's already been mentioned previously about how hard-up the club was at that time, and it's only the board that'll really know confidentially how bad things were. As staff, we were simply on a need-to-know basis, which was fine by me! I just wanted to play for Wrexham and give the fans a bit of happiness. And I know I can laugh about it now, but some of the things that happened because of our financial plight gives me more pride of how we (the players) handled the situation.

Hard to believe but, until 1984, football teams didn't have sponsors sprawled on the front of their shirts. I couldn't wait to see what sponsors I'd be wearing to face the likes of Porto. And, as it turned out, local bus company Crosville were to be the club's inaugural shirt sponsors. And as part of the sponsorship deal, the company would ship us to our away matches. We were assured that an executive coach would ferry us around.

Executive, my fuckin' arse! Yeah, sure enough it had a TV installed and a toilet for our convenience, but that counted for jack-shit on a five-hour trip to Torquay. Credit where credit's due, it picked us up from The Racecourse, as always, on time. But it didn't half fuckin' stink! It became quite obvious that bus had been used for public transport, and it fuckin' reeked of cheese and onion crisps, empty fish 'n' chips wrappers, and cigarette stubs.

I know I might sound a bit of a spoilt brat, but that's just how it was. We didn't moan, we just got on with it. You might then think that we had an on-board chef 'n' all? Well, our 'chef' was stopping at a service station armed with an envelope containing a walloping £3 food voucher from the club. So a choice had to be made – a large mug of coffee, or a greasy butty, 'cause you couldn't afford both. Fuckin' 'ell, by the time we were travelling back, I wasn't half tempted to lick those bastard fish 'n' chips wrappers!

Anyway, regardless of our regular logistic hospitality, I absolutely loved that shirt, and it makes my day when I see people walk around town or before matches wearing that retro shirt with Crosville on it, because I can proudly tell people that I actually wore that shirt every Saturday for Wrexham. I actually played against the Brazilians that played for AS Roma in that shirt, and I actually scored for Wrexham in that shirt.

"Andy Edwards – you're SHIT" … Yeah? Them comments didn't even touch the sides, 'cos I played over 150 times, played at the Stadio Olimpico against AS Roma for my club, and scored over 30 goals for my club. Oooh, hey, I loved scoring in a Wrexham shirt!

Each goal I scored for Wrexham was special. But scoring against Chester, or Cardiff City, was fuckin' immense – it was even better than extra special, because I knew how the fans felt about that team, especially as I'm good mates with a few of the Frontliners (FL) aka 'The Wrexham Firm'. Which got me into a bit of bother with the boss on one occasion, after I was called into his office.

"Right, you're getting fined a week's wages!"

So I looked at him utterly gobsmacked. "Fuck sakes! WHY?"

So he gets up from his chair and goes, "You've left tickets for THEM LOT again, haven't ya!"

I tried to play dumb, "Have I?" But I knew I was bollocked because I'd given 12 tickets to them for the main stand and then they decided to kick off and cause a bit of aggro in the same stand, didn't they? And as they're being investigated, the tickets are traced back to me. Oh shit! But there's no way I could ever turn my back on these lads, because I grew up with most members of the FL, and am still good mates with them now. And although the board feared they might tarnish the club's reputation, there were times when the FL were looked after by the club.

We'd just played Colchester United away, and the boss, Bobby Roberts, had heard that the FL were stranded, as they'd missed their bus back to Wrexham. So, fair play, he gets off the team bus, and heads towards the FL lads and offers them a lift back with the team. Well, those lads were in their element, absolutely made their day and, to be fair, all the players mixed well with them and there was a genuine camaraderie. Sound lads.

So, whenever I scored I would always have a look to see where the Wrexham fans were, and if the FL lads were also in attendance I'd give them a celebratory salute. But it was a different kind of 'salute' that I will always treasure. It's one that could've caused me a lot of bother, as after I'd scored away against Chester in the Sealand end, I gingerly jogged past their fans giving them a one-finger salute! Ha-hah-hah, they went totally berserk. Ha-hah-hah, and I loved every second of it – the bastards! Once a Wrexham fan – ALWAYS a Wrexham fan!

One special request from me please: can I say a massive thank you to Ryan Reynolds and Rob McElhenney for giving back the love, hope and belief to The Town, because what they've done for the whole of the north Wales community is beyond words.

DIOLCH O'R GALON, BOIS!

15

Waynne Phillips
Midfielder

It's always sunny in Waynne's World
1989–1998 (207 appearances, 16 goals)
1999–2003 (38 appearances, 2 goals)

Articulate, brave, persuasive, persistent, versatile. Five pillars in the world of Waynne Phillips. Whether it be as a football pundit, professional player or just doing his bit for the NHS, this 'Cofi' (Caernarfon native) has had a busy life so far. Remembered fondly as a vital cog in the Wrexham AFC engine room, memories are evoked from a right-foot rocket to nail the Hammers; being instructed to follow an opposition player to the toilet; or clearing dog shit from a training ground! With immense pride, Waynne enlightens us with his fond anecdotes and thoughts from his time at The Racecourse.

WELL, EITHER I was very persuasive with immaculate handwriting, or illiterate with unreadable handwriting – but I was 16 at the time, working long shifts in the Corona bottle factory in my hometown Caernarfon, when I wrote dozens of letters to clubs in the English Football League. Luckily for me, the chief scout and head of the YTS at Wrexham AFC, Cliff Sear, replied with an offer for a trial. Needless to say, the trial went well and I moved over to Wrexham.

Initially, though, I couldn't settle living in nearby digs and homesickness set in. So, like most Canaries, I returned home, to the land of Cofis. True to his legendary status, Cliff travelled to our home in Caernarfon and enthused to myself and my family with honourable honesty of his hopes for me with Wrexham. Needless to say, he made me feel ten feet tall, and the rest is history. And what memories I was able to create!

With Brian Flynn at the helm, assisted by Joey Jones and Kevin Reeves, the 1990–91 season will live with me for ever as the defining period of my career. They showed immense courage to regularly field a handful of youths in the first team, providing us with invaluable experience in the old Division Four. Admittedly, we lost more than we won, which eventually resulted in us finishing bottom of the League. In hindsight, it wasn't as negative as it looks on paper, as not only did we play in exciting matches against top sides like Everton in the League Cup; travelling to Copenhagen to beat Lyngby in the European Cup Winners' Cup; or battling it out against the mighty Manchester United in the next round. But the best was yet to come in the following season, as our youthful experience began to show signs of fruition.

By then I had the most precious experiences of my life, let alone my career, as I had the pleasure of sharing a lift to each training session and home matches with one of my footballing idols – Mickey T!

Each journey would be filled with laughter as he regaled me with stories that would make your mum blush, as well as offering ample advice. Mickey was such a kind and generous soul. As much as I insisted, he wouldn't take a penny of petrol money from me ... (but he didn't need to as he had hordes of dodgy tenners!).

But it was on the field that we were both to go on an epic journey together. After beating Winsford and Telford United in the previous rounds, the mighty Gunners of Arsenal were our next visitors at The Racecourse for a third round FA Cup tie. The gulf between the two clubs couldn't have been any wider, as they were the defending First Division champions ... whilst we finished 91 places below them – bottom of the Fourth Division. A real David and Goliath clash was on the cards!

As with most games, I was nervous in the warm-up. I always found it helped me feel alert and ready for the challenge ahead. Other teammates dealt with their pre-match nerves differently. Yer typical jokers like Gary 'Benno' Bennett preferred to lighten up the mood with a bit of banter ... or play sadistic pranks; whilst in complete contrast, the likes of Peter Ward could be heard being sick with worry in the cubical next door!

Considering the circumstances, we played a respectable first half. As we re-entered the changing room for the halftime interval, we were a goal down thanks to Allan Smith's opener. The atmosphere in the changing room was quite calm ... and somewhat optimistic, especially after Flynnie's positive team talk, "Lads, it's the Cup. Anything can happen. One chance. That's all it takes."

Well, I certainly fancied my chances when we were

awarded a free kick around 25 yards out, and only eight minutes remaining. But as I'd positioned myself to send myself into footballing folklore, Mickey steps in and demands, "I'm taking it!" – so I asked, "What's yer plan?" To which he nonchalantly replied, "Fucking launch it!" Moments later his missile zoomed past doomed David Seaman into the top right-hand corner. I tried to catch him to celebrate his audacious equaliser, but Magic Mickey was long gone as he dived straight into our dugout to celebrate with his best mate, Joey Jones. Unable to catch Mickey or my breath, I was however able to witness the Kop visibly rockin' in sheer elation.

The Racecourse roar was still in full voice as my fellow member of 'Flynnie's Fledglings', Stevie Watkin, slid ahead of Arsenal captain Tony Adams to send Arsenal out of the Cup and the Wrexham fanatics into ecstasy! Jubilant scenes were awash in our home changing room. "Right then, who's next!?" "West Ham away?" Bring it on!

Little did my fellow driving buddy and I know that I would find my face on the back of the national newspapers ... and Mickey's would be on the front of thousands of £10 notes!

Like every other three-hour-plus journey to an away match, we travelled to East London over 24 hours prior to the fourth round FA Cup match at Upton Park, where we'd train at a nearby football team's ground early in the afternoon, before we'd head off to the hotel. (Unlike our visit years later to Bournemouth, when we arrived late afternoon in the middle of winter, trained on a public park full of people throwing tennis balls and frisbees for their dogs to catch, whilst we scraped their dog shit off our training gear!)

Our usual schedule was somewhat thrown into disarray by the visit of none other than footballing superstar Paul 'Gazza' Gascoigne and his entire entourage at the same hotel as us. But he was as good as gold as he chatted with us in the foyer before wishing us the best of luck against the Hammers. Our itinerary was soon restored as Flynnie reminded us of our ritual overnight curfew – "You're all allowed either a half or two halves of beer tonight, lads. NO PINTS! See you early in the morning." I have to stress that not once did I take up his offer ... And that's the truth.

Personally, this exciting encounter was also a personal affair for me, as my mother was a proud Cockney from the East End regions of London. This, therefore, added to a huge increase of ticket requests from both the Cofi and Cockney side of the family!

Maybe it was fate, but as a proud Cofi, wearing the yellow jersey of Wrexham felt extra special. And even better was to finally locate the entire Phillips family at the right-hand side of the stand to the right of the travelling Wrexham red and white army. Soon after halftime, they'd all be bouncing on their feet to a right-foot rocket of an equaliser from yours truly! It's true what they say – once it leaves your foot, you know it's going in. Well, I knew too! As half-volleys go – it just sat up perfectly for me, I struck it clean and watched it fly past Luděk Mikloško to cancel out Julian Dicks' opener. Trevor Morley restored the home side's lead 13 minutes later ... only for Gareth Owen to use his peripheral 20/20 vision with a 40-yard launch into Lee Jones' path. We doggedly held on to a 2–2 draw and secured a replay at The Racecourse.

Once back in the changing rooms and in the midst of celebrations, a few players began sharing what looked like £10 notes they'd earlier acquired ... only these had Mickey's mug on them. The Hammer fans had hurled thousands of mock-up prints following Mickey's brush with the law for allegedly handling counterfeit tenners. Mickey simply laughed it off in the communal bath, before announcing – "My copies were better quality!"

Unfortunately, the replay back at The Racecourse was where our dreams came to an end, as we were defeated by a Colin Foster header in the first half. Who knows what would have happened if Tim Breaker had been red-carded for his dirty tackle on King Karl Connolly, with him clean through on goal? One thing I do know is that the spark was back at The Racecourse. More good times were just around the corner.

It's true to say that I am profoundly proud of the achievements during my career with Wrexham. Highs and lows. Promotion. Relegation. Cup exploits. Play-off near-misses. Scorer of cracking goals. A career-ending leg break. It's all there. I also almost played in every position on the field (apart from donning the gloves!).

There is one thing I need to admit, though – I wasn't the best at man-marking. Before playing Crewe Alexander, Flynnie called me to his office and said to me, "I've got a special job for you this Saturday … you're going to man-mark their danger man, Craig Hignett. Wherever he goes – you go. If he goes to the touchline – you go with him. If he goes short – you go short … Waynne, if he goes to the toilet – you go to the toilet with him!" Well, I must've been shown the wrong picture of Craig Hignett, and subsequently man-marked the wrong player … 'cos Craig Hignett scored a hat-trick! I'm still waiting for a bit of a bung off him, as he was sold for £1million to Middlesbrough following this match!

My time at Wrexham AFC wouldn't have been as pleasurable had it not been for three amazing aspects – its loyal special supporters, my fantastic teammates, and 'Mr Wrexham' himself, Joey Jones.

My teammates were more than just colleagues: I got to call them my comrades – my friends. During all my time, there was ALWAYS an excellent team spirit within the squad. A great mixture of personalities. Camaraderie characters such as Graham Cooper, Mickey, and Benno were at hand to lift the lads with their jokes and capers; then there were the steely characters such as Brian Carey, Tony Humes and Mel Pejic, who were our CHIEFS on and off the field and would set the tone for what was expected from everyone – 100 per cent commitment, being the minimum requirement.

Joey, on the other hand, was not only blessed with both humour and commitment. More importantly, he is one of THE most compassionate, warm, and kind-hearted human beings I have EVER had the pleasure of being in the presence of. One prime example of his humane qualities was to welcome me into his family home as the young and shy adolescent that I was and treat me like one of his own. I shall forever treasure the insane kindness and care I received from Joey and his family.

Yes, he could be tough to please out on the pitch; yes, he could have you rolling in hysterical laughter … but, his true thoughtful demeanour also shone through. He loved each player. He loved the fans. He loved the club. And by golly, do we all love Joey!

And as for the fans … special people deserve special times, but they deserve the best because they are THE BEST! Through the glorious to the desperate, they're ALWAYS there. It's a little wonder they sing with pride 'YMA O HYD!'

16
Billy Ashcroft
Forward

Billy in the Sky with Diamonds
1968–1977 (273 appearances, 96 goals)

Labelled 'The Golden Period' in the history of Wrexham AFC, the 1970s heralded the club as giant killers, after knocking higher division teams out from various Cup competitions.
A huge part of that success was their own giant ready to slay anything or anyone that came in the team's way. Enter – one Billy Ashcroft. Beneath his giant stature and bear gruff looks, Billy has a heart sparkling with diamonds, and a sharp Scouse wit that charmed his way out of a wrestler's headlock! With his drive, desire, and a laser eye for a goal, Billy made

several names for himself! Billy shares how he earned the nicknames – The Bear, The Yeti and King of the Kop.

EVEN THOUGH I was Everton-mad as a kid, I didn't kick a ball properly until I was 15. I was more of a swimmer. I loved that pool (the only type of pool I did like from Merseyside). I didn't even play football for the school, either. Around about this time I was a delivery boy for a grocery store, and with the money I bought a ball and thought I'm gonna be a footballer, and for hours and days I kicked and thudded this ball against a wall. To help me realise my dream, my mum helped me by buying piles of envelopes and stamps and wrote to loads of clubs for trials. Eventually I was given a trial with Tranmere. After a few sessions I was told by Dave Russell, the manager: "Go back to school because you'll never make a footballer as long as you've got a hole in your arse!"

Luckily, a lad who lived near to us was with Wrexham on training days. I was centre half at the time. We'd share a lift from Jack Daniel, a probation officer, and on the way to the first session he asked me, "What position d'you play, lad?" And my mate answered, "Centre forward!" So, I went along with it. Fortunately for me, John Neal took a shine to me, and I was offered ground staff forms in 1968. It was hard graft, a belly full of laughs ... but it could also be a long shift at times.

I'd arrive for training for 7.30am on a Monday. After getting the bus from Garston, I'd jump on a train to the centre of St Bidston, then from Bidston to Wrexham. Training wouldn't start till 10am, so I'd sit outside freezing while waiting for someone to turn up. Anyway, good old Ally McGowan found out, and he told me quietly, "Go and have a lie down in the drying room for a couple of hours." Then it was on to training and the bloody chores of cleaning boots, sorting kit out, training, collecting dirty kit, polishing boots, getting the dressing room clean, putting divots back on pitch, cutting the grass 'n' paintin' lines on it, cleaning stands 'n' brushing up. If The Racecourse pitch had frozen we'd have to use hammers to flatten down the divots.

One of the first matches I played was for the Wrexham B team at Nantlle Vale. And every bloody time the ball was the other side of the pitch or if there was a corner, Orig Williams, their big centre half, thought close marking was holding my head under his armpits and giving me a fucking headlock! I was only 15, and I was getting battered by him. By halftime, we found out he was a bloody wrestler! So my old mate Joey Duncan tells him, "If you're in the ring tonight in Rhyl, I'm comin' there to beat you up!" For the rest of the match you'd just see Orig chasing Joey around the pitch instead! Pure gold.

But that's how it was in them days. You could get away with murder on the field – there were no cameras. Get a tackle in early, and the ref would then warn you, "Right, OK, that's the last one. Next time and you're in the book. Oh, and by the way, son – expect one back!" So it's no wonder most forwards had no teeth, because you were expected to get fucking battered.

As ground staff we were on £7 a week (later upgraded to £19 a week as a first-year pro), so we couldn't afford to go out on the piss and spend on beer for 5p, maybe 6p, a pint, let alone top-of-the-range football boots. But, yeah, I suppose we could scrimp and scrape enough to buy ourselves some smokes. Quite a few players enjoyed a smoke back then. Bob Scott puffed on a cigar. Dave Smallman inherited a nickname 'Smokey' for his love of a quick smoke at halftime. I enjoyed the odd puff as well, although 'Ashtray Ashcroft' didn't stick as a nickname for long! I much preferred the nicknames that came further on in my Wrexham career, thank you!

Before long, we were joined by a pair of scallywags that would help sculpture the history of Wrexham AFC for ever.

Joey Jones and Mickey Thomas were the daftest pair of lads together – absolutely barmy. From day one, you could see the chemistry was there between them, and you'd think, "These two are gonna cause a shitload of mischief around 'ere." For instance, if we were in the middle of the tedious tasks of cleaning the first-team boots, Joey would be cleaning a pair and Mickey cleaning another, and the daft sods would be having a competition to see who could get the shiniest and finish first! We'd just look at each other, piss ourselves laughing, and be taking bets on who'd win! But, hey, they were such an infectious pair of lads and a joy to be around. Then you'd see them on the pitch, and suddenly the pissing about stopped and they'd showcase their immense talent.

FUCK ME – Joey went to the red half of Merseyside, and Mickey went to the red half of Manchester! And they weren't the only cracking, talented lads we had as ground staff. We had Bob Scott, Graham Whittle, Dave Smallman, Dave Fogg, Alan Dwyer 'n' Alan Hill ... then somewhere along the way, John Neal decided to go shopping and came back with Bobby Shinton tucked in his pocket! Geeezzz, what a team we had! Such a pleasure!

Every day you went into training, you couldn't wait to get there – BRING IT ON! Stansty training ground was a decent training ground for us. We'd get changed at the old changing rooms under the Plas Coch stand and then run the mile-and-a-half over for training.

We'd play B-team matches at the Penmaenmawr training pitch. Ooohhh, believe me mate, you'd come back from there smelling like a farmer's wellie after all the slide-tackling through sheep shit. But it was all character building and as a team we stuck together. We didn't give a fuck who we played against, we'd look after each other. Hardest games we'd play were every Thursday morning in the practice matches – ground staff/reserves v first team – because the first-team players treated ground staff/ressies as threats to their positions, so first-teamers would kick ground staff/ressies players off the park, but then the ground staff didn't mind giving a bit back. Ha, it was like a gunfight at the O.K. Corral, but that's when you learnt your trade.

That and those trips to Aberystwyth! I remember those bloody sand dunes but not for the running part of it. Ohhh nooo, my favourite part was walking back after training and enjoying the views of the seafront. I was knackered, goin' after Joey Jones up and down the sand dunes like a bloody camel and collecting a mouthful of sand as a prize! It certainly didn't help quench our thirst after our first day of training.

Unfortunately, by the time we got back, the bloody pubs were shut. It was a Sunday (back then, pubs were usually shut on a Sunday) but we found a place, don't you worry – a nice little squash club hidden away. Well, it was nice until we got there! Being the type of person he was, however, John Neal approved of it – he saw it as 'team building'.

John Neal was more than just a football manager. He was such an adorable person; you'd run through brick walls for him. For instance, if I was going through a loss of form, he'd stick by me by believing in me. In many ways he was very similar to Bob Paisley, and once told me, "If you want someone to listen to you then talk quieter," and sometimes when he spoke it was like a horror film. Ooopphh, it was like having a bollocking from a vicar during a sermon! A great example came when I was walking to the changing room one morning, and he just casually straddled beside me and says:

"I hear you scored a couple of 180s at the pub last night, Billy. Congratulations! Hey, must be all that practice you're putting in!"

WOW! That there was him saying, "Cut down on the drinking mate or your days at Wrexham are numbered!" A great man-manager and great tactician. He knew his football, and he knew his players. A bloody genius! Especially when it came to mind management.

Eddie May was our big shouter in the tunnel before a match, so John Neal had this genius idea. As we'd run out to start a match, he'd instruct Big Eddie or Gareth Davies to lead us out as our captain, then told me to be behind him! So, he made sure all the biggest/tallest players would run out first followed by the shorter players until you get to Arfon, Mickey and the rest of the Seven Dwarfs. So, as we're running out, the players from the other team would be looking at us thinking, "Fuckin' 'ell – we're playing against Gladiators!" But he loved all that stuff between the ground staff and the first team. In fact, he'd encourage it.

After most home games we'd all pile into the The Pant pub. It's where we'd have the real evaluation of the game and share our thoughts or offload our frustrations. And after a few beers it felt comfortable discussing an incident with the lads. "Hey you, you didn't do your job right today." It was a valuable release, like diffusing a pressure cooker. On the other hand, if we'd had a good day and produced a great performance, we'd praise each other. They were fantastic times for bonding together.

A fantastic time assembled with fantastic teammates. Take Gareth Davies, the brains of the team and the link between the young and senior players. Everyone respected and thought the world of Gareth. Whatever he'd say we'd all listen to him. Gareth was the classiest of people. Whenever we'd go out for a few bevvies, he would always have less alcohol than the rest of us just to keep an eye on things. But if things got a bit rowdy he'd step in with a nonchalant shake of his head, or a simple tap on the shoulder. We'd just put our hands up and say, "Sorry Skip". Mickey Evans shared the same personality traits as Gareth. If he saw something, he wouldn't bollock you or take the piss, he'd kindly help you in a manner where he wouldn't demean you.

Dave Gaskell, however, could relay a message as scary as anyone though, as I found out to my expense. I was only 17 and during a match I told Dave Gaskell to fuck off after he'd had a bit of a pop at me, and he stared at me and said, "What did you say?" Everyone stopped, and it felt like a piano face-off scene from a Western movie, with a few tumbleweeds dancing around, so I mumbled, "I'm sorry!" I FUCKIN' SHIT MESELF!

The squad was full of great characters with great attributes. Mel Sutton was unbelievably underrated. His reading of the game was that good you'd swear he'd written the entire script of the game beforehand. And what an engine he had – Aberystwyth pre-season training, we'd start off at the lifeboat in Borth and head towards what we called The Point, but Mel would've given us all a two-mile start ... and still bloody beat us. Mickey Evans was very similar to him. The day after I'd signed as ground staff, the first team were playing Man United away in the League Cup, and as part of the ground staff we were allowed to go with them and watch from the sidelines. Mickey was given the task of marking the legendary George Best, and Mickey never gave him a kick throughout the game, totally marked him out. Although we lost 0–2, it was a pure masterclass from Mickey. He was that good he could've played against some of the best in the world and given the exact performance. He could've turned over all of them. Because not only was he strong, but he'd never commit to a tackle unless he had to – you NEVER saw him on his backside. Another outstanding reader of the game.

Whereas Joey loved getting a late tackle in early! Neither the ball nor the player would get past at the same time – either one or the other, but NEVER both! Without a doubt, he was, and forever will be, the most enthusiastic person I've ever come across. That salute of the fist wasn't for show – that was just how committed he was. His first week's wages at Wrexham, he went and got an LFC tattoo on his arm and I was like, "Joey, you've signed for Wrexham, what have you got that for, mate?" and he just did that salute with his fist and goes, "Geeettt iiinnn!" But there's absolutely no doubt in my mind that Joey IS Mr Wrexham – he is what Wrexham AFC is all about.

Arfon Griffiths had a ridiculously astute football brain. Such a clever little player. The Prince of Wales could've and should've played at a higher level for a longer period in his career.

Then there's your flair players, and by gosh did we have them in abundance: Graham Whittle, Bobby Shinton, Dave Smallman, Mickey Thomas. Bloody hell they were talented and hardworking. They could create something out of nothing in a split-second and deliver it with such precision. It's no surprise that most went on to achieve big things at the leading clubs of the country.

Graham Whittle could smack a ball so hard from either foot from any distance and still fly past any keeper. It didn't bother him if the ball bobbled a hundred times before getting to him, he could still ping that ball like a missile. We'd just stand back and think, "Thank fuck I didn't have to try 'n' stop that!"

It was such a joy and a pleasure to play for Wrexham in that era. There were times when I'd think, "This must be fantastic for the fans to watch," then realise, "Hang on, I'm a part of this," and that then made me want to get more involved in the game, which would make me get just as much pleasure as creating a goal.

I'm not being cocky or big-headed when I say that it didn't surprise us as players when we started to reap the rewards on the pitch, because we fancied ourselves to batter anyone on any day. So when the big Cup games came along – League Cup, Welsh Cup, FA Cup or the European Cup Winners' Cup, we'd literally slap our thighs 'n' lick our lips and say, "Right, let's have a fuckin' go."

So here's my pick from a tasty bunch. OK, so not quite a Cup game, but who could ever forget their first-team debut?

It wasn't long though until I made my debut, for Wrexham v Reading away on 3rd December, then a week later, the same day I signed pro, we played Tranmere and beat them 4–1. I assisted three goals, and gave their centre half, Tony Knapp, a total battering. After the game, my old mate Dave Russell came looking for me, shook my hand and said, "I'm so pleased you never listened to me – well done!" The bloody cheek of him! I just wanted to tell him, "Fuck off, yer fat git!" but at least he had the decency to come in and admit he'd got it wrong and apologise to me.

Another debut, and not just for me but for the club, as we played our very first European Cup Winners' Cup encounter in 1972 against Swiss Cup winners FC Zurich. It was a massive achievement and a huge deal for the club and their amazing fans as we headed out to Zurich for the first leg. Coincidentally, it was also a first-team debut or game for Joey. Before the game, John Neal said to a few of the experienced lads quietly, "Look after our Joey out there. It's his first match, so make sure no harm comes his way." Well, I'll tell you what, after Joey's first tackle I thought Joey can come and look after me and make sure no harm comes my bloody way! Oh, we did good to get from there with a 1–1 draw, thanks to Albert Kinsey's goal. Thankfully, and proudly, we won 2–1 at home after I equalised and Mel scored the winner. You could feel the whole club and its fan base were really proud of the result and our performance.

Anderlecht away, Cup Winners' Cup quarter-final. WOW! Some people might say it was my best performance in a Wrexham shirt. Personally, I think collectively this was one of the best performances from any Wrexham side from any era. Not just because of how we played, but also because Anderlecht were a top Belgian side. But even though we lost 1–0, their players looked scared, because they knew they had to come to The Racecourse for the second leg.

Still, I hadn't expected to arrive back to see the newspaper headline calling me 'The Bear of Brussels'. Crikey, first I was nicknamed 'The Yeti' by the Wrexham fans, now 'The Bear'! Disappointingly, we only managed to draw the second leg 1–1 after Stuart Lee put us ahead and shook the whole of north Wales in the process. On a personal note, their manager put a bid in to buy me. John Neal said I was too young to go. They signed Duncan McKenzie instead, and to this day he still says, "You got me a great gig, mate!" Cheeky bastard!

And how on earth can I leave out the famous victory at White Hart Lane against First Division Tottenham Hotspur? Oh mate, that was one of those magical nights under the lights at White Hart Lane in front almost 20,000, when we absolutely destroyed them in the first half. Their players looked shell-shocked – but we weren't. John Neal wasn't either. He trusted us. And in return we gave everything back, and more! We raced to a 3–0 lead to stun Spurs; Magic Mickey scoring a cracking pair, before I pitched in to bag our third, and one of my favourite goals (perhaps not my best, but more of that later).

Then Spurs hit back with a brace, and suddenly we were defending for our lives and running our socks off. But they hadn't accounted for our high fitness levels (maybe them sand dunes came in handy after all, eh!). But no matter what they threw at us, we withstood it and made it through to the final whistle and beat the mighty Tottenham Hotspur 3–2! Oh, what a night!

So, as far as my best goal goes, it's still as clear as day in my mind, and it's so good. YouTube have been kind enough to honour the goal by not having any footage of it! But here's what happened: we were playing against Oldham at The Racecourse, 10th March 1973, so I was still a young lad learning my trade. Our keeper, Brian Lloyd, collects the ball, and launches it to me for a counter-attack. I headed the ball down to the right, into the path of Mel Sutton who was flyin' down the wing like an unstoppable train. He somehow manages to cross it out to the edge of the 18-yard area and about a yard off the floor. I then come in and just side-footed it as a half-volley. It flew like a rocket and smashed into the back of the net! Fortunately I had long ginger hair to cover my ears, because the sheer roar from the crowd was deafening! But then that was nothing new really – Wrexham fans could be heard from the moon! The atmosphere Wrexham fans could generate was incredible, and I'm one of the many lucky players that they took to. I always think it's a sign of respect if they give you a nickname – whether it's 'The King of the Kop' or 'The Yeti'!

17
Steve Massey
Forward

Vidal's hair to the throne of Euro Cup goals
1986–1988 (64 first appearances, 18 goals)

Every so often, a re-enactment goal celebration swoops the globe. Millions of fans attempt to copy superstars such as 'The Shearer' one-hand salute from the '90s, or the popular 'Shooooo' from Cristiano Ronaldo. Back in late 1986, the whole of north Wales was doing 'The Mass' in recognition of Steve Massey's celebration during a European Cup tie. With almost 400 league appearances to his name, Steve speaks of real pride 'n' verve of his two seasons at The Racecourse. So much so, he fondly describes this period as, "The most exciting time of my career." With laugh-out-loud anecdotes ranging from lashings of bird dung to sitting pretty in pink in a brothel, 'Vidal' shares his personal 'highlights' under the one and only Dixie McNeil.

I STILL HAD a two-year contract with Cambridge United, so it really surprised me when our manager, Chris Turner, said, "Wrexham manager Dixie McNeil's been on the phone enquiring about you 'n' wants to speak with you. Personally, I think it'll be a good deal for you AND for us 'cos we really need the cash! So GO, and have a chat with him 'n' see what he offers."

So next day I go with my wife at that time, Gail, to Wrexham. We were greeted with open arms by Dixie, and he took us on a tour around The Racecourse. He was such a charming enthusiast, and I was kinda in awe of him because here was this legendary prolific goal scorer, and yet he made me feel as though I was in the presence of a respected mate. Ooh by 'eck, he could've sold me a plate at a Greek restaurant 'n' I still would've bought it! Bugger that, I'd have bought the whole set!

Oh 'eck, his love for Wrexham oozed out of him, and I absolutely loved his passion. Just as we're walking on the pitch towards the Mold Road Kop, he totally poached me like a cunning fisherman.

"I think you're gonna love playing 'ere, Steve, 'n' I'll tell yer what, son – there's hundreds of players from top clubs in the First Division that haven't had, or won't ever have, the experience you'll 'ave of playing European football ... There's not a feeling quite like it." He goes on, "It's bloody magic mate, 'cos this place becomes a wall of noise, and the whole ground is absolutely rockin'!" He then swivels and points to the mile-high floodlights above the Kop end. "And yer see these floodlights? Well, there's not many grounds in the First Division with floodlights like these either, 'cos these, Steve, are fitted with specialist lamps that can only be used for those special European nights."

I kid you not ... I had goosebumps. I was nearing the end of my career and I'd never had such a strong feeling towards a club as I did that day. So as I stood on The Racecourse turf, staring at the vast Mold Road Kop end (which looked bloody massive the closer we walked towards it), the sheer size of it made me wanna grab a ball 'n' smash it into the net! 'Cos not only had Dixie seductively lured me with a sexy brand of European football, but also his vision of gaining promotion from the Fourth Division.

"I've seen the way you play, and you'll fit in brilliantly with the lads! And I'm telling ya Stevie, if you're looking for one last adventure in your career, then this is the place to be – because with these fans, and the squad we'll have – anything can happen!"

Inspirational or what? Dixie was so pitch-perfect, I didn't want to leave – I wanted to hear more stories about past glories, and the vision he had of creating more. But, anyway, time caught up with us and so we headed back towards the car park. Just as I fired up the engine, I wound the window down to thank Dixie and reassure him that I'd be in touch, to which Dixie replied, "Yeah, I appreciate that, Stevie – give me a call when you're ready," and as he's pulled his head back from the window, a bird dumped a jar load of tartare sauce on Dixie's head! SPLAT! His face mirrored mine and Gail's – absolute shock horror! Well, there was no way I was gonna say 'ta ta' to Wrexham and Dixie, so Gail said, "BLOODY HELL, you've got to sign for him now, Steve – it's muck for luck!"

Aside from the bird droppings, I'd already made my mind up before getting in the car. I knew logistically we'd have to find a property closer to Wrexham, which suited us perfectly because we'd wanted to live closer to Stockport. It was the lure of playing in front of the partisan Racecourse on a European night, being in the buzz of chasing promotion. But it was Dixie's personality, however, that was the star in the sky for me.

A manager can determine the vibe of a club and Dixie was loaded with charismatic energy and his knowledge of the game was mind-blowing. Aside from his natural charm, Dixie didn't suffer fools gladly 'n' he was a straight talker. If he thought something needed sayin' – he'd say it. But at the same time, Dixie wouldn't make it personal and didn't hold a grudge – another testament to his fantastic man-management skills.

He'd do anything to help you develope and get the best out of you. In hindsight, you could say he was ahead of the times with certain aspects of his coaching methods, especially with introducing video analysis, which at the time was pretty revolutionary.

Dixie had been around the game for a long time – long enough to know that players were always the last to blame themselves 'n' quick enough to pass the buck. So his video analysis sessions were a genius concept towards learning from what went wrong, and what went well. There was always an educational aspect to the sessions, because his intentions were never to undermine anyone and he'd never belittle anyone. Although, occasionally, it meant proving someone like me wrong.

So Dixie pulls me up me after a game:

"I thought you could've got across the centre half a bit quicker in the last attack, Mass, because as the cross comes in, you're behind him."

"NO I'M NOT," I protested.

"Yeah alright, son. Tell yer what, we'll have a look on the analysis on Tuesday 'n' we'll sort it out then, Mass!" he calmly replies,

"Yeah, no problemo!" I casually said, but inside I thought, "Ooh shit, I hope the footage backs me up!"

We were off most Mondays after a Saturday match, and if there was no match on a Tuesday, we knew it was the usual analysis sessions. So this particular Tuesday, Dixie sits everyone down and goes through various passages of play from the previous Saturday. And again he presses the pause button, "There yer are, Mass – yer behind the centre half!"

"Oh, yeah, fair enough."

SHIT! I tell ya, there's no bloody hiding place, so he continues:

"Right, so you know where to be the next time we're in this position – get in front of him, and you'll be in a better place for scoring, OK Mass? Good man, right next ..." Then he'd find the next piece of action to address. And because he treated us like responsible adults, in return he gained our utmost respect, rather than fear. That's not to say he was a softy either, because holy moly guacamole, could Dixie fly off the handle!

We were midway through the 1986–87 season, and although we're still within a shout of promotion, we were also spluttering a bit. So we're away to Halifax, 'n' Stevie Buxton equalised right at the death to make it 1–1 ... but straight from the restart, they launch an attack, and score, and we lost 1–2. Euphoria turns to despair. After the final whistle, we trudge back into changing room, and Dixie storms in, absolutely rantin' and ravin'. All the lads are staring at the floor 'n' we're all gutted and totally pissed off. So as a typically frustrated player, I slowly take my boots off.

In the middle of the dressing room there's a physio bench, and it's loaded with trays full of cups of tea 'n' plastic cups of orange juice. Then Dixie storms in, yellin' and telling us where we went wrong, then flies into a rage:

"I'M FUCKIN' SICK OF YA, YER NOT EVEN FUCKIN' LISTENING TO ME ... OI, FUCKIN' LOOK AT ME – EVERY

SINGLE ONE OF YA, LOOK AT ME – YOU DON'T CARE DO YER – YER DON'T FUCKIN' CARE!"

Just as he's waving his arms up 'n' down in a furious rage, he manages to knock these trays of hot tea and orange juice up into the air and they land like a monsoon all over him. SPLASH!

Well, bloody hell ... it was almost impossible still trying to look at him 'n' trying to hide our sniggering grins from turning into hysterical laughter! Honestly, we were biting our lips so hard they could bleed 'n' all you could hear was the eerie sound of the drips of tea and orange juice falling from Dixie's coat like a leaking tap! Then WHAM! He launches into a soft tirade.

"We've dropped VITAL points again, and all you care about is takin' yer boots off 'n' washin' yer bloody hair ... well yer better do it quickly – 'cos we leave in ten minutes, and if yer NOT on the coach, you're gonna get fined AND find yer own way home – now piss off – THE LOT OF YER."

The subject of my hair cropped up for a very different reason during that 1986–87 season.

Now, I've always thought of myself to be a man of culture as I've always strived to be in the style of the times. As a teenager in the 1970s, I'd be wearing bell-bottom flares 'n' tank tops, and then in the mid 1980s (in my late 20s/early 30s), I loved wearing those stylish suits with shoulder pads on the jacket 'n' a flashy shirt underneath. Tee-hee-hee, by 'eck, that Don Johnson 'n' his sidekick Philip Michael Thomas from the hit TV show *Miami Vice* had nothing on Joe Cooke and myself! Oh man, oh man – 'Cookey' was a stylish geezer! He always looked chic, and he would comment, "Hey, Mass, looking good my man – d'you know what, you should be a black man, because you're so cool with the way you dress." My passion for fashion didn't end there.

There was a classic scene from that era, of the sight of middle-aged men and teenage boys all huddled outside a

Dixon's electrical store shop window at 4.45 on a Saturday afternoon. They were there to catch the full-time football scores from around the country on the multitude of TVs on sale. Well, on this particular midweek afternoon, a posse caught a different kind of 'highlights'.

If it was good enough for Simon Le Bon and George Michael, then it was good enough for me! So every so often I'd spend the afternoon at the hairdresser's having my hair 'bleached' blonde (a time consuming process to say the very least). So there I was sat near the window wearing this 'dyeing hair cap' with the strands of my hair poking out 'n' bloody bleach running down into my eyes, when I suddenly noticed a huge gathering of people staring and pointing at me.

"That's Steve Massey!" Oh bugger, I've been rumbled! Soon enough, they started chanting.

"VIDAL, VIDAL, VIDAL!" Presumably after the male hairstylist Vidal Sassoon ... ah well, I thought, at least it wasn't any of the lads, otherwise my locks would be the butt of the changing room banter.

"VIDAL, VIDAL, VIDAL!" Oh bloody hell, even my teammates started chanting it in no time! It had stuck! But it was all good fun, and so typical of the changing room environment we had at Wrexham at that time. And as changing rooms go, it was one of the best I'd been a part of. Changing rooms are the nerve centre of any football team, and I'd been involved in a fair few in my career. I'd seen it all, ranging from lads holding grudges, fights escalating from throwaway comments, and plenty of personality clashes. But not one of those aspects existed during my time at Wrexham. This was the sanctum of a great group of lads, albeit with varying personalities, ranging from the quiet/unassuming, yet great companions, like Paul Emson and Mike Williams; the vocal leaders in Barry Horne and Joe Cooke; no-nonsense Big Jim Steel. And then there's yer Chris Pearces of this world, a total one-off nutcase of a fella! Bloody hell fire, there were times he'd perform his party piece of stuffing a Mars bar the size of a policeman's truncheon into his mouth in one go! I'd just look at him, shake my head and ask him "Pearcey! WHY? Honestly just WHY?"

Looking back, I was perhaps considered one of the senior players at the club, 'cos I was creeping towards my 30th. So I escaped most of the antics of the changing room pranks, usually instigated by our very own artful dodger, Barry Horne. Not for one moment should anyone be swayed by that intelligent side to him – 'cos he was a serial prankster and no one was spared when he was in the midst! Not even our big friendly Scottish giant, Jim Steel, was exempt.

And it's just as well Big Jim acquired a great temperament to deal with the banter, because the poor sod felt the brunt of most of the mickey-taking. But, to his credit, Jim could give as good as he got 'n' he was also able to back it up with his performances and his contribution to the team. Bloody hell, for such a big unit, he was an outstanding footballer. He could leap so high he had snow on his head and then follow that up with a touch so deft you'd swear his foot was fitted with a magnet to the ball. So, collectively, it was a pleasure and a privilege to be amongst these great lads, and what better way in getting to know each other, than going off for a few days to Malta?

As well as getting the chance to know my teammates, I was also still looking to register my first goal for the club. So by mid-September, I hoped to break my duck on the exciting trek to visit Maltese club Zurrieq, for a ECWC first-round first-leg tie. Could I complete a trio of firsts – first European Cup game, first time flying to a match, and first goal in Wrexham colours? Well, once again, Dixie was bang on the money with his man-management nous. No sooner had we arrived at our accommodation, he gave us an update of our itinerary.

"There's a couple of days until the match, so there will

be small pockets of time for us all to relax by the pool, or if anyone fancies a short spell of sightseeing. HOWEVER! This isn't a trip to bloody Butlin's, so let's remember we're here to win a football match! So we'll train late in the afternoon at about four o'clock, then we'll rest in the evenings."

"HANG ON GAFFER!" the lads squealed. "Surely we can't train at THAT time of the day, it's bloody roastin'!"

To which he simply replied, "Yeah, I know, and there's no better time to acclimatise to the conditions, because that's the same time when we'll kick off in a couple of days."

Ha-hah-hah, it was a light bulb moment for most of us as Dixie's theory dawned upon us.

Then came another personal first for me, and no doubt to the other lads that joined me for stroll around the 'spaghetti' streets filled with cafés and restaurants. I'd never been offered a bung to throw away a match and I'm sure it was never really considered in the lower English leagues. So, we were simply taking in the sights 'n' just sitting outside a café, suppin' on a soft drink. But, out of nowhere, we're approached by a local resident 'n' he queries if we're the Wrexham players? Like a magician, he then pulls out this brown paper bag and places it onto the middle of our table. Everyone glances at each other, wondering, "What the bloody hell?" and then he asks if we wouldn't mind taking it easy on the Zurrieq boys tomorrow? Curiosity soon turns into anger as Steve Charles and Barry Horne rage at this stange chap:

"TAKE YER FUCKIN' BAG AND DO ONE – WE'RE HERE TO WIN A FOOTBALL MATCH, AND THAT'S EXACTLY WHAT WE'RE GONNA DO!"

In the blink of an eye, the magician vanished! So did the paper bag!

Although, it was far from being a formality. We won the match 3–0, thanks to goals from Steve Charles, Mike Conroy, and myself. Yes – I finally managed to imprint my name on the scoresheet. It was a huge relief netting my first for

Wrexham. Although, midway through the second half and we're leading 3-0, I catch sight of our substitutes warming up so I give the slightest of glares to our dugout and mutter under my breath, "Don't you bloody dare take me off, 'cos I'm thirsty for more goals 'ere."

Anyway, I wasn't substituted, but I sure as hell was bloody thirsty! Oh 'eck, it was without a doubt THE hottest conditions I'd ever played a game of football in! Pheeeew, forget sun lotion – we might as well have used sunflower oil 'cos we were flamin' roastin'!"

We comfortably won the second leg 4–0 at The Racecourse. I bagged a brace 'n' Jim Steel and Barry Horne joined me on the scoresheet to set up a mouthwatering second round clash against Spanish giants Real Zaragoza – European big boys!

Brisbane Road, 18th October 1986. We've just beaten Leyton Orient at their home ground, 4–2, I've scored our fourth in the last minute, the referee blows the final whistle, and we're placed neatly at fourth in the League. Back inside the changing room, there was no talk of the game 'cos it was simply, "Let's get home and prepare for Monday's journey to face Real Zaragoza!" A real 'pinch myself' period in my career.

As you well know, I've already mentioned my taste for alluring attire and, in the weeks leading up to the second-round first-leg tie away to Zaragoza, I'd been scouting around for something a bit stylish. That was until I found out the club had splashed out on brand-new tracksuits with 'Wrexham in Europe 1986' embroidered on them. Ooohhh heeeyyy, this felt like heaven to wear, and one of my most prized possessions is a photograph of the squad standing next to our team bus in our club tracksuits before setting off to Zaragoza late October 1986. I can still hear Dixie's words swirling around my head:

"How many First Division footballers get to experience

playing against a top Spanish side like Zaragoza – let alone Fourth Division outfits like us?"

Well, it's the closest experience I've had to wearing the stylish shoes of pop stars such as Simon Le Bon, because we had a proper taste of the luxuries and lifestyles that can only be experienced by celebrities: a top-class hotel, surrounded by stunning scenery and culture. WOW!! I'd never seen so many glamorous women – every one of them dressed to impress – though I doubt they'd put on a bit of lippy just to make an impression on us lads from Wrexham in our Patrick tracksuits. BUT, they must've been aware there was something about us, with the extensive media following us. I wondered if they'd heard anything of Vidal being in town!

Another surreal moment was experiencing our impressive police escort to the match. It was absolutely fantastic being surrounded by flashing blue lights and passers-by pointing towards us and waving, and it was certainly a whole world away from our typical Saturday journey of tailgating a Ford Escort driver not giving a damn of holding us back 'n' their mates in the back seats flicking the Vs or showing their bare backsides at us! Each to their own, I suppose.

From the surreal to the 'pinch me' moment, the walk to the pitch. The changing rooms were hidden deep inside the bowels of the impressive Estadio De La Romareda stadium, and in a brief moment in time I only have to close my eyes and all my senses are transported back to when I'm striding out of the tunnel into the cocoon of noise in the partisan Spanish air ... bloody hell, it's the closest I ever felt like my hero Georgie Best did when he marched on to Estádio da Luz in 1966. Also, like Bestie, I'm even wearing the red No.7 shirt! Pinch me again!

I even came close to repeating his feat of scoring a priceless early goal for us, only to be denied seeing my name in lights on the mammoth scoreboard by a smart save from Zaragoza keeper Manolo Ruiz. That same scoreboard remained unchanged for the entire match, which didn't impress the Zaragoza faithful one jot. Displaying their displeasure towards the home side, they all stood up and waved their handkerchiefs, like a matador goading a bull. But hey, there was no 'bull' about our performance, and as we were heading towards the tunnel, those same disgruntled Spanish supporters put their handkerchiefs back in their pockets and put their hands together and joined in with our travelling fans and applauded us off as we strode down the flight of stairs and back into our proud changing room. We felt like superstars after an encore! Now all we needed was the after-party!

After such a monumental achievement of a heroic 0–0 draw at a top Spanish club like Zaragoza, we were hardly gonna head straight back to the hotel, sup on a nice cuppa 'n' say, "Nighty night" – were we buggery! We were still running on the rocket fuel of adrenaline and wanted to savour the flavour from every last drop. OCH! My oh my! It tasted mighty fine watching our fans mingling and jingling with Zaragoza fans to the music from various clubs and cafés. It was a pleasure joining both sets of supporters singing each other's terrace chants, including "VIDAL, VIDAL,VIDAL!" Ha-hah-hah, you could actually see the Zaragoza fans singing it 'n' the same time wondering, "Why the hell are we signing about a bloody hairdresser?" So, as a comical gesture, I ruffled and flicked my hair like they did in the advert – "Because I'm worth it" which had the rest of the lads in hysterics!

Absorbing the electric atmosphere, we continued to wander around the mazy streets and eventually stumbled upon a building. Was this top-notch or what? Blimey Moses, it resembled the type of five-star hotels you'd only see in the movies! So we thought it was the ideal place for us to enjoy a nice little nightcap. Although we'd already enjoyed a few drinks and were obviously a bit merry, no one was off their 'eads and making a scene. We were warmly welcomed into this extensive bar area, which looked absolutely first class, with plush leather sofas 'n' armchairs. Dangling from the ceiling were these velvet frills. But then it suddenly dawned on us that something was very much peculiar about this establishment – we were the only ones in there, which seemed oddly strange given the streets were heaving, but also, the whole decor was bright pink! Regardless, we went to order a round of drinks, but were then approached by two burly doormen (or bouncers) and somewhere in between broken English, one of the lads asked them what was the reason it was so quiet? Well blow me! The revelation had us running out of the building faster than we did during the match, 'cos it transpired we'd unintentionally wandered into a high-class brothel! I'm glad to say none of us scored off the pitch that night, either!

Far from 'job done', we knew we still had an almighty task ahead in the second leg and even though we'd certainly tamed the Los Blanquillos, the press and the media attention for the return at The Racecourse suggested there was the possibility of a major upset in store. As the match was arranged for Wednesday 5th November there were sure to be fireworks!

Now, I'm a person who likes to be attuned to my senses and surroundings – living in the moment. So the sights 'n' sounds from that Bonfire Night will stay with me for ever. As a music lover, I'm a great believer that music is a great motivator, whatever the occasion. ELO have always been my favourite band. On this occasion, Jon Bon Jovi and Simon Le Bon became my motivators, as their hits 'Livin' on a prayer' and 'Notorious' blasted out of The Racecourse PA as we warmed up during that nostalgic autumnal night. Whenever I hear either song, I stop whatever I'm doing, and inhale the vociferous atmosphere from that second leg … I can feel my ears trembling to the shuddering noise of our fans chanting, and my nose twitching to the smell of the fireworks 'n' flares from the Mold Road Kop! So let me share with you what my eyes saw in the heat of that cracking Cup tie.

In simple terms, Zaragoza should've erected a statue of their goalkeeper Cedrún after his heroic performance against us that night! Honestly, we absolutely pummelled them and how we went scoreless into extra time is purely an injustice. The only difference between us was Cedrún, he had the game of his life. And to show the gulf of finances between the two clubs, Zaragoza brought on their sub, Patricio Yañez, for the start of extra time – not bad for a cool £1million sub, eh? Bloody 'ell, I don't think our entire squad equated to his fee! And who should open the scoring for Zaragoza in the first half of extra time? Yañez! 0–1. This only added more spark to ourselves and our vocal supporters, 'n' they spurred us on with a resounding, "WE LOVE YOU WREXHAM, WE DO". Holy moly! The Racecourse was shakin' like an earth tremor when our inspiring midfield maestro, Barry Horne, got hauled down midway into their half. And from the resulting free kick, the ball pinballed towards me and without hesitation, I sent in a right-foot rocket past Cedrún! 1–1!

As soon as it hit the net, the deafening noise that erupted from our fans could've blown the roof off and landed in our garden at Caergwrle! BLOODY 'ELL! I'd never experienced a sound reaching the heights as that night. It was SO LOUD, it propelled me into such a stratospheric high, I lost all bodily control and could've quite easily sprinted through the turnstiles and carried on into the night, waving my fist and bypassing traffic! So thank the Lord for them 1980s terraced fencing, otherwise I'd still be celebrating today! In fact, I ran so fast back to the halfway line for the restart none of our lads caught up with me! And typical Barry Horne, he quips, "Oi MASS, any chance you could run that fast during the game?" But I was too excited to reply! And it was probably the reason I picked up a booking, just seconds later, for an over-zealous challenge. I desperately tried to remonstrate with the referee, but I was obviously waaayyy too pumped up and didn't intend any malice in the challenge. So in the end I agreed with my caution and actually told myself, "Calm down Mass, calm down."

Well, while the apoplectic Wrexham fans hadn't calmed down, Zaragoza instigated a swift move and that man Yañez struck a sweet volley beyond Chrissy Pearce. 1–2. Suddenly we'd gone from a wall of sound, to the eerie sound of the studs of our boots trudging back to the halfway line. Then, out of nowhere, you'd swear someone turned the dial to the speakers right to the top and our fans rose their volumes to the occasion and backed their boys. And this is when our very own 'Roy of the Rovers' made his introduction.

Far from being the 'unlikely hero' – but his contribution definitely fits the 'unlikely story' criteria. He'd actually been around the game and the club for quite a while, but Bucco (Stevie Buxton) decided not to fulfil a full-time career as a professional footballer, so struck a deal with the club and trained part-time and also worked at a local packing factory. But you would never have guessed his circumstances on a match day, 'cos he was as fit as a fiddle and brave as a lion was our Bucco. His knack of being in the right place at the right time was immaculate!

And so, on this prestigious European night, our 'Cinderella' literally came straight from the factory to The Racecourse, 'n' was still munching on his pre-match scran as he walked into the changing room just before the Zaragoza match. And, in typical Bucco fashion, he wasn't fussed about the match being beamed live across the UK and Europe – he was just 'one of the lads' and wasn't bothered by any media attention. As far as he was concerned, he was there to do a job and work his socks off for the cause.

So, in search of a spark to reignite our flames, Bucco came on as a sub for Paul Emson just before the end of normal time. With his usual gusto, hustle 'n' bustle, he soon ruffled a few of the Zaragoza players, much to the delight of our fans. And just as we were desperately in search of an equaliser, came a moment of pandemonium in their box. There's a shot cleared off the line, followed by a header cleared off the line, and the ball bounces awkwardly for Bucco 'n' somehow he manages to swivel on a sixpence, volleys the ball into the ground and it somehow bounces into the top-left corner. "YYYEEESSS!" BEDLAM! PURE CHAOS! Ooh, the scenes! 2–2, and still enough time to nick a winner and send a Euro shock wave.

It may sound totally barmy, but it's a real travesty we didn't win that night. Even though the match finished 2–2, we lost on the away goal rule to the giants of Real Zaragoza. But the reality of the story is that we REALLY should've beaten them. Being interviewed by Martin Tyler immediately after the game, I couldn't hide my disappointment. And although he announced that I was "now Wrexham's leading goal scorer in Europe", I was still upset that we'd lost the chance of coming ever so close to knocking out the greats of Real Zaragoza and progressing to the next round.

As with most sports, you tend to live in the moment – you've got to maximise it – and it hadn't really dawned on me, until a couple of days later, that I was Wrexham's leading goal scorer in Europe. I mean, come on, that's a special accolade isn't it! So, after we had the day off on the Thursday, we returned to training on the Friday in preparation for our away match to Crewe the next day. Dixie gestures to me and pulls me aside.

"You were sensational the other night, Mass, and that's the type of top-quality performances I brought you here for. I dunno if you're aware of it, but the rest of the lads were singing your praises in the changing room after the match 'n' so I want you to just feed off the buzz of that performance and take it into every match for the rest of the season. With any luck, we'll get promoted, and you'll be a legend at this club." Well, I was already living off the fumes of the buzz and adrenaline from the Zaragoza match, but now Dixie had injected me with a booster!

And if the loss to Real Zaragoza was a travesty, missing out on promotion in that 1986–87 season remains a puzzle not even the great Sherlock Holmes could fathom. In fact, it's a conundrum that should've made me bald by now, due to the amount I've scratched my head thinking, "How the 'eck did we not get promoted that season?" We acquired all the essential elements – a proper set of talented, hard-working lads; a remarkable coach in Dixie, and the type of supporters you could only dream of. But somehow, we buggered it up.

Boxing Day 1986, we drew 2–2 in a cracking match with Burnley at The Racecourse – Barry Horne and myself scored. I kid you not, we went straight home after the match, to prepare for a match THE NEXT DAY away to Tranmere Rovers ... two games in two days! But it didn't affect us, by the way, because we beat 'em 2–0, and that boosted us into fourth place. We were in great form and in a great position to mount a challenge towards promotion.

In hindsight, it could've been the 1–2 loss at home in the FA Cup third round to derby rivals Chester that started the rot, because ooohhh heck, that flippin' hurt, especially as we'd taken an early lead through Big Jim. But we just couldn't string a decent run of results after that desolate loss, and it was visibly clear to see how much our loss of form affected us. It hurt Dixie, because he genuinely believed we had the right characters to achieve promotion. You could feel his affection towards the club and the pain of a loss was written in his eyes.

And in a real testament to his character, Dixie walloped a statement of his intent in the summer of 1987 and brought in a sackfull of quality players in Brian Flynn, Jon Bowden, Kevin Russell, and ... ohhh hey, THE Joey Jones! And what a fabulous character he was, by the way – an absolutely smashing fella and a real one-off in every sense of the word. Genuinely, Joey had this amazing ability of being THE funniest guy ever, and he'd get the whole squad tripping over themselves hysterically in fits of laughter 'n' then flip the switch as soon as training or the match started, which only meant one thing – Joey the Terminator was in tow!! Phwoar – hey, he's the only person I know that could literally run through a brick wall 'n' have the audacity to look at all the bricks lying on the floor and tell them, "Fuckin' get up and stop moaning!" WOWEE!!

You can't begin to imagine how I felt, turning up for pre-season training and seeing these new guys, and they're in MY TEAM! Honestly, I couldn't wait for the new season to get started.

However ... I picked up a nasty ankle injury on a concrete of a pitch at Kidderminster Harriers and, as a result, I missed six months of the season. To keep my spirits up, Dixie arranged for me to embrace being an ambassador for the club. Although I desperately missed the buzz of playing on a match day, I actually grew into the role and embraced the meeting 'n' greeting of match day sponsors, as well as making a great connection with the loyal fans. Honestly, I found it such a cathartic experience. And who wouldn't puff their chests out whenever I was introduced. "We're joined today by Steve Massey, currently our all-time leading goal scorer in Europe!" Cooorrr blimey, that made my chest puff out like Popeye!

I eventually made a recovery, albeit a tentative one at best. I started off with a couple of run-outs with the reserves, including one against Bala Town in the Welsh National League. It was a match where I kept a wide berth from some of the tackles Joey would've relished. And when we were awarded a penalty, there was absolutely no chance of anyone else taking it but me, 'cos once a striker – always a striker.

When I gratefully converted from 12 yards, I couldn't wait to tell Dixie: "I'M BACK!"

Within a week, I was back in the first team, and scored a scrappy goal to salvage a point away at Leyton Orient. Even though the play-off positions were still a tall order, there's absolutely no doubt in my mind we'd have dominated the Fourth Division if we'd shared the end-of-season form back at the beginning as well. Hell fire, we had a crackin' string of results, which concluded with a Welsh Cup final ... and the lure of another European adventure. Cardiff City however had their own agenda, and beat us 0–2.

Obviously disappointed with the result, personally it was just magic being back amongst the lads, especially after the heartache of the ankle injury. Oh bloody 'ell, it felt good to feel that adrenaline rush again, gushing through my body like a bolt of lightning! There's no feeling like it, and once it gets inside you, it lasts for ages. But once it runs out, you can't wait for it to get pumped inside your bloodstream again! Football eh? Bloody 'ell, it's the stuff that dreams are made of, and let me tell ya, Wrexham made mine like the lyric from one of my favourite ELO songs, 'Hold on tight to your dreams'.

18
Danny Wright
Forward

The stiff bang theory
(2011–2013, 86 appearances, 25 goals)

There are a few variations of the Big Bang, 'n' most of them consist of a major event. The most notable is a theory that almost 14 billion years ago an atom exploded, thus creating the universe as we know it. Aiming to make an impact for himself, Danny Wright arrived at The Racecourse ready to send Wrexham to another universe! With a bellyful of chuckles 'n' cackles, Danny delves into his Wrexham archives and tells us about joining a club on the brink of extinction; becoming Blakey's Brute, Bootlegger's Bestie, 'n' blowing the net for the town.

"WHAT THE FUCK just happened?" I thought, as I'm standing stark bollock naked by the bar in a pub in Rhostyllen! It's only the middle of the afternoon, and on a weekday 'n' all. Only a few short hours earlier I got to meet my new housemates: Lee 'Fowls' Fowler, Adrian 'Cheesey' Cieślewicz and Glen 'Blakey' Little.

I'd only just dropped my belongings in the room and I hear Fowls shout, "Come on then, let's have a couple of pints! Hey, there's a pub just down the road."

"Yeah, awight son, but naffin too heavy, 'cos we got training tomorrow. Tel ya wot, son. I'll bring the cards 'n' all."

Blakey jumps in. "Don't worry, Brute, I'll look after ya," he says to me as we're walking towards the pub.

A couple of days earlier, mid-June 2011, I stood on the famous Mold Road terrace end (the Kop) at The Racecourse ground, imagining myself standing there being a fan during the glory days. Now I wanted to experience playin' there as a Wrexham player. I'd already played there for Histon and Cambridge United 'n' always thought of Wrexham as a big club in the wrong League, the National League. So, by the time I'd had a tour of the ground and met the manager, Dean Saunders, my view of Wrexham Football Club had changed – no longer was it a big club in that League – it was actually a 'sleeping giant' ... and I wanted to play a part in reawakening it.

Moving to Wrexham, and especially Rhostyllen, was a big deal for me. I was a 26-year-old country bumpkin from Norwich in Norfolk, and I'd never really ventured far from home, even when I was playing for Histon or Cambridge. Wrexham, on the other hand, was a four-and-half-hour drive. I was a bag of excitement and maybe curiously nervous as well I suppose, 'cos I was gonna move to a big club, with a big history, big fan base, not to mention the thought of sharing a house with my new housemates.

"Right then, bois! These are the rules," Fowls pipes up after a few card games, during that muggy June afternoon. "If you lose – you lose money, down a pint at the bar, AND take an item of clothing off!"

Being the new boy and still a little bit shy, I opted out from arguing back so just went along with it. But Blakey, being the elder statesman, thought otherwise.

"'Ang about Fowls, steady on mate! 'Ow about we just stick to the money, eh son."

A couple of hours later, we're all stripped to our boxer shorts, and contemplating nipping out to find a cash machine.

"Ah well," Fowls slurs. "Fuck the money – we'll stick to the clothes and drinks then, innit."

Soon enough we were all standing by the bar flapping like an elephant, ordering a few more pints.

"Fuckin' hell, what's Deano gonna say when we're still pissed for training tomorrow?" I said to the lads.

"Just make sure you work your bollocks off, Brutey. Oh, and try not to get too close and get in a conversation with the gaffer, 'cos he'll smell the booze on your breath straightaway," Blakey reassures me.

"Don't worry about that," Fowls nips in. "You won't get a fuckin' chance to engage in any conversation with Deano – 'cos he'll do all the talking anyway!"

Having already met Deano during my tour of the ground, I got to know the reason behind his nickname – 'Tell Us A Story Saunders' – because he was full of stories and to be fair he was a seriously good storyteller … but he didn't half sell me a different story when it came to the financial situation of the club, especially with Deano's lyrical waxing. Shit, he had fuckin' bags of it. Bags of charm? He definitely had. In fact, he was that good, he could sell Paxo to a live turkey, he could! But bags of money? Well – he definitely didn't have that.

I hadn't had much of a chance of getting to know my new teammates properly before there was a shock announcement that the club was financially in the shit, and could go bust within 24 hours. As you could imagine, all the lads were a bit confused and bewildered about what the actual fuck was going on. So our captain, Dean Keates, calls for a meeting in the changing room.

After about half an hour, we've all had a chance to say our piece, and lay out our worries. Keatesy was brilliant, 'n' it was easy to see why he was our captain. Deano was great too! He was the same Deano every day, whether it was for a match, or during training – always upbeat, and always hilarious. His Friday 'Young v Old' training match being the highlight. Always a tasty match, because the Young uns wanted to show up the Old uns, and the Old uns wanted to show they still had it and beat the Young uns. This is where Deano was in his element, giving a running commentary during the match 'n' just non-stop piss-taking. Afterwards, in the changing room, he'd pretend to be reading a match report on the Old v Young match and slating people, giving them a score out of ten, but in an impressionist's voice. 'Tell Us a Story Saunders' suited him well.

It was during this period I got first-hand experience of how much the club meant to the fans and the community. As I've said previously, I knew they had a good following, but their outpouring of unconditional love towards the players and the club just blew me away. And they deserve every success the club has, and forever will have, because they are the past, the present and the future of Wrexham Football Club. As well as the sheer amount of money they raised in such a short space of time, they also showed love and support to a level I had never experienced ... or ever will at any other club for that matter.

The house we lived in, aka Vegas, was only down the road from Colliers, our training ground, as well as The Racecourse.

Literally about a ten-minute drive from both, this helped us get to know the locals, especially with Glen around, because we'd be sat in the house and he'd give me a nudge and say, "Come on Brute, let's go for a walk and a coffee," and we'd go to the Starbucks in Rhostyllen.

It didn't take their staff long to figure out who we were, and would always greet us like a mate, "Alright Danny lad" or "Hi Glen mate, how's things pal?" or if we'd be going to Costa in Eagles Meadow for a coffee and walking through the high street in Wrexham town centre, we'd have hundreds of people shouting, "Great goal Saturday Danny lad" or "You were fantastic last night Glen, keep going!" which was something completely new to me. I absolutely loved it and loved that genuine connection with the people and the community. Even though Wrexham wasn't an incredibly wealthy area, their generosity was boundless towards us.

Blakey loved his one-shot latte coffee and, having a Starbucks within a few minutes' walk from the house, he was like a big kid living that close to a toy shop. Eventually he got me hooked on the 'one-shots' and soon enough we became great friends with the staff, and the opening line would always be the same, "Alright Danny lad, how's things Blakey? One-shot lattes? Tell ya what, I'll give you these on the house if you can get me a couple of tickets for the next match!" So me and Blakey would chuckle, and gratefully accept, "Yeah, awight, thanks!"

Getting tickets wouldn't prove too much of a problem really, because each player would get an allocation of tickets for their family and friends anyway, so we thought we'd just request a few extra for our new-found friends. In all honesty though, we would always insist on paying for our coffee and never sought to take advantage. But it would always be declined and our friends would give us a little wink and say something like, "I wish I had a ticket for the match," and again we'd let out a little chuckle and promise them tickets.

The close connection with the locals and their businesses occasionally led to a 'player's appearance' at a local establishment or business. Me and Blakey loved it and would volunteer for anything as long as we had the time – including one unforgettable experience at the local Mecca Bingo club.

We'd just finished training around 1pm, and thought we'd have a cheeky coffee at Starbucks before heading back to Vegas for a snooze, and get showered before going to the Mecca Bingo that evening. Wwweeell … that was our intentions, anyway. It was business as usual at Starbucks: two one-shot lattes for a trade of two tickets to the next match. Sorted. Blakey then goes, "Cor, I ain't 'alf starvin'! Right then Brutes, c'mon, let's go for a cheeky Nando's." And off we went to Nando's in Eagles Meadow, still in our stinking training gear.

It won't surprise you, but we'd got to know the staff there as well.

"Tell you what," they said. "You can order absolutely anything you want from the menu – in exchange for some tickets!"

Me and Blakey just looked at each other and nodded, "Yeah, that's very kind 'n' we can sort out tickets for ya. But honestly, we don't mind paying."

But they'd just start waving their arms about telling us, "Absolutely not! You're one of us now, and we wouldn't dream of charging you … so thanks for the tickets though, lads!"

Blakey gets on the phone straightaway to sort out the extra tickets – sorted! So then he gets out the cards (which he took absolutely everywhere), and in the middle of Nando's restaurant we start playing cards for a bit of money and there's people around trying to eat their meal while we're getting carried away with the cards.

Whatever we ordered to eat, I swear they must've doubled the amount, because it looked like a family feast! Honestly, it literally filled the whole of the table, and in the meantime we totally lost track of time.

"Aw fuckin' hell Blakey, we gotta go – the bingo!" So we pegged it to the Mecca Bingo and by the time we got there we were totally humming with sweat – absolutely stinking in our training gear. We arrived back at Vegas around 10pm, still in our reeking training gear, we've not spent a penny all day, and our stomachs so full we were ready to burst like a hot air balloon.

For all their love and support, there was only one way we could really repay them – do the talking on the pitch and get promoted. To do that we needed a good squad to challenge for a fight. Players that could play a bit and get stuck in. Lads with character. Each day I went to training, or to a match, I'd look around the changing room and think to myself, "Oh man, we've got a fuckin' great team of characters." Big characters like Mark Creighton, aka 'The Beast', Dean Keates, Jay Harris, Andy Morrell, Jamie Tolley, Jake Speight – all big characters, and all brutally determined to the cause. Yeah, similar to anywhere else, people wound each other up, and there'd be a bit of tension, but we had that respect at the same time, because ultimately we all wanted the same outcome – winning – and giving some love back to the amazing Wrexham fans.

Always ready to diffuse a situation with a prank were two of the biggest scallywags of pranksters I've ever met: Jay Harris and Lee Fowler. Nothing and no one was safe with them two around. One of their most notorious tricks was smudging ketchup on door handles, so just as you'd go to open the door to your car, "Oh, for fuck sakes." There's ketchup all over yer fuckin' fingers and your car, and within earshot you can hear them two pissing themselves laughing.

The door 'andle to the changing room door was always a prime target as well, and when you'd least expected it, or forget, you'd go to open it. "YOU PAIR OF WANKERS!" you'd hear someone scream, before you'd see them chasing after Little Jay or Fowls around the dressing room like a scene from *Benny Hill*, and Little Jay screeching "G'wed yer fwchin' rat!"

We had each other's back and we were a solid unit. And, sure enough, our togetherness resulted in us having a blazing start to the 2011–2012 season. We didn't fear anyone and wanted to put the fear into them. And, thankfully, it didn't take me too long before I scored my first goal for the club, at home against Kidderminster Harriers on the 3rd of September.

It was such a relief getting myself off the mark, and like many goals I scored that season, I owed much of it to our talented full back, Curtis Obeng. He absolutely flew down the right wing beating two players, before floating the ball in for me to head it beyond their keeper, to make it 2–0 for us, after Jamie Tolley's opener. We were flying high in the League and it didn't look like anyone could stop us. A couple of weeks later, Deano left us to manage Doncaster Rovers. It was quite ironic really … 'Tell Us a Story Saunders' never told us this story – him slippin' away quietly and leaving us to learn of his departure from a newspaper. Mozza (Andy Morrell) was instantly named as our new gaffer.

Although he was officially our new gaffer, Mozza was so laid-back being the boss, he insisted we'd still call him Mozza rather than Gaffer or Boss. He didn't stroll into the dressing room and give it the big, "Right, I'm the gaffer and from now on, this 'n' that are gonna change and I'm doing blah-di-blah," because that wasn't his persona. And, ultimately, he was highly regarded because of his dedication towards the club and he got on well with all the lads.

It also might have helped him that he was taking over a successful team rather than a struggling team, and he went about it in the genius way of keeping everything almost the same.

We had two great, but two totally different, goalkeepers in Chris Maxwell and Joslain Mayebi. Maxi had a more methodical 'n' organisational approach to his game, whereas Jos was perhaps more instinctive and fearless. But both were great to have in between the sticks and it was always reassuring to know you had a solid keeper that could save a game for us.

He tweaked the defence a bit and made us a bit tighter at the back, and oh my days, there were horrible monsters that could also mix it up a bit with a bit of aggression and tidy football. I mean, you ain't gonna beat Creights to a challenge; Nat Knight-Percival could read the game blindfolded; Neil Ashton would terrorise wingers like a little terrier; and nobody ever got past Curtis Obeng 'cos he even fuckin' walked at a 100mph!

Our midfield was just a nasty little engine fuelled by Jay Harris, Dean Keates, and Jamie Tolley, coupled with Fowls' creative brain. All four had the ability to fight their way out of a saloon bar, as well as dictate the play.

By far the biggest character we had was Keatesy – THE perfect captain material for us, and he led by example with his mannerisms and his personality traits. He knew when to take the foot off the pedal and when to have a laugh and piss about; but he'd fuckin' come down on ya if you stepped out of line or maybe acted in an inappropriate manner. But none of them qualities mattered if he couldn't do the business on the field ... and ooohhh, don't be fooled by his vertically challenged stature, because he was fuckin' massive for us. You wanna talk about setting standards, well there's yer man – our captain.

There were times when I'd get to bed at night and still hear his distinctive Brummie voice moaning out loud in the changing room before a match, "Awww fwcin' 'ell Wrighty! Yaw fwcin' stink!" or "Awww surprise, surprise, Pablo's in the toilet, and it fwcin' stinks in 'ere again! Yaw need to gaw 'n' see a fwcin doctor, yaw doo!"

Well ... Keatesy must've been a clairvoyant, because years later, I was diagnosed with coeliac disease. There's no wonder I was shooting my fuckin' arse off before every match, after consuming a massive pot of pasta the night before, followed by a huge bowl of porridge for breakfast and finished off with a plateful of egg and beans on toast as my pre-match meal – almost everything a coeliac shouldn't eat!

As a strike force, Mozza knew we still had plenty of goals in us, and told us he trusted us fully to carry on 'blowing the net'. Speighty would scrap and bully his way to get a goal; Mozza had an unbelievable appetite to find a goal; Adrian Cieślewicz had this astonishing speed to give defenders nightmares 'n' it's just a shame his brains weren't as quick as his feet. And I knew I could hold the ball, interlink and chip in with a few goals as well.

To help make us more of a tougher unit to crack, Mozza installed Billy Barr as his assistant. He was allowed to keep Oaksey, our goalkeeping coach, but that was his limit, because the club couldn't afford too many backroom staff. We were still relying on hand-outs from the Supporters' Trust.

Mozza, to his credit, was still full-on in training, delegating his player/manager role with ease. He'd say his piece before training and let Billy take over. They had a set routine for training, and every session was carefully scheduled. It was a bit more regimented under their supervision compared with Deano, but I still loved training and couldn't wait to get there early to sup on a hot brew and listen to the experienced lads reeling stories off, one after the other. Great times with great lads.

Those great times continued on the field as we marched on in the League, and the FA Cup, beating my old club Cambridge United in a first round replay at The Racecourse, where Mathias Pogba gave us the lead, before I made it 2–0 with a bullet header. That great result set us up for a second round tie away to League One Brentford ... two leagues above us.

Success on the field, and loving life off it, 'cos Vegas had built a reputation of being 'party central', 'n' weeell, I couldn't refuse could I? So just went along with it. We'd even inherited a housemate, young Declan 'Trigger' Walker. Great lad Trigger, and very funny.

Trigger was also quite popular with the local females and, on one successful occasion during a night out with the lads, he brought a companion back to Vegas and was eager to 'entertain' his guest in his bedroom ... but one of his housemates had a hunch of Trigger's intentions and hid inside Trigger's wardrobe. Through the slats of the wardrobe, Trigger's climaxing showcase was described by the onlooker as a "stiff bang!" But the roving reporter would later endure a long night stranded inside the claustrophobic wardrobe, as Trigger and his companion spent the next few hours chatting, before finally going to the kitchen for a coffee.

A few days later, early December, we played our second round FA Cup tie away at Brentford. We were massive underdogs and no one really gave us a chance. We didn't give a shit. If we wanted to, we'd fuckin' bash 'em about a bit. Mozza's last words before going out of the changing room doors were, "Let's have a bit of fun and let's have a fuckin' good go at them" (but I do wish he could've warned us about the door handles being lubed in ketchup again!).

A Jamie Tolley rocket from 25 yards gave us a 0–1 lead, and sent our travelling supporters into wild ecstasy. In honour of Trigger's climaxing showcase, we performed 'the stiff bang' as our goal celebration, much to the delight of our unsuspecting, yet delirious, fans! "They're doing the fish, they're doing the fish," we heard them chant.

Brentford tried to claw their way back, but we dug in and battled our way to hold on for big FA Cup scalp and, in the process, earned ourselves and our fantastic supporters another mouthwatering tie at Championship side Brighton in the third round.

It was total fuckin' madness after the final whistle. Scenes of pure elation and joy as we danced and celebrated in front of our noisy fans, which then carried on going back through the corridor towards our changing room and everyone screaming their heads off, "FUCKIN' GET IN!", or Little Jay and Jakey Speight dancing and singing, "Wembley, Wembley".

We finally reach the changing room 'n' Mozza and Keatesy settle us down by saying a few words of praise and congratulate us on a perfectly-executed celebration routine (which was authorised by them both after Fowls and Tolley had asked their permission before the game) and then BOOM! Everyone's screaming and shouting "DO, DO, DO, LET'S ALL DO THE STIFF BANG" and "WREXHAM,WREXHAM!" Brentford must've thought we'd let our fans in to join us, because the noise was deafening. But that was the level of our strong bond as a team. I'm glad to say, Trigger learnt his lesson and checked his wardrobe for the bogeyman before going to sleep at night.

Keeping me in check was a man I can only describe as a 'legend', and that 'top man' was Joey Jones. What a guy. What an absolute inspiration for anyone wanting to understand the whole ethos of representing Wrexham Football Club. Fuckin' fearless, entertaining, and the most respected person I ever came across during my career in football, and quite possibly, my life.

Like every other member of staff, you get introduced to all the coaching staff at the club. Shaking hands with Joey was like shaking hands with a pro boxer and yer best mate at the same time, because he had that personality of making you feeling like you belonged or were 'one of us', but he was also such a strong fella that I could feel his grip an hour later!

But I got lucky, and had the chance of getting to know Joey properly through Blakey ... and let me tell ya, sharing that precious time with those two could be a riot, insightful, and beautiful – all in one day. Fuckin' 'ell, they could spend hours talking football, 'n' then switch it with loadsa banter, then finish off with some pearls of wisdom.

Our close relationship only came about through Blakey getting an injury and playing a couple of games under Joey for the reserves. After that, Blakey offered to help Joey out with the reserves when he could.

"Awight Brutes! 'Aw d'ya fancy joining me and 'The Ledge' with the reserves later?" was how Blakey put it to me one morning. "You'll fackin' love it, son. 'Ere, tell ya what, bring us a couple of one-shots and we'll pick you up. Awight son."

Blakey was spot-on, 'cos I absolutely loved them days with the reserves. But it was more to do with Blakey and Joey really, and I know Blakey won't mind me saying this but Joey became like a father figure to me, whereas Blakey was more of a big brother (more on my big brother later). I do doubt, however, if Joey's mind games tactics would be approved of in any coaching manual!

So, the three of us were talking about the first-team match from the previous day, and Joey's assessment of my game was bang on:

"You were superb last night Wrighty!! And you always play better when you're angry." Then he grabs hold of me, shakes me like a fuckin' rag doll, and he's shouting, "C'MON THE BRUTES!!" before he starts shadow boxing me. "C'mon Blakey, we'll make a player out of this one yet," but Blakey's on his arse pissing himself laughing! In all honesty though, Joey was right on the money, because I'd play a blinder if something or someone had pissed me off.

January 2012, we're still battling it out with Fleetwood Town to claim top spot. We've also just secured a replay in the third round of the FA Cup, after Cheesey cracked one in away at Brighton, and we're buzzin' that we can sort 'em out back at our place. Anyway, a couple nights of hard frost postponed the scheduled original Tuesday 17th January date, so we only had 24 hours to wait to play the replay at a rampacked Racecourse.

Walking into the changing room that night, Joey bounces in, cup of tea in one hand, 'n' waving his fist with the other shouting "C'MON THE TOWN!" So I know what's coming my way as soon as he puts his tea down. So he comes my way, 'n' straightaway I start pissing myself.

"Here he is ... The Ledge! You alright Joey!" and BANG – RATTLE – WHOOSH! He starts launching at me with a tirade of flying fists, then shakes me like fuck, and does his best impression of Muhammad Ali.

"C'MON BRUTEY LAD! IT'S PACKED OUT THERE TONIGHT – YOU FUCKIN' GET THEM ON THEIR FEET LAD!"

I'm still trying to evade his swaying fists. "Fuckin' hell Joey, one of these days those rockets are gonna land one on me." I'm fuckin' ready fer this!

Whether it was down to Joey's pep talk, or if it was just one of those games, but I had a sixth sense of being on raging fire that night – almost like an outer body experience. Everything I touched and everything I tried came off. By the 23rd minute I'd already got the Brighton defence in a twist, and went on a mazy run from midfield, past two of their players, chopped the ball before laying it off beautifully for Mozza to curl it in the top corner from 20 yards ... OH. MY. DAYS! I thought my eardrums had exploded, and what a peach of a goal! As we're jogging back to the centre circle, I look for Joey and give him the thumbs-up – he just grits his teeth and shakes his fist, "GET IN, BRUTES!"

The performance of my dreams soon turned into a nightmare. An excruciating painful one, after I landed badly on my elbow not long into the second half. Lying there in absolute fuckin' agony, I could hear someone around me heaving and being sick ... turns out a couple of their players went green with sick when they saw the state of my elbow.

In a state of blur I was rushed to Wrexham Maelor Hospital, whizzed through to X-ray, had a diagnosis of a dislocated elbow, and was back at The Racecourse sporting a sling to watch us lose on penalties. Gutted.

Although we lost, there was no mistaking the sense of pride we had from our performance, and the unbelievable support yet again from our fantastic fans. I actually got a strange 'n' spine-tingling experience off the noise our fans generated when we stopped in traffic on our way back to the ground, just outside the hospital, and I had the window down. I could hear our fans chanting … I thought, "WOW, FUCKIN' HELL. LISTEN TO THAT!!"

I saw Joey straight after the game 'n' I thought, "Oh no, not now Joey," thinking he was gonna start fuckin' shadow boxing me or something.

"BRUTEY! Hey, you were sensational tonight pal, so just remember that feeling the next time you're back on the field."

I fuckin' love you, Joey. xx

Losing to Luton Town in the 2012 play-off semi-finals was a massive disappointment, and it kinda made ya scratch yer head and think, "How the fuck did we not get promoted?" It left an acid taste in my mouth throughout that summer until we finally got back to pre-season, and I'm looking around the changing room and listening to how the lads are talking, and looking at their body language, and to me it was obvious that the Luton play-off still hurt. But it probably made us all the more determined to get the job done in the 2012–2013 season, but we'd be without some key players.

Creights sustained a bad knee injury as early as August 2012, 'n' one that would keep him out for the season and probably his career. We lost Fowls to Fleetwood Town; and we lost Curtis Obeng to Swansea City. Three big players for us in the 2011–2012 season. On a personal level, I was more pissed off with the Curtis loss really, because he was the most prolific assist with the majority of my goals. His intuitive timing and quality of crosses were a striker's dream.

Undeterred, 'n' like a runaway train, we got off to another great start to the season and, quite literally, it snowballed us into March 2013. Since Christmas 2012, we knew we potentially could have a chance of at least one Wembley final ... and hopefully avoid a second.

Christmas as a professional footballer is like any other fixture list really. We trained Christmas Eve morning, loads of the usual banter and everyone wishing each other a Merry Christmas. And because Mozza's given Christmas day off, I went to see my family in Norfolk straight after I'd showered.

We had Telford United at The Racecourse on Boxing Day, so I went for a light run in the morning before we opened our gifts, ate a small and lighter than usual Christmas dinner, and finished off with another light run before my parents drove me back to Wrexham that evening.

I was always careful and conscious of keeping my parents firmly at the front door to Vegas, because this was the ultimate bachelor pad and I most definitely didn't want my mum seeing the 'leader board' hanging up on the wall ... and her disappointment at my position in it!

So they opted to stay at a nearby hotel and watched a bit of Christmas TV. They always loved coming to Wrexham to watch me play, and always complimented the warm welcome they'd receive, especially if I'd scored and the team won! That is exactly what we did in that Boxing Day encounter against Telford United, beating them 4–1! I was so pleased to score our third, and my seventh goal of the season, edging us only four points behind leaders Grimsby Town.

Less than a week later, we'd play Telford United again, away on a cold New Year's Day, for a midday kick off. I opened the scoring in the 24th minute, and Cheesey finished the game off to make it 2–0 in the 85th. We were getting closer to that top spot.

Personally, I was never fussed about New Year's Eve to be honest, 'cos I always preferred staying in. It became a routine I got used to. So, New Year's Eve 2012 was no different really, apart from the fact I was still living in a house called Vegas ... with a group of Likely Lads!

There was no cunning plan hatched, or breaking any curfews, so we went out for a nice meal at one of the local restaurants. I'm not sure what the other guests and diners must've thought when we rocked up in our tracksuits, swearing. Soon enough, we were causing a mini fuckin' riot with the cards 'cos there was always time for the cards (our own 'Fagin', aka Blakey, hated the awkward silence so much, I swear he could play cards whilst sitting on the toilet having a shit!) and to be fair to the other diners, they were all dressed in their finest clobber, and clinking expensive glasses of wine, and we didn't get a single complaint or sarcastic comment from them, even though we totally sabotaged their 'ambience' during the evening.

We couldn't have stayed too long with our fine diners anyway, as we had an evening planned with an Everton footballer back at Vegas at about 7.30. A bit of a gentleman's evening, which meant young Trigger wasn't allowed any special guests in his bedroom ... or inside his wardrobe! And by the time we got back, Tony Hibbert, the Everton footballer, was already standing and waiting for us in our living room! However, I must explain – 'Tony Hibbert' had four legs, was full of coffee and tea stains, and had about five coasters on his face ... our Evertonian 'friend' was indeed our coffee table!

Our precious coffee table was given its moniker by Blakey, not long after we moved in.

"Awww lovely! 'Ere, that's a great place to play the old cards on that! I tell ya what me ol' china, we'll give it a name

... we'll call him Tony Hibbert – after the Everton player."

I just chuckled and looked baffled at Blakey. "Yer what, Blakey? Why the bloody 'ell would you wanna give a coffee table a name, and why Tony fuckin' Hibbert?"

Sounding more like a mad scientist, Blakey coolly goes, "Yeah, good question son, and I'm glad you asked me that. But it's logic, innit? I mean ... just look at it – it doesn't actually do anything 'n' it ain't flamboyant! But it does exactly what it's supposed to do ... just like Tony Hibbert does every game for Everton! Just logic, innit," and starts tapping his finger at the side of his head as if he's cracked the code to the Crown Jewels.

So guess what we did for the next few hours? Yyeeep, we played the old cards on 'Tony Hibbert', though nothing too heavy, because young Trigger hadn't long come back from an ACL injury and was a bit strapped for cash, so we'd play the card game Crash for a quid here 'n' there, before we made sure he was tucked up nice and snug in his bed before midnight ... bless him.

Gainsborough Trinity would be our last obstacle to reaching a Wembley final, in the first-leg semi-final of the FA Trophy at The Racecourse. It was a huge relief when I slotted home to give us a 1–0 lead in the 18th minute, because it looked as though it was gonna be one of those days where we'd dominate and take advantage of our chances ... but, bloody hell, they equalised about ten minutes later, 1–1. Oh shit, there was gonna be fireworks halftime.

Credit to Mozza and Billy Barr, they didn't really go into us too heavy at the interval. "We're doing all the right things in the right way, but we're not fuckin' clinical enough when we're doing it! Listen, a blind man on a galloping horse can see they've come here to play for a draw, so let's make sure they get back on their bus with fuck all."

Gainsborough again proved a tough nut to crack, as they dug in and made it hard for us to break 'em down.

But it was only a matter of time before all our pressure would crack them open, and it was our very own 'Speedy Gonzales', Cheesey, that finally prized them open with his usual driving run down the right wing and smacked it with his right foot beyond the keeper, 2–1, and we wanted more, because we knew it was gonna be tough at their place. We had to wait until injury time for Neil Ashton, our little Tasmanian Devil, to score the all-important cushion goal and give us a two-goal advantage going to Gainsborough for the second leg.

Sometimes it's the waiting that can destroy your mind, and we were glad we didn't have too long to wait for the second leg at Gainsborough. Fortunately, I didn't have too long to give us a 0–1 lead on the day, and score maybe one of my best and favourite goals of all time, and it was best captured by a man who'd yell "Captain" whenever he saw me, aka 'The Bootlegger'.

As expected, they'd hustled and harassed us all over the pitch for the first 20 minutes, and I'd had enough, so I thought, "Fuck this," and went into Joey mode and started giving it back, and after I'd bullied their players out on the wing, I took the ball forward a couple of steps before unleashing a left-footed curler into the top corner! Then I'm running towards our fans behind that goal. Seeing the pure joy spread all over their faces made me wanna rip my heart out and throw it to them! WOW! This was probably the best feeling I've had in football ... I just wanted to jump over the barriers and go fuckin' mental with them!

"Wembley, Wembley, we're the famous Wrexham FC and we're going to Wembley," echoed the famous chant around the Northolme ground. We'd only gone and done it! But it was the bloody hard way though, as Gainsborough scored two, to make it a nervy last 11 minutes for us as we held on to a 4–3 aggregate lead. The two-and-three-quarter-hour journey home provided precious time to comprehend our achievement of getting Wrexham and our unbelievable fans to a Wembley final.

"Watch out Wembley, 'cos the Wrexham boys are on their way, and we'll be in our glory if we make history!" That's exactly how we felt travelling to Wembley a couple of days before the FA Trophy final against Grimsby Town.

Of course I was excited. I'd never been to Wembley before. It was a final, our fans had sold out our ticket allocation, and the club requested extra allocation due to the high demand (including our mates from Starbucks and Nando's ... obviously!) and I'd also have most of my family coming to Wembley, including my dear old godmother, who only had about two months to live.

Anyway, just before we arrived in London, we heard rumours and saw snippets of a heavy snowfall across most of the country. Which was hard for us to comprehend because, when we looked out through the windows of the bus, there was absolutely nothing in London. But boy were we mistaken, because the snowfall spread just as quick on social media as it did on the ground, and at one point there were doubts of the game going ahead ... yet still there wasn't a flake of snow around Wembley.

Not a flake of snow, but it was Arctic conditions 'n' bloody freezing when we went for a stroll on the Wembley pitch a couple of days before the final. Soaking up the drama of Wembley, we couldn't wait to check out the changing rooms, but for two contrasting reasons – we were freezing cold, and we were about to film and perform our very own version of 'The Harlem Shake' ... a dance craze doing the rounds on social media and YouTube.

"Yep, that's fine, but don't think for a second that any of this gets on any social media if we don't win. You only post it if we win! 'Cos otherwise we're gonna look bloody stupid!" was the response from Mozza after we'd requested his permission to shoot the video. Oh my life, ha-hah-hah, I thought we were all gonna keel over from the intense amount of laughing we had during the shoot! And I was still laughing going into my hotel room that evening, until I finally settled down to watch the TV with my roomy.

    Blakey would be my roommate for every away stay at a hotel for long journey matches. Anywhere we went that was over a couple hours' journey, we'd stay at a hotel. He took responsibility of our room. He'd suss out the conditions before saying, "Right then the Brutes, let's go for a coffee," so we'd nip out for a quick coffee, and head back to our room to watch a match or something on TV. Blakey, though, acquired the shortest attention span in history, 'n' if there was a throw-in during the match we were watching, he'd change the fuckin' channel. He'd come across a film, 'n' he'd give you a running commentary on the film! He just wouldn't stop talking and quoting stuff from the film, and suddenly he'd remember about the match we were watching and change it back ... until another throw-in, and repeat the same process, again and again, until it made me bloody seasick dizzy and I'd end up putting a pillow over me face just to stop the room from spinnin'!

    But, in all sincere honesty, Blakey was great for me. He looked after me and educated me on a lot of things, not just football, but how someone should conduct themselves, and he became like an older brother to me. Our close relationship hadn't gone unnoticed with the rest of the lads either, and they'd take the piss, saying that Blakey was grooming me! Ha! Fuckin' wankers! But I looked up to him. I was still a young footballer and he helped me and influenced me to become a man. Top man, Blakey.

    So to share this special experience of playing at Wembley with someone like Blakey was brilliant. Even more precious was seeing and hearing the noise coming from our fans going out for the match – unbelievable, absolutely unbe-fuckin'-lievable! They'd had to dig themselves out like soldiers in trenches and then travel around six hours or so to get to Wembley and still have the energy to sing their hearts out in the freezing air of the capital city.

Wembley's a big stadium to fill but, credit to both sets of fans, they created such a cauldron of noise, it just spurred us on even more … especially when we fell behind to an Andy Cook goal in the 70th minute. And this is when you need your big players the most. This is when your captain steps up, and that's exactly what Keatesy and the lads did.

"We're fine lads," he piped up. "There's still plenty of time, so just keep playin' and pushin' and we'll score," were Keatesy's encouraging words.

"C'MON BRUTES, LET'S 'AV A GO AND GET US A GOAL, EH SON!" Blakey shouts towards me. Ten minutes later – ten minutes from the end, we get a penalty after brave play from Keatesy. Our loan player, Kevin 'Bagpuss' Thornton, scores from the spot 'n' it's 1–1. I fancied myself getting the winner.

In the second half of extra time, I thought I'd actually won it for us, after I chested down a cross and volleyed it towards the top corner … but James McKeown, the Grimsby keeper, palmed it away for a corner. Anyway, we ran out of time and it went to penalties to decide the winner

Let me tell you something, yea. Taking a penalty in a shoot-out is a whole different ball game compared to talking one during a normal 90 minutes. But taking one in a final shoot-out!! Wweeell … it's crippling if you miss, but it's fuckin' immense when you score, AND your team wins! Thank fuck I got to experience the immense feeling of tucking away my penalty, before losing all control of my senses when Jonny Hunt put his penalty away, and we won the FA Trophy! I almost felt as though I could just run around in circles like a fuckin' dog, 'cos I was totally buzzin'.

Them Arctic conditions suddenly evaporated during those golden moments of celebrating with the fans. Honestly, it felt as though we were in Barbados soaking up the hot sun ... ohhh man, take me back there, please!! And then, who did we bump into when we're celebrating with the fans? Old Bootlegger, aka Karl Phillips, with his German helmet. "AYE, AYE, CAPTAIN," you'd hear him screaming! Legend.

Undoubtedly the biggest hero and legend of that beautiful day was my dear old godmother. I couldn't believe she even contemplated coming in them Baltic conditions. And to hear stories that she absolutely loved it, and was singing and chanting with our fans 'n' waving her scarf is such a beautiful story ... but it didn't end there.

It was unbelievably amazing she attended at all, considering as well the harrowing fact she only had a couple of months to live. Well, tell ya what, that freezing weather must've 'cryo-changed' her immune system, 'cos she lived for another four years! It must've literally frozen all her organs, revitalised her, and kept her going! Awww, bless her. I only wish I could've invited her on to our party bus for the journey home to north Wales ... now THAT she would've enjoyed!

However, six measly bloody minutes against Braintree at home, on Tuesday 16th April 2013, was an experience I didn't enjoy. It should've been a routine match of just getting a bit of game time before we headed into the play-offs ... again. But an innocuous injury in the sixth minute meant that my season was over. What I hadn't realised was that my time with Wrexham was also over.

We kinda stuttered after the FA Trophy final, and eventually lost ground for top spot to Mansfield Town, but at the same time we were sitting comfortably in a play-off position. It wasn't the target we'd set ourselves at the start of the season, but it was definitely a decent consolation. I found it really tough watching from the side, but the lads fought their way to another Wembley final, for a play-off final showdown against another Welsh side, Newport County.

Brett Ormerod was a top, top man. I had a lot of time and

respect for him. He'd played at a top level for the likes of Leeds United, Nottingham Forest and Southampton, and I absolutely loved supping on a brew and listening to his funny stories and invaluable advice. Brett loved his tea so much, if ever there was an ocean of tea, he'd swim in the fuckin' thing before guzzling every last drop. But, oh my days, could he moan, 'n' he is THE biggest moaner I've ever come across. No wonder he inherited the 'Victor Meldrew' nickname! "Fuckin' 'ell Victor Meldrew, are you fuckin' moanin' again?" we'd all ask him in chorus. But, as I said, a top, top man.

So, l kinda feel for Brett each time his sitter in the final minutes to Newport gets mentioned when people talk about that season ... and that play-off final loss to Newport County. Because, collectively, as a squad we'd given a monumental effort to finally get that promotion those magical fans deserved, and we came so, so close to achieving their dreams. Watching our fans traipsing back up the steps and out of Wembley was a harrowing sight, and one that still gets me now.

Those two years at Wrexham will stay in my heart forever, because there were so many great memories with amazing people, and I still get a sense of 'what if?' or 'if only' whenever I get a nudge of nostalgia.

There's absolutely no doubt in my mind that my time at Wrexham enhanced me as a footballer, but also as a person, because I learnt so much from my teammates and, most importantly, from the people of north Wales about values and the true meaning of unconditional love, not to mention the art of drinking a one-shot latte and knowing when to hold 'em ... and when to show 'em – in Vegas!

19

Andrew Morrell
Forward

Get outta this League, get into my car!
1998–2003, 2010–2014 (269 appearances, 96 goals)

If you've ever had the reassuring feeling of being a passenger on a journey, and you're overwhelmingly confident the driver of the vehicle has a strong desire to achieve their goal of reaching the destination, then you've probably met Andrew Morrell. Strongly motivated to succeed, but with an aura of humbling honesty, Andrew was adored by the Wrexham fans as one of their own. Even in his mid-20s, Morrell looked and played football beyond his years. As hard-working as a sheepdog 'n' as cunning as a fox, Mozza preferred to play like a bustling rally car rather than a Jaguar in cruise control. So, with his hands firmly on the steering wheel, he'll take us on a journey to a land called 'Nostalgia'. So, click yer seat belt in, sit back, and take in the sights.

I GUESS YOU could say I had an unorthodox pathway into professional football. Back in 1998, I was about 24 and hadn't gone through the usual route of learning the trade via an apprenticeship with a professional football club.

Then, one day, I met this guy in the gym where I was working, and he said he knew Joey Jones from Wrexham Football Club, and asked if I minded if he recommends me to them. So, he rang Joey to tell him about me playing for a team called Newcastle Blue Star, and he informed Joey of the amount of goals I'd scored, what league/level, and what my style of play was.

Joey phones me and said, "We'll look at almost anybody," and told me, "If you can get a week off work, then we'll see how you go." In the meantime, Brian Flynn knew absolutely nothing about me when I phoned to confirm, and he says: "Look, come in tomorrow morning, and you'll train with the first team, and then train with the apprentices in the afternoon. If I don't think you're good enough, I'll tell you by lunchtime ... and if I think you're alright, then there's a game on Wednesday for the reserves and I'll give you a chance to play."

So, I got through my first day and then managed to play for the reserves, and just built up a momentum from there. It also really helped that Joey really believed in me and gave me the belief to earn the chance of playing for the reserves, as well as keeping my job of working at the gym in a hotel in Leeds. My daily routine meant that I would get up at 6am, work until my shift finished at 3pm, jump in my car and then drive to join up with Joey and the reserves. After the reserves game, I'd jump back in my car 'n' get home late.

After about a month, I felt I was doing alright 'n' really enjoying it. I was so hungry to prove myself, I asked if I could come in pre-season for another month, so I could improve my fitness and my all-round game. The club granted my request and I totally loved it so much that I then booked another month off work to start the season with Wrexham. But then disaster struck on the second day. I broke my cheekbone after colliding with my teammate Robin Gibson after he unintentionally headbutted me when we both went up for a header with one of the opposition players from Connah's Quay. I couldn't work out how the fuck he did it, because Robin wasn't blessed with height, bless his cotton little socks. The injury, however, meant I had to return to work at the hotel the next day.

I eventually got the cheekbone fixed, so went back to Wrexham for another month, which went well enough for Brian Flynn to offer me the chance to carry on with the reserves on a match-by-match basis, but I said I'd love another month of training and planning full time.

Brian said, "Well, yeah, you can, but what about your work at the hotel?"

My mind was already made up, and I'd fallen in love with the club, so nonchalantly told him, "Nah, don't worry about that – I'll quit and dedicate myself here with you."

Flynnie just smiled that massive grin of his and said, "Andrew, if you can sustain that enthusiasm and attitude, you're going to have a great future at this club."

Two weeks later he offered me an official contract until the end of that season – my first-ever contract as a professional footballer – at the grand old age of 25.

Because of my age, I was a bit of a late bloomer in terms of professional football, so I was classed as a first-year professional and got the pleasure of spending most of my time learning from the great Joey Jones and his reserves.

Away from training I kept my personal life to a straight bat really, a bit like Geoffrey Boycott once he was at the crease – nothing for the front page of the papers, but enough to warrant a mention in the stats column towards the back. And that's how I liked it, because that was, and still is, my persona. I like a laugh, I enjoy a little bit of a social life with friends, colleagues, and especially my family ... but I also have an insatiable appetite for graft. So a little bit of darts in the garage, or snooker down the hall with the likes of Stephen Thomas (Ossie), was the perfect downtime for me really. Yeah, of course there'd be a little bit of mischief or shenanigans here 'n' there, but nothing to get us on the front page of *The Wrexham Leader*!

My week was prepped around playing for the reserves, combined with training for the first team. For a couple of years I was in and out of the first-team squad and getting a real insight of understanding of what it took to be a regular first-team player. I kinda hoped I'd done enough to impress after scoring SEVEN in an 8–0 win against Merthyr Tydfil in the FAW Welsh Cup on a bitterly cold night at The Racecourse in February 2000.

I kept plugging away and really worked hard on my game with Joey, Kev, and Brian. They were instrumental, alongside the other lads in the squad, in implementing essential ingredients of timing and positioning. Especially the likeable but quite shy Karl Connolly. 'King' Karl wasn't a big talker and preferred to let his feet do the talking, and boy could they talk! But he'd always share golden nuggets of advice, either in private or if requested by myself, his strong Scouse accent would always be worth listening to.

"Bide yer time lad, just keep listenin', learnin' and workin' yer bollocks off and you'll be a fwchin' legend at this place la" or "Alrice Andy lad! Ey', your positionin' was class there la', jus' remember to keep the defenders guessin' were yous are, an' that way you'll create more space for yerself, laich."

He made it sound so simple, but it was bloody brilliant advice, and when someone of Karl's calibre spoke – it made your ears prick up and listen. And I'm glad I listened and learned to all the advice I received, because by the end of the 2001–2002 season, we got relegated from League One, which resulted in an influx of lads leaving the club, including one of the main strikers at the club, Craig Faulconbridge. Good lad Craig, and a good front man as well. Scored a fair few goals for the club; either foot, or his head … which must've been bloody sore after an unfortunate altercation with a grader.

Here's what happened: For weeks he'd taken a fair bit of stick about his hairstyle, or the lack of it, because Craig's hair always looked as though he'd literally just got out of bed and walked straight through a hedge. Anyway, he finally got round to considering a haircut and 'Ossie', aka Stephen Thomas, tells him not to bother going to a barber's because he's got all the gear to give him a cut.

Craig and Ossie also happened to live in the same house, so Craig just takes a seat ready for a cut. Only thing was, Craig was as tall as a street light – but Ossie was short, so he needed to stand on a stool to perform the cut!

Acting like a pro hairdresser, Ossie shows Craig his cutting gear and digs out the grader. "Yeah, that'll do. Go for it Ossie!" So like a combine harvester zipping through a field of wheat, Ossie whizzes through the middle of Craig's head of hair "ZZZZZZZZZZZ" without realising it was on the shortest setting 'n' left it looking like a road going through the middle of his head! In total shock, Craig tells Ossie that he might as well carry on with the grader and then finish the job with a razor.

WEEELL, we should've worn sunglasses the next day, because his head looked like a fuckin' light bulb – it was so shiny! Of course, he received the usual piss-take from the lads, but the best reaction was saved until last from the gaffer.

"What. On. Earth. Has happened. To. Your. Head. Craig? Are you alright? Who did this to you? Pease tell me you didn't give consent!"

Joey just stood next to him losing total control and laughed like a hyena! He was so unrecognisable! When we went to warm up before the next match, you could hear the murmurs and notice the crowd checking their programme notes to see if we'd signed a new player and pointing towards Craig! But he took it on the chin ... and his head!

His departure in the summer of 2002 offered me the chance of stepping up and joining the other three strikers (Lee Trundle, Lee Jones and Hector Sam) and help get Wrexham promoted at the first time of asking. So Dennis Smith took all the strikers to one side one day in pre-season, and offered us a big juicy carrot.

"It's like this really, lads. I think you're all great centre forwards, and you all offer something different and unique to the squad. But obviously I can't play all four of you at the same time, can I? So there's a spot there if you want it. But you've gotta earn it every day in training, and then in every single match, 'cos goals win games 'n' you make sure you're ready to be a winner."

Pre-season went really well, 'n' I felt really good and in great shape. It must've helped because I scored in the first game of the season away at Scunthorpe United, and that form gave me the momentum for the rest of the season. Brian Flynn's coaching methods were very simple but very effective – "Just express yourself and go out and play." His team formation was slightly lopsided. He liked 4–4–2 but only played with one winger – Karl Connolly or Martin Chalk.

By the time Dennis Smith was appointed in 2001, we didn't have the personnel to keep us in League One, so he organised his team in a more structured formation and he preferred to play a 3–5–2, especially with the players he had in the squad, and that worked for us. We had a pair of brilliant wing backs in the team – the two Eddies, Carlos Edwards and Paul Edwards – we had a really industrious midfield with Daz Ferguson, Jim Whitley, Steve Thomas, Paul Barrett and later on with Scottie Green. We were then backed up with a solid defence of Big Bri Carey, Big Dennis Lawrence and the likes of Dan Bennett, and Shaun Pejic. The gaffer got the experienced Andy Dibble to wear the gloves in goal and he was a great asset for us. Although we had a decent start, we had a really strong finish to the season and battled it out for promotion with the likes of Hartlepool United and Rushden & Diamonds.

The Trinidad and Tobago lads were a great group. Hector Sam was totally off the cuff, on and off the pitch. We didn't know what he was gonna do next because he didn't know himself! This made him so unpredictable 'n' ... he was a really good substitute to have! Every team needs a great impact player and Hector defined that role brilliantly, because he could come on and change the game by going behind the defence 'n' then twist 'n' turn on a sixpence. Carlos was an exceptional player, and had this natural flow that deceived almost everyone, because he literally looked as though he was strolling, but in reality he was flying. "Nana nana, nana nana, heeeyyyy Dennis Lawrence," is what you'd hear the Kop singing when the telegraph pole Dennis Lawrence scored with his head from a set-piece – and that happened loads! For a gangly centre half, Den had tidy feet and trying to evade those extra-long legs of his was like trying to swim past an octopus!

Whether or not it was because they were still trying to adjust to the north Walian climate, every single day you'd hear all three of them screech in a squeaky voice, "IT'S FRREEEZZZINN' MAN." Even if it was a balmy 22 degrees, you'd see the three of them shivering with their hands tucked into their long sleeves. "IT'S FFFFRRRREEEEEZZZZIIIINN NN.'"

But their success worked because they had each other, so if they were struggling or if things weren't going too well, they could fall back on each other and relate to what each one was going through.

And even though they all had sticky starts to their Wrexham career, and initially didn't play much, their fantastic attitude prevailed and they eventually got the success they truly deserved and became household regulars. It's a funny ol' game: Dennis and Carlos got relegated with Wrexham in 2005 and then played for Trinidad and Tobago in the 2006 World Cup in Germany!

That's just how it was though in my early years at Wrexham, there was a conveyor belt of players. Loads of players coming in and out because the club didn't have a lot of money and couldn't afford to offer big deals and long contracts. Which is why they relied heavily on their contacts and scouting systems. But then, every now and again, they'd come across a hidden gem.

We were fortunate we had two captains in the squad – Big Bri Carey and Daz Ferguson. Daz Ferguson led with his actions as well as vocally. But what an absolute moaner! Honestly, he'd moan at anything, simply because he'd set such high standards, and rightly so, and he wouldn't ever, ever let them drop at any time. Oooh man, if you weren't at it at training, he'd tell ya without mincing his words (even though you'd be a bit confused with his strong Scottish accent), he'd proper dig into yer. But it was for the good of the team and the good of our own development, because he was so driven, he drove everyone's standards up.

Considering he was only coming in on a couple of months' loan, he obviously enjoyed his game and thought a lot of the club and its community. And what a wand of a left foot by the way, and the vision and anticipation of an owl and a hawk at the same time. Forget about his legs not being as quick as lightning, 'cos he had the two Eddies to do that for him on the wings, and then Jim Whitley and Paul Barrett to do the digging work.

Big Bri was very similar in his demeanour and ALWAYS ready to set an exemplary standard of what was expected, but in a more gruff Irish manner. Bloody hell, you didn't want to hang around if Big Bri was on the loose 'n' about to blow his head off 'cos he'd either fly at you with a mouthful of expletives, or a tray of cups flying in the air like the Red Arrows! But Big Bri was a colossus guy, not just in stature but also as a player and a person. A huge presence on the pitch, that could play a bit, score a few goals, and defend like a fuckin' brick wall. In the changing room, training, or on a night out he was one of the big characters, without being an extrovert.

The drinking was mainly left to the younger group of lads, and so it was usually their shenanigans that would be churning the rumour mill, but occasionally the whole squad would get a message from Daz or Big Bri. "Right, there's a 'do' arranged for a particular time and date – be there," and you'd make sure you were free for that specific occasion ... which was always a great time.

The main treat was the summer camp on the Isle of Man, which was always hotly anticipated and a good chance for the lads to get together and get to know each other properly, especially as there were the newly-signed players from that summer. In all fairness, we were most probably the best-behaved club at the tournament, but that's not to say that we behaved like angels, either.

Considering we were only there about four days, it was a great experience because we'd have a smashin' full-on training in great facilities; a couple of good little warm-up matches, and then have a crackin' night out on the last night. It was just a genius of a trip where we'd just get fit for the forthcoming season. Towards the end of the night our super supporters, that made the trip out there, would join in and share the experience with us.

From a personal perspective, my first trip to the Isle of Man definitely gave me a proper insight into what playing for Wrexham entailed, because I got to share valuable time and valuable lessons from the likes of Gaz Owen 'n' Waynne Phillips – local lads who'd been at the club since they were kids, and had grown up with the Wrexham AFC mantra. They gave me a real insight of what the club is about and what it meant to the town and north Wales collectively. Their words, "Wrexham Football Club represents north Wales" resonated with me personally, because I'm that type of persona and it's what I stand for really.

But if their interpretations weren't gonna sink in, then a resounding rally from 'The Town Crier' himself, the legendary Joey Jones, was certainly gonna hammer home the recipe of what it takes to play for this great club and its special fans … not to mention the expectations required to be a solid and honest professional footballer. In all honesty, I think every fan of every team expects their players to give their absolute best. I mean, it's the very least you could do. For instance, if I gave you the Wrexham shirt to play in the starting XI, well, you might be technically very good or technically inept. But, whatever your ability, THE one thing you should be able to do is to give your all 'n' absolutely wear yourself down, because you never know when you'd get the opportunity again! Not because the fans love a trier, but because you're in a privileged position of representing a club, and therefore you've gotta be willing to give everything you have to keep hold of your shirt AS WELL AS the club and fans.

With a sledgehammer of advice, Joey really hit it hard on me from the off when he said, "It doesn't matter if it's in training, or playing for the reserves, or even the first team – you never know who's watching, OK Mozza lad … because that might be a teammate, an opposition player or manager, or even someone watching from the sides – your attitude and application is what defines you as a person. And that's what people will judge you on, because HEY, if you're a lazy bastard but still score a hat-trick, you'll still give off a bad vibe – but if you work your bollocks off, do the right things, and maybe don't score, well you've given off positive vibes about you as a person."

Joey's words really resonated with me. Before long, another Welsh icon – Ian Rush! – joined the club in a player/coach role, and he was a brilliant role model and would always be ready to share priceless advice. I always listened to what Rushie had to share.

With a positive mindset, I'd like to think I got my just rewards in the 2002–2003 season, when I scored 39 goals from 51 games. Of course, I wouldn't have been able to achieve this feat without my teammates, including the incredibly talented Lee Trundle.

That's not disrespecting the other two front players I got to partner during that particular season, because they too offered an extra outlet, whether it be the sheer pace and bravery of Lee Jones, or the mesmerising trickery and unpredictability of Hector Sam. They were two great players to partner up front, but Trunds and myself just clicked as soon as we crossed the white line.

I've heard a lot saying that it was almost telepathic in how we both knew where the other one would be! Well, that's simply how it was. We both knew each other's game so well, and the fact that our styles suited each other, like a happily married couple really! We wouldn't spend hours going through sets of play on the training pitch, but we would, however, notice each other's contrasting styles and pick up little bits of ideas.

For instance, if you're gonna have two front players that are gonna run the channels, then that means you're unable to play through the thirds, or, alternatively, if you've got two front players coming in to feet, then you're not stretching the pitch. So, I loved running in behind and stretching their defence, and Trunds always wanted the ball, always loved having the ball to feet, and because he wasn't exactly a runner, he knew he could keep the ball and do something with it – either score a goal or find me in a position that could offer a goal. That was the beauty of knowing each other's game inside out.

We had a special connection. I even asked him after a few games, "Was that a mishit, or did you actually know where I was?"

And typical Trunds, he goes: "I just knew where you'd be – I always know where you'll be Mozza lad – I'll find ya 'n' I'll put it in an area where I know you'll attack it, so, let your legs do the runnin' and my feet the talking! Hey, you and me are gonna have a lotta fun this season!"

So that was Trunds down to a tee really – an exceptional player, a very funny guy and a brilliant character to have around. His attitude was unquestionable, and he was desperate to do well every day in training and in a match.

Hector was a different character. He could leave defenders seasick, dizzy 'n' clueless 'n' then slot the ball in the net as if he'd be havin' a kickabout with his mates on the beach (I bet it was 'FFFRRREEEZZZIIINNN' on that beach an' all – haha). Another funny character, though, without really trying, Hector was a pretty quiet lad but then had this ability of coming out with these one-liners and people would be crying with laughter and falling on their arses.

And what a season we all had. But all good things come to an end, and by the summer of 2003 we were on the move. We'd both been on hot form and the club desperately needed the cash to literally keep the roof over The Racecourse.

I returned in 2010 and, while I was away, it was a hard time for the club and its fans. I particularly found it difficult as a bystander watching all these heartbreaking events unfold.

But this club has got roots deep enough to be able to lift itself up and rise above any adversities to reach the top. So when Dean Saunders came calling in 2010, I did wonder if I could get the club up the leagues and give those long-suffering fans some much-needed love.

Ooohhh bloody hell, Deano didn't half pester me every single bloody day for weeks on end! Morning, noon and night, he'd phone me, message me 'n' promise me the earth, including bloody Neptune, saying how I could help Wrexham become a force again and together we could create history.

Adding to his irresistible charm, Deano was incidentally one of my heroes when I was growing up. I absolutely loved his game of being a pain in the arse to the defenders, with a phenomenal work rate, and he was a super fox in the box. In many respects, you could say that I modelled some of my own attributes on his ... just that Deano's standards were slightly higher than mine! (Ohhh, he's gonna love hearing that, ain't he!)

Let me tell you, Deano could sell sand to the Arabs – including a speedboat! So even though I was sooo tempted by his charm 'n' the thought of returning back 'home' to Wrexham, the truth was, I'd already agreed terms with Bury. That deal had been agreed long before Deano got hold of my phone number and put it on speed dial. But football, however, can be very fickle, and in a surprise twist of fate, the approach from Wrexham was given the green light from a Bury representative.

I'm no rocket scientist, but I didn't need a split-second to consider anything and was soon dialling Deano's hotline, and his greeting was as confident as ever.

"What took you so long, Andy?" It must've taken me about a minute to reply because I couldn't control my laughing so much that I almost choked. But then he jumps into his Tommy Cooper impersonation with: "Right then Andrew, ha-hah-hah, I want you to come in, just like that, and I want you to score me some goals, ha-hah-hah! And then, I want you to sit with my young right back, young Curtis Obeng, and my Polish fighter pilot, Adrian Cieślweicz, just like that, and show them 'n' tell 'em what it's like to be a top professional and help them along their way. Ha-hah-hah! Good lad."

Even though there was a comical side to his message, there was also a persuasive nature to it as well. But that didn't stop me from creasing up and rolling on the floor like an excited poodle

I was back home, and ready to make The Racecourse roar again.

Well, well, well ... I knew Deano was confident that we'd contend for promotion that season, but I hadn't realised how strong a squad he'd assembled until that first pre-season training. It was like a family-sized bag of Revels – full of different characters and each one worth savouring. Mirroring his own personality, Deano had a squad awash with entertainers, as well as proper grafters that would run the grass off the field. His main acquisition, as with every manager at any club, had to be the captain. The captain has to be the image of the club, as well as THE leader in every sense of the word, 'n' blimey, Deano must've put on a damn good show to capture his captain – OUR captain, Dean Keates, to join us at Wrexham. That's not disrespecting Wrexham in any way at all – but in fact it's entirely down to the calibre of the persona as well as the footballer that Keatesy was.

When the opposition players were lining up next to us in the tunnel, they must've thought we had two mascots in our side because of their lack of height, but in fact they were our midfield terriers – demolition man Jay Harris, and captain courageous Dean Keates. Two horrible players to play against, but two great distributors of the ball at their feet. Another advantageous asset of theirs was their voice on the pitch – albeit one a streetwise Scouse, and the other a moaning Brummie. And it worked an absolute treat. In fact, Keatesy was so authoritative, he was practically refereeing the match himself.

He'd be in the ref's ear all through the match, saying stuff in his deep Walsall accent.

"Excellent decision there, referee, well done, yaw're having a groit gaime," or "I disagree with yaw there, referee, maybe if yaw were in a better position – yaw moit 've got that one roit."

Keatesy was a clever little so 'n' so, and would use the old charm, saying stuff like, "Yeah, tawtally agree with yaw decision referee, that is a throw-in for us ... but just keep an oi on yawr linesman 'cos he's made a couple of errors in the last foiv minutes, thank yaw so much!" A true definition of talking the talk and walking the walk.

But walk, I definitely couldn't do the day after our first match of the 2010–2011 season. Was it age? Or was it my emphatic goal celebration catching up with me? The opening day of a new season is a bit like a kid waking up early Christmas morning, pounding down the stairs to see what they'd had from Father Christmas. And that's exactly how I felt driving to The Racecourse in August 2010, at the sprightly age of almost 36.

Having moved to a place just down the road, I wasn't really involved too much in the car share scheme with any of the other lads – purely logistically. Only the odd time would I get to share a lift with one of the lads. And I wouldn't say I was religiously superstitious, but I certainly displayed a few elements into my matchday routine (including the car journey). I really like music, even though I don't have a favourite genre 'n' it just depends whatever suits my mood or the occasion, to be honest. Well, on this particular occasion, 14th of August 2010, I went with the flow with listening to whatever was on the radio, and here's where superstition kicks in 'cause if I have a particularly good game, score a couple goals, or generally feel pleased with my overall performance ... I'll repeat the same song or tunes during my journey to the next match.

On my way to The Racecourse for that mid-August encounter against Cambridge United, there were tunes like 'Kickstarts' by Example; 'I'm not afraid' by Eminem, or 'I need air' by Magnetic Man being played on the radio – the latter very apt to how I felt after I scored in the 25th minute. It was a tidy lay-up towards me by Nat Knight-Percival, and I managed to chest the ball around their defender before unleashing a left-foot rocket into the bottom corner! Ooohhh man, did that feel flippin' amazing! In fact, I felt so high I almost jumped as high as the floodlights when I celebrated in front of the Tech End. "YYYYEEEESSSS, GET IN!" Ooomph! There's no feeling like it. Eventually, we held on to our slender lead and won 1–0.

Not that I had any pressure to do it, but I felt as though I'd knocked on the door of every Wrexham supporter and announced, "Hey guys, I'm back! Let's have some fun!" It felt amazing being back at The Racecourse playing in a red Wrexham shirt again, and I was more than ready to have some fun with the fans. But just give me five to gulp a bit of air!

To miss out in the play-off semi-finals to Luton Town felt so cruel, especially to our adoring fans, after we'd had a good season. Personally, I'd really enjoyed being a part of Deano's project of transitioning Wrexham from being a club in crisis to a club on the rise.

In the 2011–2012 season, we started like a snowball in an avalanche, and just bulldozed teams, aided with a bit of flair. Off the field, though, we were still running at a loss, and eventually Deano saw the writing was on the wall for him and accepted the job with Doncaster Rovers. Only a month or so into the season, I was given the task, and the honourable opportunity, of being a player-manager for Wrexham Football Club. With me behind the wheel, I was driving to steer the Wrexham bus outta trouble and onto the Yellow Brick Road of promotion.

Similar to Tim Allen in the film *The Santa Clause* (though in less dramatic circumstances), I inherited a sack loaded with talented goodies and was given the reins to deliver to the Wrexham fans. In no way did that necessarily mean it was a case of, 'It's on a plate for you – all you have to do is push the button and it'll happen.' The task, though, was a little less daunting because Deano had left the club in a good position on the field and also under his terms – whereas usually when you take over the manager role, it's because the previous person was sacked and the team are struggling. Well, it certainly helped me massively that I already knew the lads, knew what state the club was in, and knew what I had to do to fulfil my newly-appointed role – keep the ball rolling and apply just a couple of minor tweaks here 'n' there.

There was absolutely no need for any major surgery because we already had a great group of players that were more than capable of entertaining the fans and taking us to promotion. The lads' response to the transition of me going from player to manager was absolutely brilliant, which not only helped the flow of the team spirit, but also enabled me to carry out the job with ease. I'd already told them after the announcement, "Look, we already know what we can achieve, we already know we have the quality in our changing room to do it. So there's only gonna be a few minor changes 'n', other than that, I totally trust and believe in you guys, and I wanna thank you for trusting me. Ooh, and by the way, there's no need to refer to me as Gaffer or Boss, so just stick with Mozza please, 'n' that'll will do nicely!"

"Yeah, no probs Gaffer, cheers Mozza!" Typical Glen Little.

I knew I wouldn't have any hassles with the lads' attitude to training – it was always top-drawer. Then again, when you've got a Glen Little in the mix, you're guaranteed entertainment. And I don't mean that in a mocking sense – in fact he was so good, he was the one mocking the rest of us, 'cos he was just ridiculously good in those tight areas, or a five-a-side, where he was brilliant at just keeping the ball and finding the right pass to the right player.

He was a nightmare to play against, but also just as frustrating to play with, especially if he was in the same five-a-side team as Lee Fowler and Jay Harris 'cos they were so good at keeping the ball. Then I'd find myself begging them, "Erm, can I have a touch, please!" simply because they'd be zipping passes around like a pinball, and no one was able to get close to them – not even their teammates!

But Glen's performance wouldn't end on the training pitch either, 'cause he'd then hold court in the canteen for hours, talkin' about films 'n' tellin' stories of his days with other clubs. And oh my days, his knowledge of films, actors, or particular scenes from a film were incredible, and it was the same with football and stats – just incredible. He'd be like a contestant on *Mastermind*, and once he'd polished off talking with a set of lads, a few more would pull up a chair and he'd be off again! I'm surprised he never moaned of a sore throat 'cos he talked so much! But an absolute diamond geezer to have around and a great player on his day.

Well, 98 points would usually win you a League at a canter. Only five points separated us and champions Fleetwood Town. Fine margins, but too many draws entered us into the play-off lottery against Luton Town and they only went 'n' poured cold water over us again. In all truth, the quality and determination of our lads didn't deserve that outcome.

With such a tight group of lads, training and playing alongside them made my job a lot easier as a coach. What I didn't find as easy was the team selection, purely because their attitude and standards exceeded my expectations every single day of every single week. Fortunately, I had the shoulders and ears of Billy and Geraint to sometimes call upon whenever I needed to reach a final decision. Which proved to be the case for the FA Trophy final against Grimsby in March 2013.

We already knew Chris Maxwell was gonna be a good goalkeeper because he displayed all the right attributes as a young lad. But then we brought in Joslain Mayebi, initially as a solid back-up goalkeeper 'n' one we could develop and help push Chris Maxwell to reach his potential. However, Maxi got selected to play for a Welsh Under-21s game, which meant he was gonna miss two games for us. So I put the scenario to him politely.

"Firstly, congratulations on being selected for your country ... it's a proud achievement, so absolutely well done! However, just bear in mind, while you're away, we've got two games to play, which we'll be selecting Jos to play instead of you. So if he plays well enough, he'll stay in the team ... if not, then you're back in." Well, as it turned out, Jos played amazing for us, which left Maxi feeling a little bit frustrated because he wasn't starting, and eventually he went to Fleetwood Town.

But fate hadn't finished dealing with us, and in the run-up to the FA Trophy final, Jos got injured. So without hesitation I asked Fleetwood if we could get Maxi back, 'cause I knew he wasn't getting as much game time as he would've wanted, and they agreed. Credit to him, Maxi played superb for us, as was his overall attitude.

I didn't need to do much of a team talk before the final in Wembley – the extraordinary Wrexham fans did all that for me, because their tremendous support spoke volumes. Ha-hah-hah, I did have a little chuckle to myself on the coach journey from the hotel to Wembley, as I wondered how the Trinidad and Tobago lads would cope in such extremely cold conditions. "IT'S FRREEEZZZINN' MAN!" 'cos they'd have been bloody cold that day, that's for sure!

And as for the game plan, well we more or less got it spot on, didn't we? Of course I would've loved to have scored, obviously, but in a team environment, we were solid. Cheesey made his late appearance 'n' absolutely terrified their defence after coming on! Danny Wright then came agonisingly close to a deserved goal, before Bagpuss, aka Kevin Thornton, finally found the net from the spot late in the game. And what a priceless moment for young Jonny Hunt to win it for us with the final penalty in the shoot-out! At least we gave our brave fans their money's worth, eh!

The scenes after Jonny scored were ones I'll treasure for an eternity – swathes of red and white Wrexham fans just belting out of their lungs, hugging and dancing – absolutely amazing. I tried so hard to keep a lid on my own emotions, because I had to demonstrate a bit of decorum, especially in front of the Grimsby staff. But once we were up the Wembley steps, and little Keatesy lifting the trophy, well I've gone. I've lost it ... I wanna scream 'n' shout 'n' dance about! And let me tell you, it's really hard having to suppress such high emotions in such a joyous environment. So in that moment I allowed myself to let my guard down 'n' I sang, danced, and celebrated with our fans. Rebelliously, I even permitted myself to join in the frivolities on the coach back to Wrexham – ohhh, now that was a special journey! Where's that genie gone with their lamp?

Our form after the final was a little bit of a rollercoaster ride. Was it a case of 'after the Lord Mayor's show'? Or was it the rigorous fixture schedule taking its toll on the lads? Some might say it was a case of pure and simple harsh bad luck of injuries to key players at a key stage in our season.

Whichever way you look at it, there's probably an element of all three, because it's only natural in any walk of life to have some sort of deflation following a massive event. So then, the implications of us reaching a major final consequently resulted in a fixture pile-up. And the injuries? Well that's just down to bad luck, innit. I just wish we could've foreseen the true extent of Danny's elbow problems, then we could've assessed it more thoroughly and avoided the unnecessary reoccurrence he sustained against Braintree, a week before the play-off semi-final with Kidderminster Harriers.

I knew we could rely on Brett Ormerod to provide us with a different outlet, because he was a wily operator. He could play anywhere in the front three ... he was really shrewd, but a naturally unassuming guy. His experience was invaluable on and off the pitch, and he'd always look to help the younger lads through offering advice. Yeah, he could be a little bit of a moaner, hence the nickname he acquired, 'Victor Meldrew'. But he was a great signing for us in terms of his consistent standards ... which he displayed after coming back from a nasty injury he sustained during a training session on the Astro.

It was during the time when we'd had a period of sleet 'n' snow. Brett sprinted to keep the ball in play and, in the process, he's skidded off, bashed his knee hard against the concrete on the edge of the Astro, and shredded his knee to bits! The injury kept him out for about ten weeks. True to his character, he came back 'n' even scored a vital goal for us in the second-leg play-off semi-final away to Kidderminster Harriers.

I very rarely suffered hangovers ... probably because I didn't drink enough to warrant one! But there was a definite air of a hangover from the play-off final defeat against Newport County. That burning desire wasn't quite the same after that, and it was evident the fire had gone out with some of the lads. Pouring more salt on the wound, in the initial aftermath we lost a few key players due to our financial constraints, and I was instructed to recruit new players on a budget you could fit in your back pocket.

I tried in vain to regenerate a response from the lads and the club, but we just couldn't get ourselves going, which really saddened me and exasperated me. Inevitably it resulted in my resignation which, let me tell you, absolutely killed me.

But, ultimately, the club was, and always should be, at the forefront of the community, and it was with that respect I felt they needed someone else to help push the team back into the Football League, because I knew I'd given every ounce of blood, sweat and tears for the cause.

Nothing, however, will ever take away the joys and immense pride of my happiest days of being a part of the Wrexham family. It's an amazing community and one that has an enormous effect on the players that are privileged to play for them. Which is the prime reason I still go back as often as I can to this day – I love it.

20
Neil Roberts
Forward

The diary of a hatchling: Hunting Lions
1997–2000, 2006–2008 (166 appearances, 40 goals)

Not many people get the honour of sharing the same nickname as another iconic and legendary footballer. But Neil Roberts, aka 'Robbo', also displayed the same traits as his 'namesake', Bryan Robson – the fearless, committed and devoted leader! A kind soul with a heart firmly sewn onto his sleeve, Robbo speaks of great pride at hearing the chant: "HE'S ONE OF OUR OWN" serenaded to him. He also finds time to delight us with the shoulder-shakin' shenanigans of Kevin 'Rooster' Russell. Without a whiff of bull in the air, this one's as authentic as a Joey Jones salute 'n' a pint of Wrexham lager.

Neil Roberts

I'VE EXPERIENCED A range of 'I was there moments' as a fan and a player with Wrexham ... from the ultimate highs of scoring against Chester, and the hilarious high jinks with the lads – to the desolate injury blows and the heartbreak of relegation.

I'm absolutely convinced the artist L S Lowry must've painted his famous painting *Going to the Match* from the top window of the Maesgwyn pub 'cause he's got the vision from inside my mind absolutely spot-on! It's exactly how I picture the scene from my childhood 'n' adolescence of going to The Racecourse with my family, and then my mates. I loved that short walk from our home in Garden Village – on to Sandringham 'n' Edinburgh roads, past Rhosddu. We'd then make our way on to Crispin Lane to the smell of burgers 'n' fried onions. That scene of a thousand heads with red 'n' white scarfs around their necks, heading towards their turnstile or a quick pint in the pub before the match. But that's what I got to experience as a supporter during the period when Dixie McNeil was manager in the late 1980s. Ooohhh man, they were great times. A time when Marcher Sound ruled the waves with top tunes by S'Express, and Stuart Mason's was king of the sports shops with the latest must-have green 'n' yellow Wrexham away shirt.

Personally, it got even better for me 'cos I got the ultimate experience of putting on a proper Wrexham shirt; I got to train and play on The Racecourse; I was there to see Joey's tackling, sometimes even on his own teammates! I even got to share quite a few beers with some of the Wrexham FC legends when we got into a couple of hairy moments! But more of that later.

I was proud as punch when I was given the opportunity to sign as a schoolboy for Wrexham, and as well as having the best of times training a couple of times a week, I'd also have the odd chance to be a ball boy. As a stroke of luck, I was nominated as a ball boy for the famous West Ham FA

Cup match in 1992. Along with another schoolboy, we were given the task of retrieving the ball if it went into the derelict Plas Coch stand. We were about 13, and rather than keeping an eye on the match, we thought, "Fuck it – let's have a bit of head tennis" behind the hoardings. So we were there for ages until we heard a shout from one of the players "OI! BALL BOY, PASS ME THE FUCKIN' BALL!" We made sure we kept to our duties after that.

But the fun from schoolboy times had nothing on my apprenticeship era. They were THE best of times. It was a time when I couldn't wait to wake up in the morning and get to The Racecourse. I'd then 'muck in' with our daily chores of tending to The Racecourse turf with Jonny Edwards, the groundsman, or sort out the kit with Joey, Kev Reeves, and a lovely lady called Marleen. Then, once we'd completed them chores, it was straight into the changing rooms to run the communal bath, before making the teas and coffees for the first-team professionals. It all sounds a bit tedious nowadays, but we didn't think anything of it, especially when we were given half a chance to piss about.

So one day, I was busy cleaning the changin' room with a few of the lads, when the lights suddenly went off and we're in complete darkness. Then I felt someone's hand smothering something on my face before the lights went back on.

"Oh, fucking hell!" Our faces had been plastered with black shoe polish! "You Bastards!" But just then, we heard the voices of Cliff Sear and Brian Prandle coming down the corridor. "Oh BOLLOCKS!! There's gonna be SHIT hittin' the fan now!"

Good old Brian Prandle would put an arm around you or give you a bit of advice. Cliff, on the other hand, was a genius at dealing with being 'in the moment' – 'n' if you deserved being torn to pieces, he'd rip you to shreds! But if he thought you deserved praise – he'd make you feel ten feet tall. So it was just as well we had the Three Amigos (and Joey) to help us cope with the brutality of playing in the men's Wrexham and District Welsh National League.

I tell ya what, those battles against hardened middle-aged men from places like Llanuwchllyn, Brickfield or Cymau was a bloody good grounding. Yeah, some were a bit rough 'n' ready, and some of the stuff that went on was a bit naughty, but some of them could bloody play a bit as well. But I fuckin' relished it and loved that physical side of the game. Some of the other lads, however, weren't so accustomed to some of the 'dark arts' of men's football, especially when we played away.

But it wasn't just the brutality we had to get used to either ... they were just mad times! You should've seen the look on our faces when Brian Prandle turned up in this rickety old green minibus for our first away match of the season! We'd all be squealing "NO FUCKIN' WAY!" or "Are we actually going in that fuckin' thing?" Anyway, the best was yet to come, because every time we went around a corner, these shitty benches we were sat on would fling us around like the fuckin' waltzers! They hadn't even been screwed down! Honestly, you'd swear they'd been yanked out from some park and thrown into this death trap. Ha-hah-hah, a few of the lads were physically green with spew if ever we went along that winding road towards the likes of Llanuwchllyn or Bala! "SCREAM IF YER WANNA GO FASTER," someone would shout! "AAAAHHHH!" Class.

Someone must've said something, because after a few months of trekking in this wheelie bin of a minibus, we were given a brand spanking new red minibus with 'WREXHAM FC' in white writing on it. So at least we'd arrive in style at Chirk, fling open the doors 'n' inhale that sweet smell of chocolate from the factory.

That was the beauty of playing at some of these varying pitches – the likes of The Hand at Chirk had an overgrown branch leaning on to the pitch, and sometimes the ball would smack against it from a throw-in, or if someone would knock a long ball down the line! Whereas in Cymau, the pitch was like a fuckin' ski slope, and you'd need to wear walking boots one half, and ski boots for the second half! Ha-hah-hah, or there'd be the sight of the locals in Llanuwchllyn still clearing sheep shit from their pitch as we were warming up! NOW THAT was proper grassroots, 'n' we loved it!!

But, with all due respect, we were a load of lads that had just left school, most of them living in digs having moved from somewhere across the north-west of England. The rest of the squad was made up from Wrexham and District lads. Regardless of where we came from, we were a proper band of brothers and we'd look out for each other – if some gap-toothed skinhead wanted a piece, we'd all give him a piece. That's just how we rolled. I tell ya what though, we had some serious talent to match it as well.

Don't be fooled by his nickname 'Wally', because Neil Wainwright was by far the pick of our talented bunch. It didn't matter if we played on our soft 'n' flat home ground in Lindisfarne, Ruabon, or a bumpy ground elsewhere – you'd swear the ball was elasticated to his foot. Never mind Wally 'cos he should've been called 'Lightning McQueen'! Bloody hell, there were times he was so fast all you'd see was a puff of dust and the opposition players looking around, "Where the fuck's he gone?" Then he'd unleash a 30-yard rocket past their keeper. Then the likes of myself would be sayin': "Yeah, that's fantastic Wally lad, but any chance I can have a game here, mate?" 'Cos I was just exasperated at being a spectator.

That desperate feeling of wanting to prove myself and being noticed was prevalent every single day, either in training or during a Saturday match with the Wrexham Colts. I always had that work ethic in me, and I knew that being able to score goals wasn't gonna be enough to give me a chance of making the grade. A priceless bit of advice from Joey also rang in my ears every time I woke up in the mornings.

"Whatever you do in your life, Robbo, you give it 110 per cent, and you do it honestly, because if you cheat that one per cent, eventually it'll reach a 100 per cent and you'll be a fake. You've already got a great attitude lad – just keep on working hard to develop and you'll earn your chance."

So every day in training, I'd be working my bollocks off, always looking over to where the first-team players were training, and praying to hear the call from Flynnie (Brian Flynn) or his assistant Kev Reeves.

"CLIFF! WE NEED TO BORROW A COUPLE OF YOUR LADS FOR THIS SESSION!"

And I'd be thinking, "FUCKIN' YESSS! Oh choose me, please choose me."

We were so lucky when Brian Flynn instilled that 'family values' essence into the club, because we were all treated with the same importance – we were just as invaluable as the next person. So to have the apprentices training on the pitch next to the first-team professionals was a stroke of genius from Flynnie, because if and when you'd get THE CALL to join in with the first-team players, it wasn't so daunting.

Whenever there was a chance of a break in the session from either pitch, there would be a small gathering watching from the sidelines. Although, occasionally, the break in the session was caused by a bit of a scrap between players, 'n' oh my bloody days, it would get tasty with a few fists flyin' 'n' someone shouting, "FUCKIN' DO THAT AGAIN AND I'LL FUCKIN' BATTER YOU, YER PRICK!" That could've been between the apprentices or the first team, or even an apprentice and a first-teamer. Secretly, I think the coaches loved it, because it meant that the players were passionate and we were also able to look after ourselves.

Mind you, we had no choice with the likes of Tony Humes and Barry Hunter in the mix. They didn't give a shit if it a was a training session or if you were an apprentice – they wouldn't hesitate in giving you a good kickin' and you wouldn't dare complain, because they'd give you a mouthful. "Stop whining you fuckin' wimp! Ooh, watch out lads, this one doesn't fancy it!" Then WHACK! They actually fuckin' loved it when you gave a bit of physicality back – it showed that you weren't a shrinking violet. So you either sank or swam.

It's never been in my make-up to swim back to the shore if I've had to swim against the tide during some periods in my life. Getting into the Wrexham first team and earning a professional football contract was one of them periods, because this was a squad full of superstars and crowd favourites: Gaz Owen, King Karl Connolly, Waynne Phillips, Gary Bennett, Peter Ward, Stevie Watkin, Dave Brammer ... all top, top quality players.

So it was always gonna be a big shout for me to push one of these big names aside and say, "I'm here now, this is my time to shine" – because you really couldn't argue with that kind of talent, could you? However, Flynnie and the rest of the coaching team must've seen something in me, and offered me my first-ever professional contract at the age of 19, in July 1997, 'n' almost two years from my debut, a call-up with the first team for the European Cup Winners' Cup ties against Petrolul Ploieşti.

Flynnie was a shrewd operator and, to help me gain further knowledge and experience, he sent me on loan to Bangor City during that two-year absence. Whether or not he saw it as a test, but that time with Bangor definitely helped to shape me into becoming a more mature footballer, and as much as I enjoyed my time with them, it was an unbelievable feeling when Flynnie called me back to Wrexham to be involved with the first team.

Back in the mid-1990s, there was a highlights show every Sunday afternoon on HTV Wales, showing clips of Wrexham,

Cardiff City, and Swansea City from the previous days' matches. So every Sunday I'd be watching it with my family after a roast dinner, 'n' just thinkin' 'n' hopin': "We're gonna be sat here watching me play for Wrexham." So seeing my name as a substitute on the Friday team sheet late September 1997 put me one step closer to fulfilling my wish.

Sunday, 28th September 1997, was the quickest time I'd finished eating my roast dinner – jam roly-poly pudding included. We all knew the outcome of the previous day's match, because my family were there to see me making my home debut, coming on as a substitute for 'King' Karl Connolly in the 82nd minute at The Racecourse against Chesterfield. It was a massively proud moment 'n' could've been the ultimate home debut had Chesterfield keeper Billy Mercer not dived smartly to save my snap shot. "Oh shit! Hey, did someone remember to record it on the VHS?" 'Cos I kinda hoped I'd impressed enough to warrant another chance to appear on the HTV Wales *Sunday Special*.

Friday, 31st October 1997, proved to be more of a treat than a trick for me – my name was on the team sheet to start against Carlisle United away the next day. King Karl had picked up an injury and my feet were tasked to fill his boots. "Time to swim against the tide and find my flow." Well bloody hell, we couldn't have started any worse, going 2–0 down after only 17 minutes. Fuck sakes! Then I scored my first AND second goal for the first team to make it 2–2! At this stage we were flying, and to this day I'm not sure how we didn't win the game at a canter 'cos we absolutely destroyed them. But it was no surprise that we came away with something ... especially with the togetherness we had in that dressing room.

Imagine being a 19 year old sharing a changing room with the people you'd idolised – 'n' it might sound a bit surreal, but they helped make that transition for me a lot easier. I felt as though I belonged. There were no airs and graces at all – you weren't spared a bollocking 'n' you definitely weren't spared a prank. The team was full of prank merchants – and with culprits such as Gaz Owen, Dave Brammer or Kev 'Rooster' Russell around, you always 'tried' to be on your guard ... but they always found a way! The little bastards!

If sharing the *Sunday Special* experience was a proud moment, it was even better meeting up with my mates and my family in the players' lounge after a home game at The Racecourse. Over a few beers, we'd discuss moments from the match 'n' they wouldn't hold back with their opinions, either! Ranging from football to fashion, I'd get shit thrown at me like, "Bloody hell, Robbo! Can't you afford a pair of socks these days?" Then I'd start defending myself.

"Well, I did have a nice pair of socks before I went out to warm up, but when I've gone to put them back on after the game, some fucker's cut the ends off with a pair of scissors!"

I got proper done on another occasion 'n' it was bloody embarrassing when my mum asked me, "Have you got ants in yer pants, Neil? I do wish you'd stop scratching down there!"

Again I'd have to explain, "Well, I can't help it if someone's rubbed loads of bloody Deep Heat in my boxers!" And just out of the corner of my eye, I'd catch a glimpse of that rascal Rooster sniggering! This wouldn't be the last time he'd instigate an incident I'd be dragged into.

Rooster was just as quick with his wit as he was with a ball at his feet. And during one scary night out, I was just as glad his legs were just as quick. We'd become good mates very soon, and I loved being around him because of his infectious and positive personality. Yeah, he could be outrageously bonkers, but he was also generous with his time and wouldn't hesitate to help anyone out. So, whenever we had a chance, we'd go on a night out to Chester, have a few laughs and a lot of beers.

But on this particular night out in Chester, we were stumbling around the city centre 'n' going from one pub to another, when a gang of Chester fans noticed us. So they start throwing the usual abuse our way and, in a blink, start chasing after us 'n' we fuckin' leg it as fast as we can! By the time we'd reached the Chester Racecourse, we breathed a heavy sigh of relief 'cos we'd lost them.

Then someone screams, "THERE THEY ARE – THE FUCKIN' SHEEPSHAGGERS!"

OH SHIT, they'd spotted us, 'n' Rooster goes, "Shit! Leg it this way Robbo." So we set off again, our legs somehow finding the energy to sprint like fuck, even though we were pissed up out of our heads.

It felt like fuckin' ages before we reached the Posthouse roundabout near the Little Chef just outside of Chester, 'n' both of us wanted to spew our guts out! So we hid behind a bush for about half an hour until we were dead sure we hadn't been followed, and got our breath back. Honestly, we were so fuckin' knackered we booked ourselves a cab. "Hi, can we get a taxi to Wrexham town centre please ... we're behind the big bush at the Posthouse roundabout near the Little Chef just outside Chester!"

I should've learnt my lesson by the time we'd gone to the Isle of Man tournament the following summer. We'd played a few matches, so we were given the chance to go out and have a few drinks. Flynnie was very clear with his curfews – apprentices back at the hotel by 11pm, first-team players back by midnight. Anyone who was late would get a fine. Simple as that. But it was more of a case of not wanting to let Flynnie down.

As expected, along with the other first-team players, I arrived back at the hotel with about ten minutes to spare, 'n' there's Flynnie sat waiting for us in the reception.

"Exceptional timing lads. See you all at breakfast for seven o'clock – oh, and don't forget our flight leaves at ten o'clock tomorrow morning, so make sure all your luggage is ready," he goes before we all went to our rooms.

Totally wiped out, I was just about to fall into a deep sleep, 'n' there's a knock on the door – it's Rooster and the gang, including Brian Carey.

"We can't sleep – fancy sneakin' out for a couple more beers?" they asked.

So there we were, all tiptoeing out through the fire exit and heading towards the pub in taxis. Bloody hell, that was a good night, and we got well and truly bladdered!

Not sure how, but I managed to wake up for breakfast, and somehow forced a few bits of toast down me before taking about five showers to help me sober up. I jumped on the bus in plenty of time ready to catch the flight home. So, we get to the airport in good time 'n' just as I board, Rooster shoots off his chair 'n' goes, "FUCK, WHERE'S BIG BRI?" Ha-hah-hah, it transpired the coaching staff had miscounted before leaving the hotel 'n' Brian Carey was still fast asleep in his room and missed the flight home!

Such was Rooster's character, I couldn't wait to introduce him to my new teammates soon after I'd signed for Wigan in early 2000. I always loved get-togethers and saw an opportunity to arrange a house warming party once the deal was done and the house was ready to have guests round. So, the idea was to invite my closest friends and family from Wrexham and introduce them to my new teammates and the odd neighbour 'n' have a bite to eat, sink a few beers, share a few stories, and have a few laughs. I must've forgotten to send the script to Rooster.

In all fairness to him, Rooster had this insatiable energy that could outshine the moon – he was that charismatic. However, with the party in full flow, Rooster decides to introduce a personal friend of his to our guests.

"LADIES AND GENTLEMEN, I'D LIKE YOU TO MEET A VERY GOOD FRIEND OF MINE – THE WHIPPET!"

I put my hand onto my face 'n' shook with embarrassment as I quietly uttered, "Ooohhh Nooo!"

Obviously, I never really wanted to leave Wrexham, because of the love I had for the club and the community. But Wigan showed an interest in me after I'd had a couple of successful seasons with Wrexham, when I showed that I was able to chip in with a few goals as well as develop my all-round game. They told me they were going to build an exciting new future for the club, and their main intention were getting into the Premier League, and they asked if I fancied playing a part. In strictest confidentiality, I was also told that Wrexham needed the cash.

I had a fantastic experience with Wigan, that period enhanced my knowledge as a footballer as well as a person. But hey – you can take the lad out of Wrexham, but you can't take Wrexham out of the lad, and my thoughts were never far away from my town and the club. And whenever I had the chance, I'd be at The Racecourse like a shot, either sat in the Marston Ales stand, or standing in the Crispin Lane Kop, cheering the lads on, including my brother, Stephen.

Of course we'd always talk about the club and what was going on, and the conversation would sometimes edge towards the financial side of things ... which was pretty bloody bleak. And it really hurt – not just Stephen and myself, but our family and our friends, because we just felt so helpless. The situation became a lot more fraught for us as a family when Stephen sustained an injury that eventually curtailed his career at Wrexham. In a strange twist of fate, just as Stephen was limping out through The Racecourse exit, I bounced through the entrance, and back into the promise of a 'new dawn' at Wrexham Football Club.

In the early summer of 2006, there was a promising air of better times for the club as news filtered of local businesses delegating a consortium to rescue Wrexham. As it coincidentally happened, we were looking to move closer to the town for family reasons when I had a phone call from Rooster.

"Y'alright Robbo! You still runnin' away from those Chester fans, or what?" he teased.

"Rooster!" I answered. "How's the whippet?"

"Ha-hah-hah, still dangling, pal!" he continues.

"Listen mate, are you still lookin' for a club closer to Wrexham?"

"Yeah, but not fuckin' Chester!"

"Well listen, the gaffer's interested in ya 'n' if you're interested as well, he'll give ya a call later."

I didn't need to have that conversation with Dennis Smith later that day – my mind was already thinking of wearing the Wrexham shirt and my feet were back on The Racecourse turf. But, sure enough, Dennis rang me, and I was glad he phoned me – not just because of the exciting vision he had for the club, but also because it wasn't gonna affect my phone bill, 'cos honestly, it was daylight when I initially answered his call, but it was pitch-black when we finished talking ... and this was early summer!

And, to be fair, the plan seemed to be on the same page, as we got off to a great start, which included a very pleasurable away win at our despised derby rivals, Chester City. Ha-hah-hah, that felt absolutely amazin' an' it was made even better after I scored from a penalty. Another local lad, 'Jonah', aka Mark Jones, made it 2–0 after scoring another one of his collection of impressive finishes. "YYYEEESSS JONAH LAD, FUCKIN' GET IN, PAL!" I shouted to him, but typical Jonah he just went, "Aye, thanks Robbo, not bad yea?" Sound lad Jonah, and a great player.

To this day, I'm still baffled as to how and why we got so derailed? Especially with the squad we had. Because, at the beginning of the 2006–07 season, I genuinely believed we had the right characters and the ability to challenge for a promotion spot. There literally wasn't a rotten egg amongst us. So to find ourselves desperately looking for any kind of form and in the deep shit of the relegation zone by Christmas was a shocker. I have no doubt that injuries to key players, coupled with the sale of other key players may have played a major factor.

But Dennis Smith was great. He didn't waver or panic 'n' he just kept on reassuring us. "It's just a blip – I really believe we'll click things back together and put on a good string of results," he kept reassuring us. His man-management skills were bloody brilliant and every so often he'd call Daz Ferguson and myself into his office for a chat.

"Right, I think it's obvious morale is a bit low, so between you both, I want you to arrange a night out for the squad 'n' get pissed! It'll be a chance to get things off each other's chest, 'n' 'ave a good time."

"Thanks Gaffer," we'd reply, and just as we'd be heading out of his office, he'd pipe up again.

"Oh and lads! Hey, two things – make sure we don't make the front pages, and lastly, you two buy the first two rounds!"

So we'd be planning our piss-up walking from the gaffer's office.

"OK, look Robbo," Daz would command in his deep Glaswegian accent. "We'll organise two separate nights, OK pal – I'll book us a great night in Manchester."

"Sound, Daz," I'd reply. "And I'll get something going in Chester."

"FACKIN' CHESTER?" Daz squealed "ARE YOU FACKIN' SMOKIN' SOMETHIN' WEE MAN – WE'LL GET FACKIN' BATTERED MAN!"

"Aye," I sniggered. "But at least a good scrap might help us get that frustration out of us an' all, eh?"

But them nights out were like putting a finger to stop a gaping leak, because by March 2007, we looked odds-on to sink into the abyss of non-League football. And, in the meantime, Daz Ferguson left, Dennis Smith had been sacked and replaced by the popular, yet inexperienced, Brian Carey. As a result of Daz's departure, I was installed as club captain. A huge honour and a proud moment for myself, as well as my friends and family. However, we were under no illusions about the massive task of avoiding relegation and we needed to puff our chests out and show our Wrexham colours – because the folk of Wrexham and north Wales don't just buckle under pressure – we fucking roll up our sleeves, stick together and fight like hell.

Which is exactly what we did, and by the end of April we were within hope of avoiding relegation, after an ecstatic midweek win at our other despised derby rivals, Shrewsbury Town, when Michael Proctor swooped home late on and sent our apoplectic fans into pure ecstasy. And that feeling continued on the coach home. On the journey, I gathered the lads and announced: "Hey, look, we're so fuckin' close boys – 'n' I reckon we need to chill, so I'm throwing a BBQ at my gaff in a few days' time – every single one of you is gonna be there, so bring yer wives or yer partners. It's fancy dress – so there's a crate of beer for the best dressed."

There must've been something in them burgers, because we succeeded in avoiding relegation by beating fellow struggling Boston United 3–1, and it was more of a huge wave of relief than a celebration really. I just kept on thinking, "Phew! Right then, we have to learn from this 'cos things can only get better."

I only wish our form for the 2007–08 season matched my own enthusiasm, because by February '08 we were favourites for relegation again, and by now I was absolutely sick of it. Nah, scratch that, I was fuckin' fumin'! And I woke up one mornin' 'n' decided I was gonna have it out. So I marched to the manager's office, occupied by our new gaffer, Brian Little, knocked on his door 'n' didn't bother waiting for him to invite me in.

"Can I have a word please, Gaffer?"

"Yeah, sure Neil, take a seat."

"No thanks, I'd rather stand to say what I've got to say."

"Rrriiiiggghhhtt, OK, what's on yer mind?"

"I'm absolutely fuckin' pissed off with the attitude of some of the loan players the past few months," I announced.

"Well, I'm sorry you feel like that."

"SORRY? HEY! THEY JUST DON'T GIVE A FUCKIN' SHIT ABOUT THIS CLUB!" I protested. He tried gesturing for me to calm down, but I wasn't finished. "IT'S LIKE A FUCKIN' REVOLVING DOOR FOR ANY OLD TOM, DICK 'N' HARRY 'N' IT'S JUST NOT GOOD ENOUGH!"

It was nothing personal towards the lads we'd had on loan, but I just felt they honestly didn't give a shit. It looked as though they just turned up, picked up their wages and fucked off. The fans and the club deserved better than that kind of blasé attitude. It's no surprise there were more punch-ups in training or in the dressing room during that period than any other time during my career at Wrexham, deriving from lads like myself towards the fuckers that didn't care!

And, ultimately, my despondent mood didn't alter, because after a harrowing away defeat to Hereford United, we lost our once proud League status. It hurt. It still does, to the pits of my stomach. Even the fact that I'm the last player to score in front of the old Crispin Lane Kop, the famous terrace where a whole host of iconic players have scored iconic goals, it's still tinged with sadness for me, because I care so SO much about this club and this community, it still hurts like fuck whenever I think of that period.

But this old place never surrenders and my heart will forever beat to the sound of The Racecourse roar!

Afterword

So THERE WE have it. We hope you've enjoyed the ride. It all started with a casual conversation after a morning run. Before we knew it, we had the title – *There's Something About Wrexham*. And then we had the format. A bit of a biog followed by a few anecdotes. It sounded simple but none of this would have been possible without some of the players who not only contributed but also worked as 'fixers' on this project. Thank you once again. Another thank you goes out to Debs 'n' Karen – our suffering partners who have propelled us along with *panads* and Mars Bar cakes. Debs' Mars Bar cakes deserve more than just a mention, but we can't keep going on about them or else she'll think we're taking the piss!

Which brings us to YOU, the readers – if you've enjoyed the book, please leave us a review with Amazon or Google or whatever forum works for you.

Rick and Deborah from North Carolina, Kathy from Kansas and Tom from Wisconsin – everywhere we go – we can't stop meeting new friends from across the Atlantic. Is it the small leathery ball that brings us all together? Or is it just that sense of belonging to a crowd or a tribe ... it must be in our DNA. They say football is a universal language, and they're right – it weaves us together, bringing people closer through shared excitement. It promotes teamwork and inclusion, making it a powerful tool for connection. And in a time of political unrest around the world, boy can we do with building bridges and striving for unity and understanding!

Afterword

We hope that you've enjoyed reading this book as much as we've enjoyed putting it together.
Diolch eto
Oddi wrth Deio ac Iestyn
xxx

Also from Y Lolfa:

£9.99

£9.99

£9.95

£14.99